Scotland's Foreshore

**Scotland's Land**
**Series editor:** Dr Annie Tindley



This series presents the latest scholarly work to academic and public readers on Scotland's land issues. Predominantly focusing on the history of Scotland's economic, political, and social and cultural relationships to land, landscape, country houses and landed estates, it also brings in cutting-edge approaches to explore new methodologies and perspectives around this politically contentious but stimulating issue. As an interdisciplinary series, it will necessarily contain a wide range of approaches, including history, law, economics and economic history, philosophy, environment/landscape studies, and human/cultural geography. The aim of the series is to bring together and publish the best work on land issues across a wide range of disciplines for a diverse set of audiences.

**Published and forthcoming titles**

*The Land Agent: 1700–1920*
Lowri Ann Rees, Ciarán Reilly and Annie Tindley (eds)

*Scotland's Foreshore: Public Rights, Private Rights and the Crown, 1840–2017*
John MacAskill

edinburghuniversitypress.com/series/slf

# Scotland's Foreshore

## Public Rights, Private Rights and the Crown, 1840–2017

John MacAskill

EDINBURGH
University Press

Edinburgh University Press is one of the leading university presses in the UK. We publish academic books and journals in our selected subject areas across the humanities and social sciences, combining cutting-edge scholarship with high editorial and production values to produce academic works of lasting importance. For more information visit our website: edinburghuniversitypress.com



Edinburgh University Press Ltd
The Tun – Holyrood Road
12 (2f) Jackson's Entry
Edinburgh EH8 8PJ

First published in hardback by Edinburgh University Press 2018

Typeset in 10.5/13pt Sabon by
Servis Filmsetting Ltd, Stockport

A CIP record for this book is available from the British Library

ISBN 978 1 4744 3691 5 (hardback)
ISBN 978 1 4744 3692 2 (paperback)
ISBN 978 1 4744 3693 9 (webready PDF)
ISBN 978 1 4744 3694 6 (epub)

# *Contents*

# *Preface and Acknowledgements*

When, as a young child, I played on the beach and among the rock pools at Reiff in Wester Ross, it is no surprise that it never occurred to me wonder who owned or managed the beach or whether it was lawful for me to make sandcastles, swim, fish, collect seaweed, play beach cricket or paddle a boat, or even to be there at all. And as an adult playing with my children on the beaches at Clachtoll and Achmelvich in Sutherland, it still never occurred to me to question, or even to think about, issues of ownership and management or our right to be on the beach or to enjoy recreational activities there. If I had thought about it at all, I am sure I would have assumed that the beach was, as it were, neutral territory, not owned by anyone and open to everyone to be, and to do what they liked, there. I certainly had no idea that the ownership and management of Scotland's foreshore had been a matter of prolonged controversy. It was only when I began the research for my doctorate on which this book is based that I appreciated the fascinating questions of rights, ownership and management, and how it was that the ownership and management of the foreshore had been so controversial; all of which undermined my rather innocent assumption of the foreshore being land owned by no one and available to everyone. I hope that this book will prove as interesting to those who have shared my assumption – and indeed to the better informed – as it has been for me to write it.

I am sincerely grateful to the editorial, production and marketing teams at Edinburgh University Press who worked on and supported this book, especially the copy-editor Eliza Wright whose attention to detail far exceeded my own. There are many people who have helped me in my research and in writing this book, but I would like to single out and thank the supervisors of my PhD, Professor Donald Meek and Mrs Janet Hunter, and my examiners, Professor Ewen A. Cameron and Professor John Bryden. Ewen Cameron has been unfailing in his help, encouragement and support to me in my academic endeavours, as has Dr Annie Tindley, the editor of the series that this book forms a part of. I am very fortunate indeed to count them as my friends and it is a huge pleasure to acknowledge their help and support. Dr Jill Robbie was extremely kind to give me the benefit of her time and knowledge. I would also like to thank the staff and curators of the many repositories and libraries in which I have undertaken research for this book: the National Records of Scotland; the National Register of Archives for Scotland; the National Archives in London; Dunvegan Castle, Isle of Skye; the National Library of Scotland; the British Library; and the libraries of the Universities of Edinburgh and Cambridge. While I have received much assistance from those mentioned above, any errors of fact or interpretation remain mine alone.

Part of the material in this book first appeared in the *Scottish Historical Review*, 85:2:220 (October 2006) under the title '"The most arbitrary, scandalous act of tyranny": the Crown, private proprietors and the ownership of the Scottish foreshore in the nineteenth century', and in chapter 21 of M. A. Mulhern (ed.), *Scottish Life and Society: A Compendium of Scottish Ethnology. Vol. 13: The Law* (Edinburgh, 2012).

And finally, of course, I owe a huge debt of thanks to my family and especially to my wife Gwyneth who probably thought that the long disappearances to my study would come to an end after my book on the Highland Destitution of 1837 was published, but graciously accepted further periods of my absence as this book was taking shape!

# *Glossary of Legal Terms*

The explanation of the terms in this glossary is largely derived from Law Society of Scotland, *Glossary: Scottish Legal Terms and Latin Maxims* (Edinburgh, 1992).

| | |
|---|---|
| *Absolvitor* | A final civil judgment in favour of the party against whom a civil action has been raised. |
| *Actio popularis* | An action brought by a member of the public for vindication or defence of a public right. |
| *Alveus* | The bed of a river. |
| Barony | A direct grant of an estate in land from the Crown. |
| Closed record | A document comprising the final written pleadings of the parties to a civil action. |
| Conclusions | The statement in a summons in civil proceedings of the precise remedy asked for. |
| Condescendence | Statement(s) of fact by the person instituting or suing in a civil action. |
| Court of Session | The supreme Scottish civil court. It is comprised of the Outer House that determines cases at first instance and the Inner House having primarily an appellate jurisdiction. |
| Crown Counsel | Advocate(s) instructed on behalf of the Crown. |
| Declarator | A declaration by the court of a person's rights made in an action for declarator. |
| Decree | The final judgment of a court in civil proceedings. |
| Decree in absence | A final order granted to the pursuer in a civil action where the defender has not lodged a notice of intention to defend or has not lodged defences. |
| *Ex adverso* | Opposite to; describing the position of land or buildings. |

| | |
|---|---|
| *Habile* | Admissible; valid; competent for a legal purpose. |
| Interdict | A judicial remedy granted by the court forbidding an act or course of action. |
| Interlocutor | The official and effective expression of an order or judgment pronounced by the court in the course of a civil action. |
| Law Officers | The Lord Advocate and the Solicitor General for Scotland. |
| Lord Advocate | The senior Law Officer of the Crown in Scotland. |
| Lord Justice-Clerk | The holder of the second-highest judicial office in Scotland. He presides over the Second Division of the Inner House of the Court of Session. |
| Lord Ordinary | A judge of the Court of Session who sits in the Outer House of the Court of Session and determines cases there at first instance. |
| Lord President | The first in rank of the judges who constitute the Court of Session and the High Court of Justiciary. He is the presiding judge of the First Division of the Inner House of the Court of Session. |
| *Obiter dictum* | An opinion expressed by a judge, in giving judgment, on a point which is not essential to the decision. |
| Parts and pertinents | Everything which passes with the actual land on its transfer or disposition. |
| Precognition | A preliminary written statement of the evidence which a witness may be expected to give. It is not signed and is not binding. |
| Prescription | The rule of law by which certain rights and obligations are established or extinguished or the modes of proving them are limited by lapse of time. |
| Prescriptive period | The requisite period of time during which possession must be proved for a claim to prescriptive possession to succeed. |

| | |
|---|---|
| Prescriptive possession | In the context of the foreshore, the doctrine under which ownership may be acquired by possession of the foreshore for the prescriptive period founded on a *habile* title. |
| *Regalia* | Rights which under feudal law attach to the Sovereign. |
| *Regalia majora* | Royal rights of the Sovereign which are personal or pertain to the Crown as guardian of the public interest and consequently inalienable without parliamentary sanction. |
| *Regalia minora* | Royal proprietary rights which the Crown may exercise as it pleases and which it may alienate. |
| *Res judicata* | A case or matter decided. |
| Servitude | An obligation attached to land. |
| Sheriff | The judge of a sheriff court. |
| Sheriff court | The principal inferior court in Scotland presided over by the sheriff. |
| Sheriff principal | A judge, formerly known as a sheriff, who hears appeals from sheriffs in civil cases. |
| Sheriff substitute | The title, from 1746 to 1971, of the sheriff. |
| Solicitor General for Scotland | A Law Officer of the Crown who assists the Lord Advocate. |
| Summons | A document requiring a person to appear in court to answer a claim made against him. |
| Suspension and interdict | A procedure in the Court of Session to prevent injury to a right by a deliberate act which is threatened or being performed. |
| *Ultimus haeres* | The last heir. |

For my Schatz,
my darling wife Gwyn
7 June 1953 – 3 April 2018

# 1

# 'A matter of prolonged controversy in Scotland'

## INTRODUCTION

THIS BOOK IS ABOUT the part of the land in Scotland which is 'neither always wet, nor always dry due to the ebb and flow of the incoming and outgoing tide':[1] the foreshore. It is the part of the shore that is wholly covered by the sea at high tide and wholly uncovered at low tide, in each case by reference to ordinary spring tides.[2] The foreshore in Scotland is 19,509 kilometres in length and accounts for some 61 per cent of the total coastal length of Great Britain.[3] Under the modern law Scotland's foreshore is, in very simple terms, considered to have been originally owned by the Crown but it can be acquired by a grant from the Crown or other owner. The grant need not make express mention of the foreshore; it is sufficient if the foreshore is included within the boundaries of the grant, whether the boundaries are express or where the boundaries of the grant are explained by possession as including the foreshore. It can also be acquired by prescriptive possession. Whether in Crown or private ownership, the entire foreshore in Scotland is subject to public rights held inalienably by the Crown in trust for the public.[4]

[1] T. Bennion, M. Birdling and R. Paton, *Making Sense of the Foreshore & Seabed* (Wellington, 2004), p. 5.

[2] Fisherrow Harbour Commissioners v. Musselburgh Real Estate Co. Ltd (1905) 5 F 387; D. J. McGlashan, R. W. Duck and C. T. Reid, 'The foreshore: geographical implications of the three legal systems in Great Britain', *Area*, 3 (2004), pp. 338–47.

[3] The Highlands and Western Isles have 8,911 kilometres of foreshore (45.6 per cent of the Scottish coastline); Report of the Crown Estate Working Group, 2006, available at <http://www.orkney.gov.uk/Files/Council/Publications/2007/CERWG07MAR22.pdf> (last accessed 25 October 2017), p. 62. In England and Wales the extent of the foreshore is measured by reference to mean low and high water marks.

[4] J. Robbie, *Private Water Rights* (Edinburgh, 2015), paras 2.96, 2.97, 2.100–2.102, 3.40–3.41; K. G. C. Reid, *The Law of Property in Scotland* (Edinburgh,

It is said that today only around 50 per cent of the foreshore remains owned by the Crown, the remainder being in private hands.[5] Scotland's foreshore in Crown ownership has, since 1 April 2017, been managed by a body corporate appointed by the Scottish government.[6]

It may seem that the ownership and management of Scotland's foreshore is an unremarkable subject. But this is far from so: the ownership of the foreshore 'has been a matter of prolonged controversy in Scotland', a controversy in which the debate centred on whether the shore was owned by the Crown or by adjacent proprietors and on how, and by whom, Crown-owned foreshore should be managed.[7] The Crown owns the foreshore that is not in private ownership, in a representative or public capacity as head of state,[8] and so managing the foreshore in the public interest is a critical part of the management responsibility. This book looks at the controversy. It tells the story of the battle that took place during the nineteenth century and into the early twentieth century between the Crown and private proprietors over the ownership of the foreshore and, in particular, the role played by the Association of Seaboard Proprietors of Scotland; the modern law as to ownership of

1996), paras 314–16, 524–6; Parliamentary Papers [hereafter PP], 1911, XIV, Royal Commission on Coast Erosion and Afforestation [hereafter Royal Commission], vol. 3 (part 1), Cd 5708, para. 6. The public rights over the foreshore are considered in Chapter 9. In Orkney and Shetland owners of udal land have rights of ownership to the adjoining foreshore; M. Jones, 'Udal law', in M. A. Mulhern (ed.), *Scottish Life and Society: A Compendium of Scottish Ethnology. Vol. 13: The Law* (Edinburgh, 2012), p. 391.

[5] Crown Estate – A Consultation on the Long Term Management of the Crown Estate in Scotland, 2017, available at <http://www.gov.scot/Publications/2017/01/8661> (last accessed 25 October 2017), p. 7. How accurate this figure is remains, however, doubtful; see Chapter 6 and Robbie, *Private Water Rights*, para. 3.41. In evidence to the Scottish Affairs Committee it was accepted as 'possible that there are in relation to the foreshore third party ownership rights of which the Crown is not aware, which have arisen under the Prescription & Limitation (Scotland) Act 1973'; House of Commons Scottish Affairs Committee – The Crown Estate in Scotland – Seventh Report of Session 2010–12, HC 1117, Evidence 190). There has been a political commitment to complete Scotland's Land Register by 2024 and to register all public lands by 2019; it will be interesting to see how, without a detailed investigation of hundreds of titles and associated possession, this commitment can be met in relation to the foreshore. The expression 'private hands' can include local authorities.

[6] The Crown Estate Transfer Scheme 2017, SI 2017/524, as discussed in Chapter 9.

[7] Robbie, *Private Water Rights*, para. 3.14.

[8] Scottish Law Commission Discussion Paper on Law of the Foreshore and the Seabed, No. 113, April 2001 [hereafter SLC Discussion Paper], para. 3.2.

the foreshore was forged in the crucible of this battle. It shows the different motivations of the Crown and proprietors towards the ownership of land and the importance, for proprietors, of the 'sacred and inviolable' right of private property, and discusses the issues that arose concerning which body should manage the Crown-owned foreshore and how the responsibilities should best be carried out;[9] the potential for conflict between the public interest and financial considerations which may have to be taken into account is an important part of this discussion.

By the early years of the nineteenth century the view, indeed the assumption, had grown up that the foreshore was owned by the adjacent proprietors as a pertinent of their land, and that any interest of the Crown was simply to protect basic public rights to use the foreshore for navigation and commerce.[10] The extensive use of the foreshore by the adjacent landowners during the years that the kelp industry had played such an important part in the Highland economy played a significant part in the growth of this view, and the case law, such as it was, appeared to support it. The early relevant litigation had mostly been concerned with the right to collect seaware from the shores, and the cases are often unclear as to whether what was being fought over was ownership of the foreshore or the servitude of wreck and ware.[11] There is no suggestion of any challenge to this view by the Crown; the cases had been fought between proprietors without the involvement of the Crown.[12] Indeed, as the Lord Justice-Clerk, Lord Moncrieff, said in the Agnew case discussed in Chapter 5:

> Along the coasts of Scotland, especially in the west, the possession of the sea-shore by adjoining proprietors was, during the last century, practically universal. A large and lucrative manufacture – that of kelp – was carried on . . . The Crown never pretended right to interfere with the owners in this use

[9] As it had been described by David Hume (P. Stein, 'Law and society in eighteenth-century Scottish thought', in N. T. Phillipson and R. Mitchison (eds), *Scotland in the Age of Improvement* (Edinburgh, 1970), p. 155) and by the Duke of Richmond in 1876 (J. S. Blackie, *The Scottish Highlanders and the Land Laws* (London, 1885), p. 107). Issues as to the ownership and management of the foreshore are not, of course, solely of interest in a Scottish context; there is a valuable comparative law survey to be found in Appendix 2 of the SLC Discussion Paper.

[10] N. Whitty, 'Water law regimes – the foreshore', in K. Reid and R. Zimmerman (eds), *A History of Private Law in Scotland* (Oxford, 2000), vol. 1, p. 434; Reid, *Law of Property in Scotland*, para. 314.

[11] Robbie, *Private Water Rights*, para. 3.17.

[12] Robbie, *Private Water Rights*, paras 3.30, 3.17–3.21; J. Rankine, *A Treatise on the Rights and Burdens Incident to the Ownership of Lands and Other Heritages in Scotland* (4th edn, Edinburgh, 1909), pp. 257–61.

> of the shore, simply because it never had occurred to the Crown to be doubtful that the charter to the land included the shore also; and this accounts for the fact that . . . it seems to have been assumed that the Crown had, and could have, little interest in the matter, excepting as trustee for the public.[13]

In this introductory chapter we see how the historiography has reflected this view that the *ex adverso* proprietor owned the foreshore as a pertinent of their land. But as we shall see in Chapter 2 and in the succeeding chapters, this view came under challenge from the 1830s onwards when the Crown began to assert its rights to the ownership of the foreshore.

While the controversy over the ownership of the foreshore may have centred on the legal debate over whether the shore was owned by the Crown or private proprietors, it is important to appreciate that the battle over the ownership of the foreshore and rights to the seaware on it was more than just a legal dispute between the Crown and private proprietors, and was more than the case law. The protagonists were not just the proprietors and the Crown; the people who lived and worked on the land should be seen to be important players, and custom should be seen as an important component. And so in this introductory chapter we contrast the exercise of proprietorial rights in relation to the foreshore and seaware with the position in Gaelic Scotland, with the position of the foreshore as a place of customary land use, and seaware as a communal asset in the late eighteenth and nineteenth centuries. The contrast should be made to remind us when in later chapters (especially Chapter 7) we note the reactions of crofters and others who lived and worked on the land to the exercise of these proprietorial rights, that whatever the law might actually provide, there was historical justification for regarding the foreshore and seaware as belonging not to an individual proprietor or even the Crown, but to the community. Finally, we look at an intriguing exception to the view that the foreshore belonged to the *ex adverso* proprietor as a pertinent of their land, in the unlikely context of the disruption of the Church of Scotland in 1843.

## 'THE SHORES WERE PART OF HIS LAND'

The main contemporary sources that reflect the view that the foreshore was owned by the adjacent proprietors as a pertinent of their land appear to be works by Sir John Carr in 1809, John Macculloch in 1819 and B. Botfield in 1830. In a section describing the kelp business on the

[13] Agnew v. Lord Advocate (1873) 11 M 309 at p. 324.

island of Ulva, Carr says: 'in most cases, through the whole Highland properties, the landlords usually reserve the kelp to themselves, and it is in very few instances indeed that kelp is now let with the farm to the tenant'.[14] Macculloch, writing about North Uist, makes a similar comment when he says: 'In general, it may be remarked, that the kelp is reserved by the proprietor, and manufactured on his account; a very questionable piece of policy in some points of view.'[15] Botfield, in his description of the isle of Mull, says: 'the value of a kelp estate is regulated principally by the linear extent of the shores . . . Under the present system, the landlord usually reserves the kelp to himself.'[16] Now, in none of these examples is there an express statement as to the ownership of the foreshore but rather an indication that the *ex adverso* proprietor had, at the very least, complete control over the seaware on the foreshore. But the secondary works which draw on these and other sources include statements that refer to ownership of both the foreshore and the seaware found on it without any clear distinction between them. So, for example, Gray refers to the fact that 'it was by the ownership of the land that a few magnates were able to rivet their hold, not only on the produce, but also on the details of production', and 'The raw material . . . was, by legal construction, at the sole disposal of the proprietors of land', and the landlords 'are found letting *their* kelp shores'.[17] Other modern writers on the Highlands and islands have made similar statements. Hunter in his work on the creation of the crofting community says that 'landlords . . . stepped in and took over the industry, establishing legal rights to the seaweed on which it was based', and in more recent work he says: 'Seaweed, it was declared by landed proprietors and agreed by government, belonged to the owners of the coastline off which the seaweed grew.'[18] In his dissertation on the kelp industry, Thomson

[14] Sir J. Carr, *Caledonian Sketches on a Tour through Scotland in 1807* (London, 1809), p. 491.

[15] J. Macculloch, *A Description of the Western Islands of Scotland* (London, 1819), p. 121.

[16] B. Botfield, *Journal of a Tour through the Highlands of Scotland during the Summer of 1829* (Norton Hall, 1830), pp. 242–3.

[17] M. Gray, 'The kelp industry in the Highlands and islands', *The Economic History Review*, 4 (1951), p. 200 (emphasis added). Similar references are to be found in M. Gray, *The Highland Economy* (Edinburgh, 1957), pp. 124–41.

[18] J. Hunter, *The Making of the Crofting Community* (Edinburgh, 1976), p. 16; J. Hunter, *Last of the Free* (Edinburgh, 1999), p. 248. The same point about ownership of the seaware is made in A. J. Youngson, *After the Forty-Five* (Edinburgh, 1973), p. 136 and in D. S. Thomson (ed.), *The Companion to Gaelic Scotland* (Glasgow, 1994), p. 142 in the entry referring to kelp making.

quotes from Hunter as evidence of the establishment by landlords of the legal ownership of the seaweed.[19] Devine makes reference to the profits from the kelp industry accruing to the landlord 'simply because of his rights of ownership'.[20] Richards refers to the 'monopoly of the supply of' kelp, which the landlords had.[21] Macinnes draws attention to the feature of control: 'By reserving proprietary control over the manufacture and marketing of kelp, landlords in the islands made extortionate profits.'[22] A more specific reference to landlords assuming ownership of the foreshore is to be found in Duncan's work on the island of Scarp where, in speaking of the peak years of the kelp industry from 1748 to 1822, he says: 'In those days the landlord claimed the shore, as well as every reef and rocklet, and no seaweed could either be cut or gathered to manure the land. It all went in the kelp trench.'[23] There was no doubt in Bumsted's mind as to the issue. In his work on Highland emigration he states unequivocally:

> Moreover the landlord had ultimate control over the raw material. The shores were part of his land; he could either reserve the kelping rights to himself in his leases or fix the price of burnt kelp when setting lands to tenants.[24]

There are other examples to be found that show how the extensive use of the foreshore by adjacent landowners during the boom years of the kelp industry contributed to the view that the foreshore was owned by adjacent proprietors. The *Inverness Courier* wrote in 1822 that 'The proprietors of the Western Hebrides derived a large annual

[19] G. W. Thomson, 'A Hebridean industry: kelp manufacture in the Western Isles, c. 1760–1846' (MPhil thesis, University of Strathclyde, 1994).

[20] T. M. Devine, *Clanship to Crofters' War: The Social Transformation of the Scottish Highlands* (Manchester, 1994), p. 44; repeated in T. M. Devine, *The Scottish Nation, 1700–2000* (London, 1999), p. 186.

[21] E. Richards, *A History of the Highland Clearances* (London, 1982), vol. 1, p. 133. Richards says (in Richards, *Highland Clearances*, vol. 2 (London, 1985), p. 11) that Samuel Johnson 'was fully familiar with the sacred right of property' and quotes from Johnson: 'as any man may be said to give, what he gives the power of gaining, he has certainly as much right to profit from the price of kelp as of anything else found or raised upon *his* ground' (emphasis added).

[22] A. I. Macinnes, 'Scottish Gaeldom: the first phase of clearance', in T. M. Devine and R. Mitchison (eds), *People and Society in Scotland: Volume I 1760–1830* (Edinburgh, 1988), p. 85.

[23] A. Duncan (ed.), *Hebridean Island: Memories of Scarp* (East Linton, 1995), p. 12.

[24] J. M. Bumsted, *The People's Clearance: Highland Emigration to British North America 1770–1815* (Edinburgh, 1982), p. 43.

revenue from licensing their tenantry as kelp-burners, and the boast of one of them is still recollected that his shores were lined with a silver fringe.'[25] In their appeals to government for the continuation of the fiscal protection of the kelp industry in 1827, the kelp proprietors had claimed 'protection for the produce of our real estate'.[26] A further example may be found in the 1914 Scott Report on Home Industries in the Highlands and islands, which, in its discussion of the kelp industry, reported that 'The landowners rejoiced in "the golden fringe" of their estates.'[27]

The degree of control exercised by the estate proprietors over the seaware for the kelp industry was a feature in many of the examples discussed above, and the fact that the proprietors exercised such control may perhaps be taken as further evidence that the proprietors assumed that the foreshore belonged to them.[28] The granting of leases of the shores on which the seaware was found is the classic example of this control. Evidence of leases of the kelp shores abounds. In his note on the kelp industry in North Knapdale, Rymer refers to the shores being let to independent contractors in the late 1770s and that 'As the industry became increasingly important, the people bidding for the shores came from further afield and increased in number', and he gives a number of examples of the terms of such leases which clearly indicate an assumption of ownership on the part of the landlord.[29] The control exercised by estate proprietors over the kelp shores is also, as the following chapters

[25] J. Barron, *The Northern Highlands in the Nineteenth Century* (Inverness, 1903), vol. 1, p. 204.

[26] NRS, GD 46/17/74, Resolutions of the Kelp Proprietors, 12 December 1827.

[27] PP, 1914, XXXII, Report to the Board of Agriculture for Scotland on Home Industries in the Highlands and Islands, Cd 7654, p. 26. The words came after a statement about the profits of 'the owner of the kelp-shores'.

[28] The 5th Duke of Argyll was concerned in 1796 that the kelp shores of his estate had fallen outside his control and he determined 'to recover the property of my kelp shores'. This he proposed to do through issuing instructions to the tenants who did not have leases that all the kelp which they made was to be delivered to him and that all new leases should contain such a provision; see E. R. Cregeen (ed.), *Argyll Estate Instructions* (Edinburgh, 1964), pp. xxxiv, 185–7.

[29] L. Rymer, 'The kelp industry in North Knapdale', *Scottish Studies*, 18 (1974), p. 128. Rymer also draws attention to Samuel Johnson's remarks on the battle between Macdonald and Macleod for ownership of the rocks of Grianam (Lord Macdonald v. Norman Macleod (1781) 2 Pat App 583) and of how the growing importance of the value of kelp had led to litigation over ownership; see L. Rymer, 'The Scottish kelp industry', *Scottish Geographical Magazine*, 90:3 (1974), p. 143; A. Morrison, 'The Grianam case 1734–1781, the kelp industry and the clearances in Harris, 1811–1854', *The Transactions of the Gaelic Society of Inverness*, 52 (1980), pp. 20–89.

show, a significant element in the proof of the required degree of possession to establish a claim to title through possession and an important part of the story told by this book.

While in each of the above examples there are differences of emphasis, each seems to accept at least control by the proprietor of the shores of his estate and/or the seaware on those shores, and in some of them specifically ownership, but the crucial point is that in none of them is there any indication that the basis for this assumed ownership and control might have been questionable, and certainly there is no mention of any challenge by the Crown. The historiography, therefore, reflects the view that the foreshore was owned by the adjacent proprietor as a pertinent of his land, or at least does not question it. This, so far as commentaries before the mid-nineteenth century are concerned, is not surprising given that it was not until the 1830s that the Crown began, as we discuss in Chapter 2, to assert rights to the foreshore; until then the proprietors' claims to the foreshore and the seaware had not been challenged by the Crown. But what is perhaps surprising is that the facts and implications of the challenge by the Crown and the reactions of the proprietors to the challenge from the mid-nineteenth century onwards that form the subject of this book have been neither examined nor, in general, commented on since then. The bare facts are to be found in the work by the Scottish jurist, John Rankine, on the law of land ownership in Scotland where he mentions the existence of 'a Foreshore Association'.[30] And there are two brief but notable exceptions to the historiographical silence on the Crown's challenge: in his book on Canna, Campbell, in a footnote to a reference to the kelp industry on the island, says:

> Up to 1840 in Scotland the foreshore where the kelp was to be found was the property of the adjacent landowner, whereas in England it was the property of the Crown. In Scotland the rights of the proprietors to the foreshore were undermined by a decision of the House of Lords in that year, and since then Scottish law on the point has been assimilated by legal judgments to that in England.[31]

[30] Rankine, *Ownership of Lands* (4th edn), p. 274. The modern work of Niall Whitty mentions the organisation of a Foreshore Association; Whitty, 'Water law regimes', p. 434.

[31] J. L. Campbell, *Canna: The Story of a Hebridean Island* (Edinburgh, 1994), p. 154. While this is not a wholly accurate representation of the situation, as will be seen in Chapter 2 below, Campbell's footnote does at least draw the attention of the reader to the fact that there was a dispute over the ownership of the foreshore as between the Crown and private proprietors.

Canon R. C. Macleod in his comments on the kelp industry in his book on the Macleod muniments in Dunvegan wrote:

> The kelp, of course, was found upon the foreshore, i.e. the shore between the high and low water marks. It was a very fortunate thing for Highland proprietors that it never occurred to the Government to make claim to the foreshores of Scotland during the palmy days of the kelp industry.[32]

The kelp industry had played a significant part in the growth of the view that the proprietors owned the foreshore as a pertinent of their land. As Lord Moncrieff said in the Agnew case: 'the commercial manufacture of kelp was a direct assertion and enjoyment of the right of property in the shore which produced the sea-ware'.[33] As we shall see in subsequent chapters, especially in Chapter 8, it was also to play a significant part in the resolution of the battle that ensued between the Crown and private proprietors over ownership.[34]

## THE FORESHORE AND SEAWARE IN GAELIC SCOTLAND AND CUSTOM

While the sources of early Celtic law in Scotland are not easy to find, we are able to look to Celtic law in Ireland for an understanding of Celtic law in Scotland because 'There is every indication that the law of the Gaelic-speaking Scots . . . was similar to that of their compatriots in Ireland.'[35] The sources of Celtic law in Ireland are to be found in the Ancient Laws and Institutes of Ireland, commonly called the Brehon Laws. It would be wrong to believe that under the Brehon Laws there was no concept of private property; indeed, 'early Irish society clearly attached great importance to the principle of the private ownership of property'.[36] So far as the foreshore was concerned, it appears that

[32] Canon R. C. Macleod, *The Book of Dunvegan* (Aberdeen, 1939), vol. 2, p. 116.

[33] Agnew v. Lord Advocate (1873) 11 M 309, p. 325.

[34] See also the examples given in J. MacAskill, '"A silver fringe?" The Crown, private proprietors and the Scottish kelp shores and the Scottish foreshore generally, c. 1800–c. 1940' (PhD thesis, University of Aberdeen, 2003), ch. 9, especially pp. 250–2.

[35] M. C. Meston, W. D. H. Sellar and Lord Cooper (eds), *The Scottish Legal Tradition* (Edinburgh, 1991), p. 32; J. Cameron, *Celtic Law* (Edinburgh, 1937), p. 168; J. Hunter, *On the Other Side of Sorrow* (Edinburgh, 1995), p. 59.

[36] F. Kelly, *A Guide to Early Irish Law* (Dublin, 1988), p. 105. But William Skene, in his work on Celtic Scotland, took a somewhat different view as to the early existence of the private ownership of property. He thought it was 'tolerably certain

privately owned grazing rights on the foreshore were recognised by the Brehon Laws but that 'In general there seems to be a common right to the seaweed cast up on the shore, though one text refers to privately owned seaweed.'[37] The importance of seaware to the life of the agrarian economy of Celtic Ireland and Gaelic Scotland and the customary right of gathering and collecting seaware was reflected in this provision of the Brehon Laws.[38] As to anything else cast up by the sea on the shore, the Brehon Laws provided that it belonged to the owner of the shore.[39] This communal right to seaware was later reflected in Scotland in how the land was worked on the old run rig system. Fenton suggests that these communal rights and, in particular, the division of seaware on the shores amongst different communities were 'obscured and modified' by 'the great emphasis of kelp burning in the late eighteenth – early nineteenth centuries',[40] and that the recommendations of the Napier Commission on, and the provisions of the Crofters Holdings (Scotland) Act 1886 as to, crofters' rights to seaweed might be viewed as an attempt to return to this customary position.[41] When Charles Fraser Mackintosh MP attempted in 1891 to introduce legislation which would provide for free public access to the foreshore for the collection of seaware (as we discuss in Chapter 7), he was simply attempting to take the position back to what had existed from the time of Gaelic Scotland.

Neeson has examined the place of custom in the use of the Scottish

. . . that private property in lands did not exist at first, but emerged from a right of common property vested in the community'; W. F. Skene, *Celtic Scotland: A History of Ancient Alban. Volume III: Land and People* (Edinburgh, 1880), p. 137. For a discussion of the private/communal property argument, see E. MacNeill, *Celtic Ireland* (Dublin, 1921), pp. 144–51.

[37] Kelly, *Guide to Early Irish Law*, p. 107; F. Kelly, *Early Irish Farming* (Dublin, 1997), p. 305. As to the reference to privately owned seaweed, Kelly draws attention to the fact that it is not clear whether such ownership is permanent or temporary; see Kelly, *Guide to Early Irish Law*, p. 107, n. 51.

[38] See T. P. O'Neill, 'Some Irish techniques of collecting seaweed', *Folk Life*, 8 (1970), p. 15 where O'Neill also says: 'The sea wrack of every strand was regarded by the ancient laws of Ireland as the inherent right of every territory and was the property of every person.'

[39] Kelly, *Guide to Early Irish Law*, p. 108, n. 55.

[40] A. Fenton, *The Shape of the Past 2: Essays in Scottish Ethnology* (Edinburgh, 1986), pp. 74–5.

[41] For the Napier Commission recommendations, see PP, 1884, XXXII–XXXVI, Report of Her Majesty's Commissioners of Inquiry into the condition of the crofters and cottars in the Highlands and Islands of Scotland [hereafter Napier Report], vol. XXXII, pp. 22–3, and Chapter 7 below.

foreshore.[42] The legal writers have largely neglected the role of custom in describing the entitlement to seaware in Scotland.[43] But while this may suggest that custom has little place in a history of the ownership of the Scottish foreshore, the practice (which, of course, is part of custom) of those who lived and worked on the land would suggest otherwise, and one has only to turn to the Napier Report to find considerable testimony as to what the crofters believed was their customary right to the use of common pasture, heather, peat and seaware.[44] The idea of a customary or communal right to seaware is really only a specific example of the ideological belief which the Gaelic word *duthchas* describes: '[a] collective heritage of a holding, in which it was believed that any holding or plot, having been held and continuously worked by a family group over four generations, belonged by customary right to those tenants'.[45] It was the notion that legitimised the belief of crofters and cottars that they had a right to use and occupy land and which, as an ideology, lay behind their nineteenth-century protests against land shortage.[46] Put more simply, it was the belief that 'Whatever be the legal theory [the crofters] feel [the land] to be their own.'[47] There is a letter in the files of the Board of Agriculture for Scotland (BoAS) that gives a fascinating insight into the belief of crofters in their customary rights to seaware; the writer of the letter said he was

> astonished to learn that the Board of Trade were now claiming as their property all the seaweed on the foreshores of [the Hebrides] and that no person could carry away or use the same without their consent . . . Any interference with what the people undoubtedly consider their rights in this matter will be strongly resented. So far, the impression I formed was that the people do

[42] J. M. Neeson, 'Coastal commons: custom and the use of seaweed in the British Isles, 1700–1900', in S. Cavaciocchi (ed.), *Ricchezza del Mare, Ricchezza dal Mare Secc. XIII–XVIII. Atti della 'Trentasettesima di Studi', Istituto Internazionale di Storia Economica 'F. Datini', Prato, 11–15 aprile 2005* (Florence, 2006).

[43] When the history and importance of gathering seaware for the crofting community was, as we discuss in Chapters 7 and 9, examined in 2001 by the Scottish Law Commission (SLC), the SLC did not appear to give any recognition of, or to mention, any of the customary communal rights to seaware; SLC Discussion Paper, paras 6.6–6.24.

[44] There are further discussions of rights to seaware in Chapters 6–9.

[45] C. J. Withers, *Urban Highlanders: Highland–Lowland Migration and Urban Gaelic Culture 1700–1900* (East Linton, 1998), p. 54.

[46] C. J. Withers, '"Give us land and plenty of it": the ideological basis for land and ownership in the Scottish Highlands', *Landscape History*, 12 (1990), pp. 49–51.

[47] PP, 1953/54, VIII, Report of the Commission of Enquiry into Crofting Conditions, Cmd 9091.

> not regard the action of the Board of Trade as one worthy of their serious consideration. They would regard an order to prohibit them from breathing as being much in the same category.[48]

The importance of seaware to the crofting community and the conflicts that were created by the insistence of landlords in asserting their rights to it are vividly brought out in the 2015 novel set in the 1860s, *His Bloody Project*.[49] Neeson says that while crofters may have known what the landlords believed to be the legal position as to seaware, this did not destroy the crofters' view that their practice over generations had given them a customary right to it and crofters did not concede, at least in their own minds, the ownership of it to anyone else: 'Crofters believed the seaweed . . . belonged to them long after landlords had captured [this commodity] and impoverished or even evicted [its] users, and long after the decision of the court in Macalister v. Campbell.' As Neeson puts it, 'The law of the foreshore [the crofters] obeyed as a matter of course . . . may have been their own.'[50] But crofters' memories of former uses and their insistence on continued use were pitted against what Neeson describes as the superior economic and police power of landlords. It was never likely that this custom would be anything other than remaining unwritten, as the crofters would have neither the incentive nor the ability to try a custom in court. Despite this, the evidence of practice

> suggests that crofters retained some access to common shores, and, where that was insufficient, met their needs by buying or taking seaweed as they could. This practice and the ritual recorded in their stories suggest that they regarded the foreshore as theirs.[51]

The huge irony is that while the crofters may have regarded the foreshore and seaware as theirs, this book shows that their use of the foreshore and their collection of seaware actually had the effect in law of helping in many instances to secure the title to the foreshore to the *ex adverso*

[48] NRS, AF 70/444, Letter MacDonald to Mackinnon, 9 March 1925. For the Board of Trade's practice that is referred to in the letter, see Parliamentary Debates [hereafter PD], Fifth Series, vol. 181, House of Commons, cols 1099–100 (10 March 1925).

[49] G. M. Burnet, *His Bloody Project* (Glasgow, 2015), pp. 72–81, 214–16.

[50] Neeson, 'Coastal commons', pp. 361, 364. The decision of the court in Macalister v. Campbell (1837) 15 S 490 was followed in Paterson v. Marquis of Ailsa (1846) 8 D 752 and Lord Saltoun v. Park (1857) 20 D 89 which affirmed that there was no public right to collect seaware on the foreshore; see further in Chapter 9.

[51] Neeson, 'Coastal commons', p. 367.

proprietor. While, as this book shows, the crofters may have played an unwitting role in the battle over ownership of the foreshore, it is important to appreciate that the crofters were not, in this sense, the unwilling cause of their own misfortune, but rather actors in their own defence.

## THE PREACHERS ON THE SHORE

One of the consequences of the disruption of the Church of Scotland in 1843 was the problem which the new Free Church ministers found in being able to secure sites for their churches, in particular coming up against the obstacle of estate proprietors whose support for the established Church of Scotland resulted, in many cases, in their refusing a site on their estates for the Free Church. The Free Church ministers thus had to resort to a number of different, and enterprising, tactics, the floating church of Loch Sunart being the most notable.[52] Open-air services of the Free Church were frequent and some of them were held on the foreshore. Holding the services here would, clearly, have presented the minister and his congregation with the obvious problem of the rising tide, but the reason for holding services in such a seemingly impractical and inhospitable place was that this was the one place to which the hostile proprietor could not, it was thought, object. It was the place 'where his writ could not run'.[53] It seems reasonably clear from the examples we have of services being held below the high water mark that the minister and his congregation felt they were outwith the jurisdiction of the estate proprietor who was hostile to their services, thus running counter to the view that the *ex adverso* proprietor owned the foreshore as a pertinent of his estate. In his reminiscences of his life in the Highlands, Joseph Mitchell recalled a conversation he had with Mr Gunn, the Sutherland estate factor, over the instructions Gunn had received from James Loch as to how the estate was to deal with the Free Church ministers. Mitchell suggested to Gunn that the Duke of Sutherland should provide facilities for the ministers and their congregations: '"No" said Mr Gunn, "the recusants shall not have an inch of land in the County to build either house or church."' Mitchell continued, 'meetings for worship were consequently forbidden on any part of the Duke's territories. What was the result? On the road sides and on the sea beach between high and low

[52] See L. A. Ritchie, 'The floating church of Loch Sunart', *Records of the Scottish Church History Society*, 22 (1985), pp. 159–73.

[53] J. Macleod, *No Great Mischief if you Fall: The Highland Experience* (Edinburgh, 1993), p. 56.

water mark, the Free Church clergy held worship and preached to the people.'[54] At Kilmallie, the minister was excluded by interdict from the churchyard and reported, no doubt with a fine sense of irony given the close proximity of a statue of Cameron of Lochiel, the proprietor who had excluded them from the churchyard, that 'we took up our next position on a little green spot upon the seashore, within high water mark . . . opposite the monument of Colonel John Cameron'.[55] At Torosay on the isle of Mull the proprietor refused a site for the Free Church, and the minister and his congregation were 'driven to shift as best they could [and] met ordinarily for worship in a gravel pit which during spring tides was under high water mark'. The exigencies of services on the foreshore are brought starkly into focus by the account of services at Torosay:

> For sometimes the tide rose so high during worship that preacher and people had not only to quit the tent but the gravel pit as well, and thus continue the service, in spite of all restrictions above high water mark.[56]

We do, however, have one example of an *ex adverso* proprietor objecting to the erection of a church on the foreshore. The Free Church had applied to the Office of Woods and Forests for a Crown grant for a church site on the foreshore at Lerwick in Shetland. The proprietor, John Scott, objected on the ground that he had the title to the relevant piece of foreshore. The Solicitor to the Office of Woods advised that the ownership was uncertain and the proposed grant to the Free Church was not proceeded with.[57]

It was not only the fledgling Free Church ministers who took refuge on the foreshore. The Baptists were also forced, in certain cases, to worship in the open air. The Baptists of the Ross of Mull were driven out of their first meeting-house in around 1830. In his article about them, Meek draws attention to the significance of the fact that they had to worship on the shoreline: '[it] implies that they were apparently meeting below the high water mark, most probably because they were banned from

[54] J. Mitchell, *Reminiscences of my Life in the Highlands (1884)* (London, 1884), vol. II, pp. 97–8.

[55] The Rev. T. Brown, *Annals of the Disruption* (Edinburgh, 1884), p. 238.

[56] Brown, *Annals of the Disruption*, pp. 424–5; see also D. Ansdell, *The People of the Great Faith: The Highland Church 1690–1900* (Stornoway, 1998), p. 80; J. Hunter, 'The emergence of the crofting community: the religious contribution 1789–1843', *Scottish Studies*, 18 (1974), p. 110.

[57] NRS, CR 11/559, Letter Horne to the Office of Woods, 29 April 1848. This was, of course, an issue subject to udal law.

the land by their feudal superior, the Duke of Argyll'.[58] But perhaps the most fascinating of accounts of ministers preaching from the supposed safety of the foreshore is that concerning the Baptist preacher the Reverend Donald McArthur. The account of how, in 1805, McArthur was press-ganged into the Navy, released and won a case in the Court of Session against the landlord Colonel Campbell of Southall is told by Meek[59] but the significance of the case for this book lies in the fact that because Campbell refused permission to McArthur to preach on his estate, McArthur took his service on the foreshore below the high water mark and it was from here he was seized by Campbell's men and handed over to the press gang. The interesting point for us is that while Campbell had prohibited McArthur from preaching on his estate, it seems to have been accepted by the Court of Session that this prohibition did not extend to the foreshore. It would also appear that Campbell might not, indeed, have considered that the foreshore formed part of his estate as a matter of law, because his successors, in 1866, approached the Office of Woods with a request to purchase the title to the foreshore from the Crown.[60]

The question whether the public right to use the foreshore for recreation might have extended to the holding of church services on the foreshore is discussed in Chapter 9.

## THE STRUCTURE OF THE BOOK

Chapter 2 considers how the increased interest on the part of the Crown in asserting its rights in the foreshore from the 1830s and the manner in which the Office of Woods exercised its management responsibilities for the foreshore clashed with the assumption of the seaboard proprietors that they owned the foreshore and that any interest of the Crown was limited to protecting public rights to use the foreshore. This led to the formation in 1861 of the Association of Seaboard Proprietors in Scotland whose objective was to have it settled, by the courts or legislation, that private proprietors had the absolute property in the foreshores *ex adverso* of their estates. The chapter looks at how, in the period up

[58] D. E. Meek, 'The Baptists of the Ross of Mull: evangelical experience and social change in a West Highland community', *Northern Studies*, 26 (1989), p. 31.

[59] In D. E. Meek, 'The preacher, the press-gang and the landlord: the impressment and vindication of the Rev. Donald McArthur', *Records of the Scottish Church History Society*, 35 (part 2) (1994), p. 256.

[60] W. Buchanan, *Reports of Certain Remarkable Cases in the Court of Session* (Edinburgh, 1813), p. 62; NRS, CR 11/127, Letter Crawford & Simson to Office of Woods, 8 January 1866.

to the end of 1866, the Association crossed swords with the Office of Woods, at the leadership of the Association by Norman Macleod of Macleod and George Loch QC and at the work of its law agents Skene & Peacock. It considers the legal advice given to, and cases taken by, the Association, and the motivations of the proprietors to become members of the Association.

The antagonism that had developed by the end of 1866 between the Association and the Office of Woods led to the transfer, by the Crown Lands Act 1866, of the responsibility for the management of the foreshore from the Office of Woods to the Board of Trade. Chapter 3 examines the reasons behind the transfer and its implications, and explores the way in which the final form of the Crown Lands Act was largely influenced by the Association and its law agents Skene & Peacock, leaving a legacy that would be relevant to the issue of how, and by whom, Scotland's foreshore should be managed, into the twentieth century and, indeed, in the context of the 2017 devolution of the management of Scotland's foreshore to the Scottish Parliament. It also explores the important memorandum produced in 1866 by the permanent secretary to the Board as to how the Board should exercise its responsibilities for the foreshore, with particular reference to the public interest; a memorandum that was still being referred to in 1958 as providing 'excellent guidance'.

Chapter 4 considers the important contributions that the 8th Duke of Argyll made to the debate during the 1860s over the ownership of the foreshore. The chapter looks at how the Office of Woods challenged the duke's ownership of the foreshore of his estate at Rosneath while it still had management responsibilities for the foreshore, and at the extensive correspondence the duke had with the Treasury about the conduct of the Office of Woods, and his criticism of the Board of Trade memorandum discussed in Chapter 3.

Chapter 5 looks at the actions of the Association and the attitudes and actions of the Board of Trade towards the Association in pressing the Crown's claim to the foreshore from the beginning of 1867 that culminated with the landmark Agnew case in 1873 which finally decided the issue as to ownership of the foreshore as between the Crown and private proprietors. It looks at the very important 1868 legal opinion of the Law Officers of Scotland and England over the ownership of the foreshore, discusses the negotiations that took place between the Crown and the proprietors over legislation that the proprietors proposed should affirm their assumed title to the foreshore, and examines the deliberations of the Crown lawyers and officials over the Agnew case.

With the resolution of the basic issue over whether the foreshore was owned by the Crown or the adjacent proprietors decided in the Agnew case, Chapter 6 sees the focus after 1873 passing to the important role of possession of the foreshore to establish title as against the Crown. The chapter examines the Crown's attempts during the first forty-five years or so of the twentieth century to alter the law as to how prescriptive possession of the foreshore would establish title as against the Crown, starting with the recommendations of the Royal Commission on Coast Erosion in 1911. The rise and fall of the various legislative proposals and the opinions of the Law Officers are considered in detail.

Chapter 7 examines the debate over the provisions as to seaware in the Crofters Holdings (Scotland) Act 1886, and Charles Fraser Mackintosh MP's Sea Ware (Crofting Counties, Scotland) Bill 1891, and whether crofters, and the public, should be given legislative rights to seaware and access to the foreshore. The reaction of the proprietors and the Association of Seaboard Proprietors of Scotland and their law agents Skene Edwards & Garson (the name by which the firm Skene & Peacock was by then known) to this further threat to the proprietors' sacred right of property and their economic interest in the foreshore is also examined.

Chapter 8 tells the story of the dispute between the Crown and the 9th Duke of Argyll over the Tiree foreshore at the beginning of the twentieth century. The eventual success of the duke in establishing title to the Tiree foreshore derived predominantly from the fact that the crofters and cottars had collected drift seaware for the manufacture of kelp and that the duke and his predecessors had purported to regulate this activity. The chapter provides a detailed case study, indeed a blow-by-blow account, of how the Crown's representatives went about considering a foreshore claim in the aftermath of the Agnew decision. The Tiree case study is an important example of the significance of the kelp industry to, and of the role played by crofters and cottars in, the battle for the ownership of the foreshore.

Chapter 9 traces the evolution of the shifting departmental responsibility for the management of Scotland's Crown foreshore between 1832 and 1961 and then looks at the devolution of its management provided for in the Scotland Act 2016. The Chapter concludes with a discussion of the Scottish Law Commission's proposals in 2003 for changes in the law of the foreshore relating to public rights and to crofters' rights to seaweed.

# 2

# 'Illegal encroachments of the Crown on the rights of proprietors'

## INTRODUCTION

As we saw in Chapter 1, by the early years of the nineteenth century the view, indeed the assumption, had grown up that the foreshore was owned by the adjacent proprietors as a pertinent of their land, and that it had never occurred to the Crown to doubt that the charter to the land included the foreshore. But this position was to change; after years during which the subject had 'scarcely been stirred' it had 'of late years sprung into life again'.[1] In 1829 all the possessions and land revenues of the Crown in England and Ireland, including the foreshore, were put under the management of the Commissioners of Woods by the Crown Lands Act 1829. In 1833 the management and control of all the possessions and land revenues of the Crown in Scotland, including the foreshore, were transferred by a Treasury warrant under the authority of the Crown Lands (Scotland) Act 1832 from the Barons of His Majesty's Court of Exchequer in Scotland to the Commissioners of Woods in London, and a further Act passed in 1833 gave to the Commissioners the same management powers with regard to land revenues and possessions in Scotland as they had in England, and all the provisions of the 1829 Act were extended to Scotland.[2] It is, perhaps, a statement of the obvious that the transfer of management responsibility for the Crown foreshore did not change its ownership: it remained vested in the Crown and not in the body responsible for its management but, in

[1] Anon., 'Title of the Crown to the seashore', *The Law Magazine and Law Review*, 6 (November 1858–February 1859), pp. 99–100.

[2] The Crown Lands (Scotland) Act 1833; see further in Chapter 9. The Board of Admiralty retained responsibility for protecting the public right of navigation over the foreshore and in 1862 this responsibility was passed to the Board of Trade under the Harbours Transfer Act 1862. In this book the Commissioners of Woods are also referred to as the Office of Woods or the Office of Woods and Forests.

the light of some comments made in 2009 that suggested otherwise, it is a statement that is worth emphasising.[3] The Acts of 1829, 1832 and 1833, then, were concerned with the management of the foreshore and not its ownership;[4] but they had implications for ownership. In his work on the history of the foreshore, Moore says that after the passing of the 1829 Act 'the Commissioners . . . began actively to raise the claims of the Crown to foreshore which had practically laid dormant for upwards of a century',[5] and Marston says in his work on the practice of the legislature, executive and judiciary concerning the bed of the sea adjacent to the dry land of the United Kingdom:

> Although it made no specific mention of the Crown's claim to the ownership of maritime territory, [the passing of the 1829 Act] marked the beginning of a sustained effort by the Crown to assert the rights which it claimed to the foreshore and the bed of the sea.[6]

Marston also draws attention to the fact that just one year after the 1829 Act was passed, Robert Hall published his essay on the rights of the Crown in the seashores, which supported the Crown's claims in vigorous terms.[7]

The increased interest on the part of the Crown in asserting its rights in the foreshore was based on the underlying understanding on the part of the Crown, and in particular the Office of Woods, that the Crown's rights in the foreshore extended well beyond merely a right as trustee for the public; this understanding was, of course, diametrically different to the assumption of the *ex adverso* proprietors discussed in Chapter 1 that they owned the foreshore as a pertinent of their estates, and that if the Crown did have any rights in the foreshore, they were limited to protecting public rights to use the foreshore for navigation and commerce.

The position as to ownership of the foreshore in Scotland was not, however, quite as clear as the Crown and the proprietors may have assumed. Robbie has very helpfully summarised the four possible

[3] See the discussion in A. Wightman, *The Poor Had No Lawyers* (Edinburgh, 2010), pp. 138–53.

[4] As were the Crown Lands Act 1866, discussed in Chapter 3; and the Crown Lands Act 1927, the Coast Protection Act 1949 and the Crown Estate Act 1961, discussed in Chapter 9.

[5] S. A. Moore, *A History of the Foreshore and the Law Relating Thereto* (London, 1888), p. 461.

[6] G. Marston, *The Marginal Seabed: United Kingdom Legal Practice* (Oxford, 1981), p. 22.

[7] Marston, *Marginal Seabed*, p. 22; R. Hall, *Rights of the Crown and the Privileges of the Subject in the Sea-shores of the Realm* (n.p., 1830).

situations regarding the status of the Scottish foreshore that the works of the institutional writers and decisions of the courts revealed.[8] First, the foreshore was *inter regalia majora* as to trusteeship for public rights and possibly also *inter regalia minora* as to ownership and so would require an express grant to transfer it to private persons; this was Erskine's view. Second, it was *inter regalia majora* as to the trusteeship for public rights but was not *inter regalia minora* as to ownership but carried as a part and pertinent with a grant of the adjacent lands; this was Bell's view but it was one that he developed over the various editions of his book. Third, the foreshore was *inter regalia minora* as to ownership but with continuing obligations on the transferee in respect of public rights; transfer required either an express grant, an appropriate bounding description or a *habile* title with possession for the appropriate prescriptive period.[9] Fourth, the foreshore was not *inter regalia* in any sense and it was carried as part and pertinent of adjacent lands but the owner could not interfere with public rights; this was the view that appeared to be supported by the case law and, as we saw in Chapter 1, is the view reflected in the historiography.[10]

It was against this confused backdrop that in 1840 the Crown took the positive steps of asserting ownership of the foreshore in Scotland which were to lead to concerted protests on behalf of the private proprietors, to the formation of the Association and, finally, to clarification of the prolonged controversy as to the ownership of Scotland's foreshore.[11] The battle lines were drawn.

[8] Robbie, *Private Water Rights*, para. 3.28.

[9] This was Hume's view. Robbie points out that when the foreshore issue was finally decided in the Agnew case discussed in Chapter 5, the outcome was very similar to Hume's analysis of the requirements of possession, and that one of the judges, Lord Cowan, mentioned that he had been a student of Hume; Robbie, *Private Water Rights*, para. 3.39.

[10] E.g. Innes v. Downie (1807) Hume 552 (Robbie suggests that the Lord President's decision in this case may have had an economic agenda to help the kelp proprietors at a time when the kelp industry had reached its zenith; Robbie, *Private Water Rights*, para. 3.24); Whitty, 'Water law regimes', p. 434.

[11] There was considerable resistance in other parts of the UK to the Crown's attempts to assert its rights over the foreshore. In Wales there was resistance from several landowners but the opposition did not lead to consolidated action comparable to the Association; H. Pryce and G. Owen, 'Medieval Welsh law and the mid-Victorian foreshore', *The Journal of Legal History*, 35:2 (2014), pp. 172–99.

## THE ORIGINS OF THE ASSOCIATION OF SEABOARD PROPRIETORS OF SCOTLAND

The Clyde Navigation Trustees had, from time to time, narrowed the channel of the River Clyde to obtain a greater depth of water. Undertaking these operations resulted in a large part of the channel being reclaimed as dry land and the question arose for the first time as to who owned the reclaimed *alveus*. A proprietor, Mr Todd, raised the question by bringing an action against the Clyde Navigation Trustees in the Court of Session to have it declared that the reclaimed *alveus* belonged to him. The court decided against Todd, basing its decision on the particular wording of the Clyde Navigation Acts. Todd appealed to the House of Lords where he was again unsuccessful.[12] The significance of the case lies in the fact that the Office of Woods had their attention drawn through the court proceedings to the valuable ground which had been acquired through the reclamation and the Office of Woods secured the inclusion in the Clyde Act of 1840 of a clause which preserved the rights of the Crown in the *alveus* of the Clyde. On the Act being passed the Office of Woods claimed from the Clyde Trustees all the ground reclaimed. This claim was settled out of court, but in 1852 the effect of the clause in the 1840 Act was finally determined by the courts and although the decision turned on the particular provisions of the Act, both the Court of Session and the House of Lords stated that the *alveus* or bed and soil of all navigable rivers belonged to the Crown.[13]

The increased interest on the part of the Crown in asserting its rights to these hitherto marginal areas of property was accompanied by a new deference in the courts.[14] The River Clyde cases were followed by two cases, which were argued and decided by the Court of Session consecutively in 1846, in which the court said that the Crown had a full patrimonial interest in the foreshore and that an express grant was required to transfer ownership, suggesting, although this was not expressed, that the foreshore was *inter regalia* as to ownership.[15] Robbie

[12] Todd v. Clyde Trustees (1840) 2 D 357, aff'd (1841) 2 Rob 333.

[13] Lord Advocate v. Hamilton (1852) 1 Macq. 46.

[14] For possible reasons for the Crown becoming more active in the assertion of its rights, see Robbie, *Private Water Rights*, para. 3.32.

[15] Officers of State v. Smith (1846) 8 D 711; aff'd (1849) 6 Bell's App 487; Paterson v. Marquis of Ailsa (1846) 8 D 752. In both these cases Robert Hall's powerful 1830 essay referred to above was cited by counsel in support of the view that the Crown had a full patrimonial interest in the foreshore; Robbie, *Private Water Rights*, para. 3.35.

says that the *dicta* in these two cases largely contradicted both the trends in previous case law and also the beliefs held by adjacent proprietors and that the result was even more confusion and uncertainty.[16] The Office of Woods began to extend the Crown's claims to the foreshore in Scotland in various ways and to a degree which was said seriously to compromise the interests of the *ex adverso* private proprietors:

> They not only in some cases deny the rights of proprietors to the foreshores of their estates, but they are understood to assert their power to grant the foreshores to any third party, and for any purpose, which might even lead to the exclusion of a sea-side proprietor and the public from access to the sea, as well as to their deprivation of the 'fruits of the shore' . . . such as sand, gravel, stones, shells, sea weed etc.[17]

The claims of the Office of Woods were thought to derive strength from the fact that a number of proprietors, although denying the claims of the Crown, had taken leases and charters of the foreshore from the Crown for the erection, for example, of piers, in order to avoid the expense and uncertainty of litigation against the Crown.[18] The actions of the Office of Woods had prompted Mr Augustus Smith MP to raise the issue in the House of Commons on a number of occasions, including a request in April 1860 for a select committee of the House of Commons to be set up

> to inquire into the rights of the Crown as connected with the Foreshores, Tidal Rivers, and Bed of the Sea round the Coasts of the United Kingdom, and the manner in which the Commissioners of Woods and Forests are dealing with the same.[19]

A motion for such an inquiry by a select committee into the rights of the Crown was very unusual, and was rejected by the House. However, Smith tried again in April 1861 and was supported by Alexander Finlay, the Member of Parliament for Argyllshire.[20] Finlay said that the question

[16] Robbie, *Private Water Rights*, paras 3.33–3.35. Robbie suggests (para. 3.35) that it is difficult to explain the change of view in the courts shown by these decisions other than as a reaction to the increased assertiveness on the part of the Crown.

[17] DVGN 551/3 and TNA:PRO, MT 10/139, Memorial for a Committee of Proprietors of Estates in Scotland whose lands are bounded by the sea, for the opinion of counsel, 4 November 1862 [hereafter 1862 Memorial].

[18] DVGN 551/3, 1862 Memorial, p. 6.

[19] TNA:PRO, CRES 36/4, Memorandum, March 1860; PD, Third Series, vol. 158, House of Commons, cols 25–37 (24 April 1860).

[20] Finlay was the Member of Parliament for Argyll from April 1857 until 1868 and was a Commissioner of Supply for the County of Argyll and held the influential

of the claims of the Crown to the foreshore 'was exciting in Scotland a very great deal of dissatisfaction and especially in the County he had the honour to represent . . . [where] . . . its inhabitants naturally feel very keenly the evils arising from the unjust interference from the Crown'. This further attempt to have a select committee appointed was also rejected. The Attorney General was singularly dismissive of the attempt and critical of the motives of those who were seeking to have the issue examined: 'There was nothing to complain of in the conduct of the Commissioners, except from some disappointed persons, who thought they might make great gains from the foreshores if the Crown did not vindicate its rights.' And he gave a warning to the barrack room lawyers in the House: 'persons who read works of law without, in the first instance, obtaining a clear apprehension of the meaning of the words were apt to be led away by their own crude conceptions from the true nature of the propositions laid down in such volumes.'[21]

While parliamentary efforts to have the issue of Crown rights to the foreshore investigated were not making any progress, the proprietors were beginning to take concerted action at the local county level, and it was the confrontation between the Commissioners of Supply and the Road Trustees of Argyllshire (the Argyll Commissioners) and the Office of Woods in 1860 which proved the catalyst for the formation of the Association of Seaboard Proprietors of Scotland.[22] The fact that the Argyll Commissioners took up the issue of Crown rights in the foreshore was an important development because it was the beginning of a concerted and organised effort by the Scottish proprietors to assert what they believed were their rights.

The Argyll Commissioners had, for some years, had their attention drawn to the fact that expensive damage to sea walls had been caused by gravel, sand or rock being taken from the foreshore by various parties and they had tried, in a number of instances, to stop this with the help

position of Convener. As we shall see, he also became a member of the committee of the Association.

21 PD, Third Series, vol. 162, House of Commons, cols 644–66 (16 April 1861). Sir Thomas Riddell of Ardnamurchan applauded Finlay's contribution to this debate. In a letter to Finlay after the debate, he said: 'Allow me to take this opportunity of thanking you for your speech the other night in the House, on the subject of the attacks made by the Crown on the rights of Proprietors of the foreshores'; DVGN 570/1/3, Letter Riddell to Finlay, 20 April 1861.

22 The Commissioners of Supply have been described as 'the chief organ of the politicized Scottish landowners'; A. E. Whetstone, *Scottish County Government in the Eighteenth and Nineteenth Centuries* (Edinburgh, 1981), p. 89.

of the *ex adverso* proprietors. They had, however, found difficulty in obtaining damages or an interdict in such cases after the alleged publication in Dunoon and Kilmuir of a handbill with a letter from the Office of Woods which apparently gave a licence permitting the extraction of gravel and asserting the right of the Crown to the foreshore. It seems the publication of the handbill and letter had encouraged the general public into believing that there was a public right to take sand and gravel from the foreshore and this had, in the view of the Argyll Commissioners, led to considerable depredations of the foreshore.[23]

The result of this was the presentation by Alexander Finlay MP, Colonel Malcolm of Poltalloch and a Colonel Campbell of a memorial from the Argyll Commissioners to the Office of Woods. The memorial stated:

> Government officials in Scotland have recently claimed a right of property to the whole shores of the Country up to the usual high water mark, and are attempting to establish this right in a sense, and to an extent, which the Memorialists believe to be unprecedented and illegal by granting titles to individuals which your Memorialists have reason to believe are contrary to the usage and law of Scotland and which are very prejudicial to the public interests which as Road Trustees they are bound to protect.[24]

Finlay wanted the Commissioner of the Office of Woods, James Howard, to be in no doubt as to the seriousness with which the Argyll Commissioners viewed the situation. He said that he was to be accompanied to the Office of Woods when he presented the memorial by: 'one or two other Members of Parliament who have taken a deep interest in this question' and he wanted to know from the Office of Woods 'whether it is their intention to persevere in the vexatious and hazardous course which has of late years been adopted'.[25] The 1860 Memorial is important because it is the first formal statement on behalf of private proprietors that makes clear the extent of their claim to absolute ownership of the foreshore. It stated that the Argyll Commissioners understood that under Scots Law proprietors had a right to the seashore *ex adverso* of their estates, subject only to a right held by the Crown as trustee

[23] DVGN 551/3, 1862 Memorial, p. 7. This was not, in fact, one of the public rights; see Rankine, *Ownership of Lands* (4th edn), p. 272; J. Ferguson, *The Law of Water and Water Rights in Scotland* (Edinburgh, 1907), pp. 53–4.

[24] NRS, CR 11/95, Memorial of the Commissioners of Supply and Road Trustees, for the County of Argyll to the Commissioners of Woods and Forests, May 1860 [hereafter 1860 Memorial].

[25] NRS, CR 11/95, Letter Finlay to Howard, 23 May 1860.

for the public to use the shore for navigation and similar purposes. This public right certainly did not, however, challenge the 'proprietors' right of property and the profitable use of all things on the shore that are valuable and saleable'. The 1860 Memorial also stated that it was understood that the claim of the Crown was very generally disputed and that it was 'neither expedient nor becoming on the part of the Officers of the Crown to vindicate a right . . . in a manner so little profitable to the Crown and so injurious to the lieges as has been above described'.[26]

Howard responded to the 1860 Memorial in an uncompromising letter to Finlay in June 1860 that did nothing to allay the concerns of the Argyll Commissioners but, rather, exacerbated them. Howard rejected all the claims and allegations made in the 1860 Memorial and asked Finlay, if the Argyll Commissioners wished to press their complaints further, to provide full details of any alleged illegal or unprecedented acts of the Office of Woods. Howard also sent to Finlay a copy of a memorandum that he had read out to those present at the meeting when the 1860 Memorial was presented. This memorandum made clear the view of the Office of Woods that the interest of the Crown in the foreshore was not limited simply to rights as trustee for the public but extended to a right of property and gave the legal foundation for this claim including passages from such institutional writers as Erskine. The memorandum explained that a split of Crown responsibilities had led to confusion over the extent of the Crown's rights:

> The right of property . . . is under the charge of the Commissioners of Woods, the guardianship of public rights is under the charge of the Board of Admiralty. It is probably owing to the distinct character of these two rights having been lost sight of that the Crown has been sometimes loosely said to hold the Sea shore as trustee for the public.[27]

Howard's response to Finlay ended with what was probably an inflammatory suggestion that the Crown would be happy to consider any applications from proprietors to obtain a lease of the foreshore *ex adverso* their properties.[28]

[26] NRS, CR 11/95, 1860 Memorial.

[27] NRS, CR 11/95 and TNA:PRO, MT 10/139, Memorandum on Memorial from Argyllshire as to Crown's rights in the seashore, p. 2.

[28] NRS, CR 11/95 and TNA:PRO, MT 10/139, Letter Howard to Finlay, 29 June 1860. We shall see, in Chapter 5, that Howard's letter to Finlay and the memorandum explaining the Office of Woods' views of the law of Scotland as to ownership of the foreshore were considered by the Board of Trade in 1867 when the Board was dealing with the representations of the Association.

The committee of the Argyll Commissioners considered Howard's letter and memorandum on 26 September 1860. Not surprisingly the committee took the view that the statements in Howard's memorandum were not conclusive as to the law. In particular the committee rejected what it saw as a selective use of Erskine. The committee obtained its own statement of the law of Scotland that confirmed the committee's view of the ownership issue. The statement began by saying that the foreshore in Scotland had, 'until recent times, been regarded as the private property of the owners of the coterminous ground, as part and pertinent of the adjacent lands under burden of the Crown's right as Trustee for the public use of navigation' but that recently the Office of Woods had 'asserted a claim to the Scottish Shore, as the patrimonial estate of the Crown, a claim that previous to 1840 was unknown'. After a summary of the views of the institutional writers and the case law, the statement said: 'it is still the opinion of eminent Scotch Lawyers that the claim of the Woods and Forests is not well founded in law'.[29] Finlay wrote on 17 December 1860 to a number of the relevant Scottish proprietors enclosing a copy of the statement, inviting them to join together in an association to fight the Office of Woods:

> This Committee . . . consider it most important that immediate and combined efforts should be made by those interested, for the purpose of resisting this aggression; and they suggest that an Association be formed and funds subscribed for trying a case, to be carried if necessary to the House of Lords, in order finally to determine the rights of proprietors, and for adopting such other measures as may be deemed expedient.[30]

## THE WORK OF THE ASSOCIATION

We will now look in this section first at the administration of the Association – its management, organisation and membership – and second at the steps the Association took to achieve its objectives, including the legal opinion obtained and the cases taken up by it up to the end of 1866. The activities of the Association and the cases taken up by it after 1866 are discussed in Chapters 5 and 7.

[29] DVGN 549 and NRS, CR 11/95, Statement relative to the Proprietorship of the Foreshore of Scotland as affected by claims of the Commissioners of Woods and Forests on the part of the Crown, and the recent decisions of the Law Courts, December 1860 [hereafter 1860 Statement].

[30] DVGN 549/1–3, Letter Finlay as Convener of the Committee of Argyll Commissioners, 17 December 1860.

## *Management, organisation and membership*

The first formal meeting of a committee of the Association took place at the apartment of George Loch QC at 12 Albemarle Street in London on 24 May 1861. Norman Macleod of Macleod was asked to take on the role of honorary secretary. The other persons who attended the meeting were Alexander Finlay MP and Colonel Malcolm of Poltalloch. Henry Baillie, the Member of Parliament for Inverness-shire, was also appointed to the committee. Macleod had succeeded his father as chief of the clan in 1825 but he came into a reduced and heavily burdened inheritance and his financial position appears to have been made perilous by expenditure during the famine year of 1846 and years following, and the un-entailed estate and personal property not protected by the entail were all sold. Macleod left Dunvegan and moved to London where he obtained employment as a junior clerk with the science and arts department of the civil service. He gradually moved up the promotion ladder in the department, becoming assistant secretary in 1858.[31] Macleod, therefore, lived in London and, as a relatively senior civil servant, might have been expected to move in political and administrative circles that the Association might find of use. As a civil servant he would also have been a man well used to the preparation and drafting of documents and to possess the organisational skills and abilities necessary for the secretary of the Association. As a prominent, if somewhat financially reduced, hereditary proprietor and a man with this civil service experience and contacts, Macleod was an obvious choice as secretary. But it is the role of George Loch that is perhaps the most interesting. Loch was the eldest son of James Loch who had coordinated the management of the Marquis of Stafford's estates in England and Scotland and he succeeded his father as commissioner to the Sutherland estates in 1855. Richards has described James Loch as 'probably the most influential estate administrator of his day',[32] and the experience George Loch would have gained from his father and from his own years running the Sutherland estates and also as managing trustee of the Keith estates would have been invaluable to the committee of the Association and Macleod in particular.[33] It is probably no coincidence that the

[31] The Rev. R. C. Macleod, *The Macleods: Their History and Traditions* (Edinburgh, 1929).

[32] E. Richards, 'The landed agent', in G. E. Mingay (ed.), *The Victorian Countryside* (London, 1981), p. 451.

[33] For George Loch's position as commissioner of the Sutherland estates, see

Duke of Sutherland's £200 guaranteed subscription to the Association was the largest single contribution. While Macleod, as the secretary of the Association, was to take the main responsibility for the day-to-day administration of the Association, he appears to have relied most heavily on George Loch for his knowledge and experience as a barrister, for his experience as Commissioner for the Sutherland Estates and for his business skills. James Mitchell, in his reminiscences of his life in the Highlands, described George Loch as being 'an excellent man of business',[34] and Loch's brother William Adam Loch characterised him as 'a man of much ability and . . . a manager and organiser by nature'.[35] Loch undoubtedly played a very important role on the committee.[36] It does not appear that Henry Baillie, the other original member of the committee, played a particularly important role and, indeed, he may, as we shall see in Chapter 3, have rather blotted his copybook by purchasing from the Crown a disputed piece of foreshore.

The meeting determined that Macleod should prepare a circular letter that would invite proprietors of foreshore in Scotland to join an association 'for the purpose of determining their rights against claims brought forward by the Commissioners of Woods on behalf of the Crown'.[37] There was clearly some debate as to what, if any, publicity should be given to the names of proprietors who had shown an interest in joining. Baillie believed a list of names would encourage others to join, but Loch had reservations. Indeed, Loch was against the issue of any sort of circular letter at all and thought that the members of the committee should carry out the enlisting of members privately. He wanted to 'avoid anything like canvassing or display of force'. If the committee received a large level of support, there was no need to advertise and if support was not forthcoming, 'it will be as well not to publish it'.[38]

A. Tindley, *The Sutherland Estate 1850–1920: Aristocratic Decline, Estate Management and Land Reform* (Edinburgh, 2010).

[34] Mitchell, *Reminiscences of my Life*, p. 216.

[35] G. Loch, *The Family of Loch* (Edinburgh, 1934), p. 275.

[36] Loch was born in 1811 and died in 1877. He was called to the English bar in May 1847 and was appointed a QC and a Bencher of the Middle Temple in 1863, becoming Treasurer in 1875. He was appointed the Attorney General to the Prince of Wales in 1873 and was the Member of Parliament for Wick Burghs from 1868 to 1872; F. Boase, *Modern English Biography*, vol. II (Truro, 1897). Loch had a close relationship with the monarchy: he was visited by the Queen on his death bed (the author is grateful to Dr Annie Tindley for this insight).

[37] DVGN 543/2/1, Minutes of meeting, 24 May 1861.

[38] DVGN 570/2/3, Letter Loch to Macleod, 12 June 1861. As we shall see below, at least one proprietor was impressed by 'such a formidable array of names' but

A further meeting of the committee was held on 20 June 1861 at which the draft circular produced by Macleod was considered. Loch's views as to publicity were partly overruled and the committee decided that a circular should be written and that the members of the committee should ask as many personal friends as possible to join the Association so that a list of such names could be attached to the circular.[39] The circular referred to the claims which the Office of Woods had been making, claims which the circular described as 'entirely inconsistent with the absolute property in the Foreshores which has hitherto been enjoyed and exercised by the heritors with whose lands they are coterminous, and at variance also with the law'.[40] The circular proposed that there should be formed

> an Association of Proprietors interested in the question, who may each, in proportion to his interest, contribute to a common fund, by means of which to meet the expenses of such law proceedings as shall, on consideration, seem best adapted to raise and try the question fairly and fully between the Crown and the Sea Coast Proprietors.[41]

Macleod was asked to write to the clerks of supply in Scotland for the names of foreshore proprietors in their areas so that as comprehensive a list as possible could be compiled and to whom the circulars could be sent. Not surprisingly, given his position with the Argyll Commissioners, it was Finlay who had suggested to Macleod that the clerks of supply should be used.[42] Macleod compiled a list of some 600 Scottish proprietors from the information provided by the clerks of supply. Macleod was also asked by the committee to enquire as to appropriate law agents for the Association and he wrote, immediately after the meeting, to William Brand in Edinburgh, 'a great personal friend of mine, a WS and a man of good sense'.[43] Macleod was to turn to Brand for advice on a

one other proprietor, the Earl of Selkirk, did not want his membership to be made public.

39 DVGN 543/2/1, Minutes of meeting, 20 June 1861.

40 DVGN 543/2/2, Circular letter, June 1861. An interesting manuscript change appears on one of the printed draft circulars in the Macleod muniments: the words 'subject to public rights' are added after the words 'absolute property in the Foreshores'.

41 DVGN 543/2/2, Circular letter, June 1861.

42 DVGN 570/40/2, Letter Finlay to Macleod, 3 June 1861.

43 This was how he described him to Loch; see DVGN 570/3/1–6, Letter Macleod to Loch, 10 November 1863. This was a letter written some two years later and it does not appear that Macleod revealed he was taking Brand's advice on Association matters until this point. Brand (1807–69) was the Secretary of the Union Bank of Scotland.

number of sensitive issues, including his own personal involvement in the Association, and he was clearly a man whose judgement Macleod respected. Brand was apprehensive as to the outcome for the Association in taking the issue to court:

> The question is a very important one and should certainly be tried . . . [but] . . . you will have difficulties in the House of Lords which of late has shown a tendency to adopt English rules in regard to Crown rights although different from Scotch law principles or authorities. But I still see no alternative to having the matter tried.[44]

As to law agents, Brand recommended that the committee should appoint Skene & Peacock in Edinburgh. Brand considered that the firm 'would be as well suited as any other agents – Mr Skene's antiquarian knowledge being of use in a matter of this kind'.[45]

Towards the end of 1861 some 600 circulars had been dispatched but the response was disappointing. Macleod reported that, by the beginning of December 1861, only fifty replies had been received, most of which were favourable, but not all. There was uncertainty over the amount of the subscription. Macleod reported to the committee that 'there is evidently a hesitation about joining owing to the uncertainty of the contribution. I think it is most desirable that some definite plan should be prepared with respect to subscription.'[46] It was only at this stage that the subscription that the Association was looking for was considered, which is somewhat surprising given that the issue had been recognised as one of some difficulty and sensitivity in June of that year. Skene & Peacock had told Macleod that it would cost in the region of £3,000 to try a case, but that the sum of £5,000 might be a better target. Macleod suggested that proprietors should contribute proportionately

[44] DVGN 572/5, Letter Brand to Macleod, 22 June 1861.

[45] It is apparent from these words that Brand's recommendation of Skene & Peacock was influenced by the fact that William Forbes Skene, who was the senior partner, was a man who had already gained an important reputation as an archaeologist and a historian. Skene would also have been well known to a number of the proprietors of Highland estates through his work as the Secretary of the Edinburgh Section of the Central Relief Board during the famine year of 1846 and thereafter. Skene did, in the early stages, give advice to, and correspond with, Macleod, but it was his partner William Peacock who was principally responsible for acting for the Association in these early years. Skene & Peacock was founded in 1858 and in 1872 the firm's name was changed to Skene Webster & Peacock, in 1878 to Skene Edwards & Bilton and in 1890 to Skene Edwards & Garson. Before its merger with Morton Fraser in 2008 the firm practised under the name Skene Edwards WS.

[46] DVGN 572/40/6, Letter Macleod to Finlay, 6 December 1861.

on the basis of the total coastal mileage comprised in their estates. He also thought contributions should be paid in full.[47] It appears that this was considered over-complicated and in March 1862 a further circular letter was sent to those who had responded to the June 1861 circular informing them that a committee had been formed and that the committee believed that action could no longer be delayed. The members of the Association were told that the Crown was claiming 'to establish a proprietary right to the shore, under the power of selling it at the highest price'. This was, of course, inconsistent with the Association's claims on behalf of its members to their 'absolute property in the Foreshores' and so 'steps should now be taken to determine the rights of Proprietors under the Law of Scotland'. The circular recommended a modest subscription, without naming a specific amount, and asked proprietors to respond stating what amount each of them proposed to subscribe. It also printed the name of eight of the proprietors who had already subscribed, showing individual amounts ranging from £10 to £100.[48] The concern over the wording of the circular as to subscriptions was well founded because the issue was one that a number of proprietors referred to in their letters about joining the Association. It appears that the wording of the 1861 circular suggested, at least to some, that proprietors were being asked to provide a kind of guarantee of the Association's liabilities and, indeed, the fact that members were asked to subscribe to a letter of guarantee must have reinforced this concern. The 1862 circular used the term 'a moderate subscription' and Sir John Forbes picked this point up:

> I see that the word subscription is exchanged for guarantee meaning I suppose that no one is liable for more than he guarantees and only for that in the extent of his share of the whole cost when divided proportionately, but on the other hand in the small paper it is said that the whole expenses are to be divided proportionately leading to the inference that each is to be liable for the proportion of the whole whatever it may be.[49]

Others took up this worry over liability extending beyond the amount subscribed. Captain Fraser of Kilmuir told Macleod that 'you may place twenty pounds against my name as my subscription towards the object stated subject that I shall not be called upon for more'.[50] The concern was, moreover, not limited to proprietors who may have been of limited resources; Charles Morrison of Islay, a man of considerable wealth,

47 DVGN 572/40/6, Letter Macleod to Finlay, 6 December 1861.

48 DVGN 543/8/1, Circular letter, 28 March 1862.

49 DVGN 572/93, Letter Forbes to Macleod, 3 February 1864.

50 DVGN 572/83, Letter Fraser to Macleod, 6 January 1864.

made it clear to Macleod that in subscribing his £50 he wanted 'to be certain that in the event the litigation fails, the members will not be responsible beyond their subscription'.[51] The Earl of Cawdor's agents similarly wanted it clearly understood 'that he is not to be responsible for any further sum in respect of his subscription',[52] as did H. G. Murray Stewart who stressed that he was not to be liable for more than his £5.[53] The Marquis of Breadalbane did not want to pay his subscription in advance and asked that 'it should only be paid on the question being actually tried in the Courts'.[54] But while these examples are interesting in showing the concerns of a number of proprietors at what they were letting themselves in for, what is, perhaps, more interesting is that the majority of proprietors who joined did so without expressing any concerns over their liabilities. While this may be explained by the fact that the majority understood the circulars to say that their liability was limited to the amount of their subscriptions, it is more likely that it simply did not occur to the majority of proprietors that their liabilities could be unlimited.

The response to the 1862 circular was an improvement over the 1861 circular, although not all the proprietors approached wished to join. But while the membership of the Association had reached eighty-one by the end of 1864, there was still some feeling that more could be persuaded to join if 'the real effect of the Crown's claims [could be] brought to their knowledge through the medium of the public press'.[55] Skene & Peacock asked the Association's junior counsel, Donald Crawford, to prepare a draft article for publication in the *Edinburgh Evening Courant*, which had a large circulation among landed proprietors. The editor had agreed to publish the article as a leader in the paper, and Skene & Peacock hoped that the public would see it as the work of the editor and not of the Association. The committee received this proposal enthusiastically and the drafts were reviewed by committee members and by the Duke

[51] DVGN 570/1/3, Letter Morrison to Macleod, 23 November 1863. Morrison was clearly a man who was astute enough in financial affairs to be very careful, notwithstanding – or perhaps because of – his immense wealth, about what he was signing up for; he was a man who 'habitually kept several million pounds in gold bullion, selling it judiciously whenever a general panic threatened the British economy'; see W. D. Rubinstein, 'New men of wealth and the purchase of land in nineteenth century Britain', *Past and Present*, 92 (1981), p. 132.

[52] DVGN 572/87, Letter Cawdor's agents to Macleod, 12 January 1864.

[53] DVGN 570/1/3, Letter Stewart to Macleod, 30 January 1865.

[54] DVGN 572/45, Letter Breadalbane to Macleod, 21 April 1862.

[55] DVGN 570/4/56, Letter Skene & Peacock to Macleod, 30 December 1864.

of Argyll who was mentioned in it. Loch thought that the article was 'remarkably well done' and Argyll was most enthusiastic about the 'steps we are taking in directing public attention to the question through the press'.[56] The article was published on 9 January 1865 at a time when 'there is no stirring public question pre-eminently occupying the public mind' and so that 'County Gentlemen are likely to read [the] article with more attention during the present lull'.[57] The article gave a full account of the origins of the Association and of its successes thus far, mentioning the Duke of Argyll's case over his estate at Rosneath on which the Association had obtained a judgment in default of the Crown's appearance and mentioned that the case involving Maclean of Ardgour was proceeding.[58] The article ended with a powerful indictment of the actions of the Crown and gave a clear indication that it was the protection of private interests and amenities, and the value of private estates – the sacred right of property – which were at stake, even if there was also a rather odd suggestion why the public would wish to support the Association in the fight against the Crown:

> the public will indulge the hope that the association of heritors will be successful in their resistance. The amenity, and even the value of many estates, depend on their command of the sea and shore. To deprive them of that would amount to sheer mutilation . . . The right asserted [by the proprietors] is and must be absolute. The proprietors may at pleasure be excluded from the shore altogether; factories or fish curing establishments may be erected under their drawing room windows.[59]

The article had attached to it a list of the members of the Association who had guaranteed subscriptions, giving the amount of each guarantee. A copy of the article was sent to proprietors who had not yet joined the Association with a simple pre-addressed and printed reply to Macleod authorising the Association to add the sender's name to the list of guaranteed subscriptions. The article proved successful, raising the profile of the Association and producing further members so that, by the beginning of 1872, the total number of members had risen to 130 guaranteeing,

[56] DVGN 570/2, Letter Loch to Macleod, January 1865; Letter Skene & Peacock to Macleod, 7 January 1865. It was, of course, at precisely the same time that the Duke of Argyll was conducting his own correspondence about the foreshore with the Treasury which was later to be made public; see further in Chapter 4.

[57] DVGN 570/4, Letter Skene & Peacock to Macleod, 4 January 1865.

[58] These cases are discussed below.

[59] 'The foreshore', *Edinburgh Evening Courant*, 9 January 1865, p. 4; also found at DVGN 543/10.

between them, a considerable sum of money.[60] One particular proprietor, the Earl of Zetland, had been concerned that the Association was not acting in the interests of all the proprietors but it seems that the article satisfied him and he sent in his guaranteed subscription for £100. Skene & Peacock reported that after the copies of the article were sent out, 'the question has been very much agitated and discussed since, and noticed by the Law Professors in their lectures in the University'.[61] The 130 members of the Association owned, between them, over five and a half million acres of Scotland and so over 28 per cent of the total area of Scotland. While this statistic is, in a way, somewhat meaningless in the context simply of the foreshore, it does show that the membership of the Association comprised a significant segment of the land-owning proprietors of Scotland.[62]

Later in 1865 the members of the Association were sent copies of the correspondence between the Duke of Argyll and the Treasury over the Rosneath case, which is discussed in Chapter 4. In the accompanying circular letter the members were told of the importance of not complying with the demands that the Office of Woods was making. And the circular expressed the hope of the committee that

> the publicity given to the course taken by the Woods and Forests by the Correspondence now sent will prevent any further self-sacrifice by proprietors of their Foreshore Interests and that the operations of the Association will command their approval and support.[63]

Thus far the members of the Association had not been asked to pay any part of their guarantee, but in July 1866 a further circular was sent out reminding them of the success achieved in the Duke of Argyll's

[60] The list of members is in MacAskill, '"A silver fringe?"', Appendix 1. A total of 130 members guaranteed, between them, a total of £3,047 3s. 0d. The subscriptions vary from £200 guaranteed by the Duke of Sutherland to £1 by Mr W. Campbell of Dunmore. There were four dukes, thirteen earls, one viscount, six lords and eleven baronets who, between them, guaranteed comfortably over half of the total. The total subscriptions of £3,047 3s. 0d. in 1865 is equivalent, in terms of the purchasing power of £1 in 2016, to £267,400; the £200 contribution by the Duke of Sutherland equates to £17,550 in terms of the 2016 purchasing power of £1; L. H. Officer and S. H. Williamson, 'Five ways to compute the relative value of a UK pound amount, 1270 to present', *MeasuringWorth*, 2017, available at <https://www.measuringworth.com/ukcompare/> (last accessed 25 October 2017).

[61] DVGN 570/4/62, Letter Skene & Peacock to Macleod, 3 February 1865.

[62] The acreage owned by the members is based on J. Bateman, *The Great Landowners of Great Britain and Ireland* (London, 1883).

[63] DVGN 543/11, Circular letter, 29 September 1865.

Rosneath case, informing them that the Crown had decided not to take any further the Maclean of Ardgour case after its defeat in the Outer House of the Court of Session, and making a call for the members to pay one-quarter of the guaranteed amount.[64] The communications with members after the end of 1866 are discussed in Chapter 5.

We can take it from the papers and the correspondence that the Association was very much the creature of two men, Norman Macleod of Macleod and George Loch, although Alexander Finlay, who had, of course, been instrumental in the formation of the Association, kept a continuing interest in the work of the committee and the Association's affairs, as did Colonel Malcolm of Poltalloch. Macleod's life was not made easy by men such as Finlay who seems to have proposed, with the backing of his fellow Member of Parliament Henry Baillie, changes to the management of the Association at the end of 1863 which would have involved a paid agent having responsibility for the administration of the Association. Finlay believed the running of the Association lacked the proper degree of professionalism; the fact that it was not until the beginning of 1864 that the Association was seen to be taking action against the Crown had been bothering members of the Association. In October 1863 Loch was warning Macleod of this concern. He told Macleod: 'I hope to be in London by the end of the week. I should like to see you, and talk over our Foreshore matters – some of our friends are becoming impatient.'[65] Loch was supportive of Macleod and very much against the proposal. He considered that the whole character of the Association would be changed and that they would quickly lose all

[64] DVGN 543/12, Circular letter, 2 July 1866. The amount received on the call came to £754 17s. 1d. The amount of Skene & Peacock's legal expenses to 31 December 1866 came to a total of £321 2s. 3d. (DVGN 544/3/7) and the expenses of the secretary and other administrative expenses came to £109 4s. 10d.; see DVGN 543/15, Foreshores. Total Subscriptions as per Book, 7 June 1869 (see further below).

[65] DVGN 570/2/1/44, Letter Loch to Macleod, 26 October 1863. It is likely that Finlay's concern over progress was influenced by the fact that he was having an unsatisfactory correspondence with the Office of Woods over alleged acts of trespass on the foreshores of his Castle Toward estate. Finlay had, apparently, asked the Office of Woods to take action over these trespasses but the Office of Woods had interpreted Finlay's request as implicitly accepting the Crown's ownership of the foreshore: if the Crown did not own it, why was Finlay asking for the Crown to take action over the trespassers? Finlay vehemently denied this and his personal experience of the policy and practices of the Office of Woods no doubt encouraged his anxiety to have the issue as to ownership settled as soon as possible; see NRS, CR 11/132, Correspondence Finlay and the Office of Woods, November 1863.

control over it if it were to be run by a paid agent. Indeed, he believed that if the proposal was accepted, proprietors such as the Duke of Sutherland would not want to commit themselves to the Association. Loch wrote to Macleod saying that 'it is at all times tiresome to have to act with fussy people, who at the same time have little real experience in business – our friend Finlay is one of these'.[66] Macleod was, it seems, distressed by Finlay's proposal and wondered if he could, or should, remain in his position, but Loch pressed him to stay:

> I can assure you, for my own part, were you to cease to hold your present position with reference to the foreshore movement, my confidence in it would cease. I could not tell Finlay in writing to him how very unwise his suggestion seemed to me, but I should be extremely sorry were you to suppose that I shared in his feeling in the remotest degree.[67]

In the event, Loch and Macleod prevailed and nothing further was heard of Finlay's proposal. But it is interesting to note that, while the proposal to have a paid agent responsible for the management of the Association was not accepted, the Association's legal agents, Skene & Peacock, did assume a role that was more than a simple responsibility for the management of cases. Loch, on one occasion, considered that Skene & Peacock were acting in too independent a manner. In relation to a suggestion from them that the letter of guarantee signed by members should be made public, Loch made his feelings plain to Macleod:

> Let me recommend you strongly to write and forbid them from printing the letter of guarantee – they have no business to take a step of this kind, except by your instructions – their province is strictly limited to managing the law plea, and not to deal with measures of general conduct.[68]

But Skene & Peacock undoubtedly had a role that was not limited as Loch suggested. They were proactive in a number of membership matters which lay well outside a simple responsibility merely for the cases taken up by the Association. They rendered business accounts to the Association in respect of work done for the Association in each of the years 1861–74 and the successor firm of Skene Edwards & Garson, as we shall see in Chapter 7, rendered an account to the

[66] DVGN 570/2/17, Letter Loch to Macleod, 29 November 1863.

[67] DVGN 570/2/18, Letter Loch to Macleod, 1 December 1863.

[68] DVGN 570/2/16, Letter Loch to Macleod, 26 November 1863. Loch also believed that such a publication would be 'injurious and ill judged . . . I can't help thinking we should diminish and "vulgarise" our position by any such demonstration.'

Association for 1891. These business accounts show that the firm was not merely engaged in 'managing the law plea', but that it dealt with more wide-ranging matters. The firm had discussions with the editor of *The Scotsman* and of the *Edinburgh Evening Courant* about the publication of articles, procured proprietors to join the Association and corresponded with, and gave advice to, members of the Association on issues concerning such members' own foreshore matters; and the costs and expenses of such correspondence and advice were rendered to the Association and not to the individual members. So, for example, in 1866 just under a quarter of that year's account from the firm was in respect of individual members' personal issues.[69] The committee of the Association clearly understood the Association's role to be one where all matters that affected the foreshore were worthy of consideration and Skene & Peacock's role was similarly extended. So, for example, the Oyster and Mussel Fisheries Act was, as we shall see in Chapter 5, given close consideration by the firm in 1866 and they were also to give important advice to the Association on the Crown Lands Bill 1866 which is examined in Chapter 3.

The extent of the role of both the Association and Skene & Peacock might, perhaps, have come as something of a surprise to proprietors who had subscribed to the Association on the basis of what the circulars had said. When the first call on the subscription moneys was made in 1866, the explanation for the call was that

> The chief part of the charges in the litigation of [the Duke of Argyll and Maclean of Ardgour] cases has fallen on the Crown, but some extra judicial expenses will have to be paid by the Association, and in order to defray them and retain a sum in hand for the purpose of taking up any other case that may arise and of watching the future proceedings of the Board of Trade, to which the management of Crown lands is about to be transferred, the Committee propose that each Subscriber shall now pay one fourth part of his guaranteed subscription, an amount of £794-17-1.[70]

The total business accounts of Skene & Peacock for the years 1861 to the end of 1866 amounted to £307 1s. 0d. but of this only £75 11s. 8d. was in respect of the costs and expenses of the two cases which had not been recovered from the Crown. The secretary's expenses came to £109 4s. 10d. The members were, therefore, being asked for a very healthy balance to fund the future activities of the Association. For the years

[69] DVGN 544/3/6, Business Account of the Association for vindicating rights of Seaboard Proprietors to Foreshore in Scotland.

[70] DVGN 543/12, Circular letter to members, 2 July 1866.

1866–74 the total business accounts of Skene & Peacock amounted to £214 3s. 3d., none of which was in respect of the cases taken up on the Association's behalf. The members may also have been surprised that a large part of the funds provided by them were used to pay Skene & Peacock for advice given to individual members of the Association and not, as they might have thought, for the payment of the costs and expenses of litigation on the Association's behalf. We might note that the Association bore the expenses of individual members' cases.[71]

### *The legal opinion obtained, and the cases taken up, by the Association up to the end of 1866*

One of the first steps taken by the committee was to obtain an opinion from counsel as to the law on the foreshore question. Macleod's friend William Brand had warned him of the difficulties the Association faced in finding a case which would embrace all the legal points which had to be determined. It seems Macleod suggested putting forward a case involving the Dunvegan foreshore, but Brand did not think this was sensible:

> Perhaps your own [foreshore] would be as comprehensive as any, but in your position it would scarcely be desirable that you should appear in front of the battle, for although the question is partly one of Civil Rights, the Crown will not be apt to look with complacency on those who raise it.[72]

Brand also predicted that what was to follow would be 'a feast for the lawyers'.[73]

Skene & Peacock recommended that the committee should seek the joint opinion of three counsel: George Young, A. R. Clark and J. M. Duncan; the choice of counsel was approved by Loch.[74] The

[71] NRAS, 3583/Bundle 10, Letter Tods Murray and Jamieson to Ardgour, 19 January 1864.

[72] DVGN 572/41, Letter Brand to Macleod, 12 March 1862.

[73] DVGN 572/41, Letter Brand to Macleod, 12 March 1862. In fact, the Board was still disputing the ownership of the Dunvegan foreshore as late as 1926 but eventually decided not to contest the Macleod claim to it; NRS, CR11/386A, Letter Board of Trade to Commission for Crown Lands, 23 October 1926. Brand's concerns about Macleod being involved in a court case with the Crown were, as we shall see later, echoed by the Earl of Selkirk and others.

[74] DVGN 570/4/10, Letter Skene & Peacock to Macleod, 8 July 1862; DVGN 570/2, Letter Loch to Macleod, 10 July 1862. George Young was Solicitor General from 1862 to 1866 and 1868 to 1869, Lord Advocate from 1869 to 1874, a Lord Ordinary from 1874, and 'one of the most brilliant and successful court pleaders

memorial for counsel, which drew heavily on the 1860 Statement, was submitted in July 1862 and counsel were asked five questions, the most important of which was 'Generally to whom does the Scottish foreshore between high and low water belong in property? Whether to the proprietors whose estates are situated *ex adverso* thereto, or to the Crown?' Counsel were also asked to give their views on the rights of the public in the foreshore.[75] The opinion of counsel was given in November and, as to the main question, it was, from the point of view of the proprietors, less than satisfactory. Counsel said that as the Crown had not been a party in any of the cases which held that the foreshore could be regarded as a pertinent which passed with the *ex adverso* lands without a special grant, these cases could not be considered as conclusive of the main question of law. The three counsel were only prepared to say:

> While we would wish to express a very qualified opinion on the question, which, as presented in this memorial, raises for decision new and undecided points of law, we are, on the whole, inclined to think, in the case of those of the Memorialists who hold Crown grants of land adjacent to the sea, and bounded seaward by the 'sea' or by the 'sea shore', the solum of the shore *ex adverso* of their lands belongs in property to them, subject to the burden in favour of the public already mentioned.[76]

As to the rights of the public, the opinion of counsel was that whatever the situation as to ownership was, it was clear that whoever owned the foreshore did so 'under burden of the full use by the public of the foreshore for various purposes, among those connected with navigation are the most common and important'.[77] Counsel also said that if a case went to the House of Lords, they were even less confident of the result.

This was unsatisfactory for the Association. Macleod wrote a memorandum on the opinion in which he said that the proprietors had not wanted an opinion on the effect of specific words in a charter, or on what the House of Lords might think. The simple question which the

of his day'; G. F. Miller, 'Young, George, Lord Young (1819–1907)' , in *Oxford Dictionary of National Biography*, Oxford University Press, available at <http://www.oxforddnb.com/view/article/37074> (last accessed 25 October 2017). A. R. Clark was Solicitor General from 1869 to 1874, Dean of the Faculty of Advocates from 1874 to 1875 and a Lord Ordinary from 1875.

[75] DVGN 551/4, Memorial for a Committee of Proprietors of Estates in Scotland, whose Lands are bounded by the Sea, for the Opinion of Counsel, and Opinion, 4 November 1862 [hereafter 1862 Memorial and Opinion]; this can also be found at TNA:PRO, MT 10/139.

[76] DVGN 551/4, 1862 Memorial and Opinion, paras 1 and 2 of the Opinion.

[77] DVGN 551/4, 1862 Memorial and Opinion, paras 1 and 2 of the Opinion.

Association wanted answered – did the foreshore belong to the *ex adverso* proprietor by implication without an express Crown grant or possession? – had not been given a firm answer by counsel. Indeed, the inference he read into the opinion was that counsel were doubtful on the point. Other members of the committee were similarly dissatisfied that counsel had not reached a firm view.[78] Malcolm of Poltalloch thought that the opinion was very guarded but he took the three counsel to be saying that they thought the law of Scotland was with the Association on the question and that if the question was finally to be decided by the Scottish courts, the decision would probably be in the Association's favour, but as the House of Lords was guided entirely by English lawyers, they had doubts over the outcome: 'This latter part we all of us know before and in this as in so many other points we suffer from the final Court of Appeal being constituted as it is.' Malcolm had serious doubts over what the correct course of action should be but he favoured 'trying the question thoroughly for anything would be better than the state of uncertainty we are now in'.[79]

Some months then passed while the committee decided what the Association's next steps should be in the light of this rather unsatisfactory opinion. The members were divided on what should be done, but Macleod eventually wrote to Skene & Peacock saying that although the opinion was 'so little of an encouraging nature', steps should be taken in the courts towards finally deciding the main question – did the

[78] DVGN 550/1, Memorandum on Counsels' opinion respecting foreshores. It is interesting to note that Macleod, in the light of the opinion, for a time considered accepting the proposition that the Crown owned the foreshore in return for the agreement of the Crown that the *ex adverso* proprietor had title to the seaware on the foreshore. Finlay said that he regretted that the opinion was not more satisfactory; see DVGN 572/40/13, Letter Finlay to Macleod, 20 November 1862; DVGN 572/40/15, Letter Malcolm to Finlay, 25 November 1862.

[79] DVGN 572/40/15, Letter Malcolm to Macleod, 25 March 1862. There was considerable dissatisfaction in Scotland with the performance by the House of Lords of its responsibilities as the final Court of Appeal from the Scottish courts in the period down to 1876. There was, until 1876, no Scottish judge who sat as part of the court and this exacerbated the English Law Lords' ignorance of Scots Law and practice. There was, among the English judges who comprised the House of Lords, a common assertion that the law must be the same in both countries, and the Law Lords frequently reversed a unanimous decision of the Court of Session. The value of an appeal from the Court of Session to the House of Lords down to 1876 was much doubted because the appeal would be considered by a tribunal of judges 'whose judgments frequently betrayed gross ignorance of and disregard for the principles, traditions and practices of Scots Law'; D. M. Walker, *A Legal History of Scotland* (Edinburgh, 2001), vol. VI, pp. 313–20.

foreshore belong to the *ex adverso* proprietor by implication without any express grant or possession?[80] Skene & Peacock agreed that the opinion was, as they put it, 'very awkwardly phrased'. Unfortunately, William Peacock had not been able to attend the consultation and 'had he been present he may have been able to get a more direct opinion upon the general question'.[81] Skene & Peacock went on to suggest that rather more sinister forces had been at work:

> We may be wrong but we cannot help thinking that the counsel consulted may have been to some extent influenced by political views. Mr Young was then in the expectation of being, and is now, Solicitor General, and all of them, though eminent counsel have been more or less connected with the Whig party by office or otherwise and we had it in view to suggest whether it might not be expedient to take the opinion of two eminent counsel on the other side of the bar such as Mr Edward Gordon . . . and Mr George Patton who was for some time Solicitor General under the Conservative Government.[82]

Finlay did not agree that there should be another consultation with counsel of allegedly more correct political views; this, he thought, was not the main problem. Interestingly, he believed that the Association's case might be more sympathetically received if it stressed more the public interest than the interest of private proprietors.[83] He wanted to see the Association take a broader approach and to resist the claims of the Crown on public grounds. He accepted that the respective rights of the public and the private proprietors were different but thought that both had been infringed.[84] While the Association did attempt in its communications with members and the Crown to stress that the Association was, indeed, acting in the public interest, it is difficult to conclude from the proprietors' letters that the expressions of interest by the Association on the part of the public were any more than half-hearted. The concluding lines of the *Edinburgh Evening Courant* about

[80] DVGN 572/40/13, Letter Macleod to Skene & Peacock, 19 June 1863.

[81] DVGN 570/415, Letter Skene & Peacock to Macleod, 22 June 1863.

[82] DVGN 570/415, Letter Skene & Peacock to Macleod, 22 June 1863. George Young, in fact, advised the Crown as Solicitor General in the Maclean of Ardgour case discussed below.

[83] As to the interest of private proprietors, we might note that the economy of the Highlands and islands was under severe pressure in the 1860s, and so arguments based on sympathy for the proprietors may have been regarded as insensitive; A. M. Tindley, '"Actual pinching and suffering": estate responses to poverty in Sutherland, 1845–1886', *Scottish Historical Review*, 90:2 (2011), pp. 236–56.

[84] DVGN 570/40/19, Letter Finlay to Macleod, 5 August 1863.

the effects of the Crown policy on private estates and their enjoyment by private proprietors betray the real concern of the private proprietors.[85] In the event, no further consultation was arranged, but the Association gave instructions to Skene & Peacock to find a case or cases that could be taken up by the Association to test the main question. It is interesting to note that there had obviously been some debate as to what really was the main question which the Association wanted to have settled; we find Loch writing to Macleod in April 1862 about a proposal which would involve some acceptance that the Crown did have a right of property in the foreshore. Loch was adamant, however, that this line of attack was not the right one:

> it can hardly be suggested at the present moment, that we should acquiesce in this view, for it involves the whole question at issue . . . we are much more logical in denying property altogether with all its attendant circumstances, and merely admitting that the Crown possesses certain fiduciary powers.[86]

Given the lack of success in the choice of counsel for the 1862 opinion, rather more thought was given to the choice of counsel to fight the chosen cases for the Association. There was a lengthy correspondence between Skene & Peacock, Macleod and Loch as to suitable names and by late 1863 and early 1864 there were expressions of disquiet from Finlay, Malcolm and the Duke of Argyll that no progress had been made in agreeing the counsel and finding a case. We find Loch again writing to Macleod about Finlay's interference; Finlay, said Loch, 'continues to urge "decisive action" and this, that and the other, as if you were not already a long way ahead of him – these busy bodies are very tiresome'.[87] Skene & Peacock believed that George Patton and John Millar 'would make as good a bar as we can have apart from Counsel more or less connected with the Crown', although they agreed that the choice between Patton and Edward Gordon was very close.[88] Loch did not feel able to advise on the issue because he had so much less acquaintance with the Edinburgh bar than he had with the London bar. He stressed, however, the importance of the choice and told Macleod that he 'should hardly be disposed to rely alone on the recommendation of Skene & Peacock. Do you know anyone in Edinburgh whom you could

[85] This was also the conclusion of the Crown's representative in the Judicial Factor proceedings for the eventual winding-up of the Association, as discussed in Chapter 7.

[86] DVGN 570/2/6, Letter Loch to Macleod, 15 April 1862.

[87] DVGN 570/2/6, Letter Loch to Macleod, 11 November 1863.

[88] DVGN 570/4/26, Letter Skene & Peacock to Macleod, 3 November 1863.

consult confidentially?'[89] Macleod turned again to William Brand who suggested that, while the counsel recommended by Skene & Peacock 'are perhaps as good as you can have for pleading when your action has been raised', the Association should also instruct one or more counsel who would advise on the law, but not appear in court. He suggested George Moir and James Anderson, and he preferred Gordon to Patton.[90] Macleod's thoughts about the suggestion of Anderson provide another example of the concern over Scottish appeals to the House of Lords noted above. Macleod told Loch: 'As to Mr Anderson, consulting him depends on whether we desire to know what the House of Lords will say to us and I rather fancy we know that too well already.'[91] Loch had some sympathy with Brand's recommendation to have a combination of a specialist advocate and a more academic lawyer. He also agreed with Brand over the choice of Gordon rather than Patton.[92] Macleod reported these feelings to Skene & Peacock who replied that they still preferred Patton but agreed with the suggestion of instructing a counsel to advise purely on the law and were quite content with Moir for such a role.[93] Eventually a decision was taken to instruct Patton, Millar and another junior counsel who had drafted the 1865 article in the *Edinburgh Evening Courant*, Donald Crawford, with Moir to advise on the law but not to be used as an advocate.[94]

The Association decided to adopt the Duke of Argyll's dispute with the Crown over the Rosneath foreshore as its leading case not just

[89] DVGN 570/2/14, Letter Loch to Macleod, 6 November 1863.

[90] DVGN 572/63, Letter Brand to Macleod, 9 November 1863.

[91] DVGN 570/3/1–6, Letter Macleod to Loch, 10 November 1863. James Anderson was also a member of the English bar and was Examiner of Court of Chancery from 1873 to 1876.

[92] DVGN 570/2/15, Letter Loch to Macleod, 11 November 1863.

[93] DVGN 570/1/3, Letter Macleod to Skene & Peacock, 12 November 1863; Letter Skene & Peacock to Macleod, 16 November 1863.

[94] George Patton had been the Solicitor General in 1859, Lord Advocate from 1866 to 1867 and Lord Justice-Clerk in 1867. John Millar was Solicitor General from 1867 to 1868 and from 1874 to 1876. Donald Crawford served as Secretary to the Lord Advocate from 1880 to 1885 and was appointed Sheriff of Aberdeen in 1895. George Moir was the Professor of Rhetoric at Edinburgh University from 1835 to 1840, the Sheriff of Ross from 1840 to 1858 and of Stirling in 1858 and was appointed to the Chair of Scots Law at Edinburgh University in March 1864. While 'good at opening a case [Moir was] not so good at replying'; B. Hillyard, 'Moir, George (1800–1870)', in *Oxford Dictionary of National Biography*, Oxford University Press, available at <http://www.oxforddnb.com/view/article/18891> (last accessed 25 October 2017).

because it involved such a high-profile proprietor, but also because it was considered by Skene & Peacock as very favourable.[95] The progress and result of the case are discussed in Chapter 4. It was a success for the Association but of limited value because it had not been fought by the Crown.[96] At the same time as the Argyll case was being considered, the Association adopted the defence of the claim by the Crown against another member, Maclean of Ardgour.[97] This claim arose out of the refusal by Maclean to pay for the transfer from the Crown of the relevant piece of foreshore for the construction of a pier. It was a case that the Crown considered a good one for trying the Crown's right to the foreshore. The Crown also believed that it was 'desirable from the agitation which the assertion of the Crown's right to the foreshore is occasioning in some parts of the Country that the question should be definitively settled'.[98] While George Young and Thomas Ivory[99] advised the Crown in February 1864 that the case was a favourable one, a less enthusiastic view was given in May 1865 by an English barrister, W. M. James QC, who had been asked to look at the case by Horace Watson, the Solicitor in England to the Office of Woods.[100] James thought that if the case

95 DVGN 570/4, Letter Skene & Peacock to Macleod, 9 December 1863. Loch himself thought that it was impossible to consider the duke's case too favourable; DVGN 570/2/15, Letter Loch to Macleod, 12 December 1863. But, as we see in Chapter 4, it was not considered to be so favourable by the duke's own lawyer.

96 The Association had also intended to take up the case of another member, MacFie of Airds, in which the Crown was to take an action of declarator to establish the Crown's ownership of the foreshore. But before the summons was executed, MacFie paid the Crown for a transfer of the relevant piece of foreshore so that he could start the construction of a pier, and the Crown dropped the case.

97 NRAS, 3583/Bundle 10, Letter Macleod to Ardgour, 14 January 1864.

98 NRS, CR 11/75, Case for the Commissioners of Her Majesty's Woods for the opinion of Crown Counsel, and opinion, 17 February 1864.

99 Young had given the 1862 opinion to the Association before his appointment as Solicitor General. Thomas Ivory was the standing counsel to the Office of Woods in Scotland between 1862 and 1882.

100 William Milbourne James; during his career he was junior counsel to the Treasury in equity, the Office of Woods, the Inland Revenue and the board of works; he became vice-chancellor of the court of chancery in 1869 and in 1870 was made a Lord Justice of Appeal. 'He was thought a good judge by his contemporaries, being educated, shrewd, and firm, and was remembered for his terse and clear enunciation of legal principles'; J. A. Hamilton, 'James, Sir William Milbourne (1807–1881)', rev. H. Mooney, in *Oxford Dictionary of National Biography*, Oxford University Press, available at <http://www.oxforddnb.com/view/article/14630> (last accessed 25 October 2017). James was one of the team of Crown Counsel that gave the opinion on the ownership of the foreshore discussed in Chapter 5.

was tried in England, it would be perfectly hopeless because there was very persuasive evidence of possession by the gathering of seaware for manure and kelp. Notwithstanding this, the Crown continued with its action. In his opening speech for the Crown, Thomas Ivory explained very clearly what was at stake:

> In this case the question is, for the first time, raised in a pure and direct shape: what is the proper legal character of the Crown's right and interest in the shores of Scotland? Is it a right of exclusive property in the Crown, and therefore such that the proprietor of an adjacent estate, unless he has an express grant of the foreshore, or has a barony title, combined with prescriptive possession, has no rights in the foreshore except as one of the public; or, on the contrary, is the right of property in the foreshore *prima facie* in the proprietor of the adjacent estate to such an extent that any proprietor, without proof of prescription but simply by the fact of his possessing an adjacent property, can use and appropriate the foreshore as his own property, unless the Crown shall be able to shew that such use and appropriation is detrimental to the public?[101]

The Lord Ordinary, Lord Jerviswoode, decided in favour of Maclean in January 1866 based on the fact that Maclean had a barony title to his estate and that this, coupled with the very substantial possession of the foreshore for over forty years, gave him title to the foreshore.[102] The judge did not decide the main proposition of the proprietors that the *ex adverso* proprietor owned the foreshore by implication without express grant or proof of possession; indeed, in his reply on behalf of Maclean, John Millar told the judge, somewhat surprisingly given the avowed aims of the Association, that he need not decide the main proposition:

> It is true that we have a plea on record, that by virtue of our titles alone, and without possession we have that which entitles us to judgement in our favour. But if your Lordship comes to be satisfied that it is not necessary to deal with that question, because we have at all events a title which, when fortified by possession, is sufficient, then my client has no interest to insist on judgement on the abstract question. All that he desires to have is a judgement in his favour, on whichever of the two grounds that judgement may be placed.[103]

101 TNA:PRO, MT 10/139, Report of Debate in action of declarator the Lord Advocate against Alexander Maclean of Ardgour, p. 2.

102 Lord Advocate v. Maclean (1866) 38 Scot. Jur. 584 and 2 Scottish Law Reporter 25. Discussed in Ae Mackay, 'The foreshore question', *Journal of Jurisprudence*, 11 (1867), pp. 75–88.

103 TNA:PRO, MT 10/139, Report of Debate in action of declarator the Lord Advocate against Alexander Maclean of Ardgour, p. 40.

The Crown initially intended to appeal the decision but the Lord Advocate advised against it on the basis that no decision was given, or opinion expressed, on the main question affecting the Crown's rights to the Scottish foreshore and also because of the imminent transfer of the responsibility for the management of the foreshore to the Board of Trade discussed in Chapter 3.[104] We shall see that this decision not to appeal was one that came to haunt the permanent officials at the Board in 1871, who believed that this acquiescence in the decision had exacerbated the problem with the proprietors.

In addition to these two cases and three further cases taken up by the Association in 1869, discussed in Chapter 5, there were a number of other cases fought between 1851 and 1869 that did not involve the Association, which showed that there continued to be a variety of opinion as to the question of who owned the foreshore.[105]

## MOTIVATIONS FOR MEMBERSHIP OF THE ASSOCIATION

Out of a total membership of 130, the Macleod muniments contain correspondence relating to the membership of all but eleven of the members. About half of the proprietors who joined the Association did so in an informal manner, simply sending back the pre-addressed and printed reply which accompanied the *Edinburgh Evening Courant* article distributed in January 1865, or by merely writing in brief terms that they wished to join without giving any reasons. The correspondence from this half, therefore, tells us nothing of the motivations for membership other than, perhaps, that the proprietors who joined in this way were not sufficiently motivated to explain why they joined or that they implicitly accepted and agreed with the reasons for the formation of the Association, and in this half of the correspondence there are a number of messages of support and good wishes for the success of the Association. However, the correspondence of the other half, together with correspondence from proprietors who decided not to join, provides an interesting insight into the motivations that proprietors had for joining or not joining the Association.

There are three broadly defined categories of motivation for mem-

[104] NRS, CR 11/77, Letter Donald Horne to Office of Woods, 9 May 1866; PP, 1866, LX, Return of Correspondence between the Treasury and the Board of Trade as to the transfer of the Management of certain rights of the Crown in Tidal Lands, p. 3.

[105] Robbie, *Private Water Rights*, paras 3.37–3.38.

bership. The first, and the one into which most of the members fell, may be described as a wish that all proprietors should unite to defeat what were seen as the unjust claims of the Crown which were conducted in an unfair manner by the Office of Woods. A belief that the proprietors should present a united front appears to have been strong. James Baikie of Orkney, whose foreshore had been conveyed to him by the Crown 'from the lowest ebb to the highest tide' and who, therefore, was in a strong position, nonetheless thought that 'it is becoming to unite in opposing the "Dog in the Manger" attempt of Her Majesty's Woods and Forests'.[106] Further examples of expressions of unity include that of Augustus Clarke of Nairn who wrote:

> I think it right to tell you that I am the owner of but a few yards of coast so that my contributing to a common fund in proportion to my interest would I fear be a drop in the ocean. At the same time should it be thought by the Committee desirable that all, however little interested, should unite, I have no objection to joining the Association.[107]

Another is that of Viscount Hill who said: 'My interest in the foreshores is very trifling – but to show my concurrence with the objects of the association I shall be happy to have my name placed among the list of subscribers for £25.'[108] Kenneth Macleod of Grishernish believed that 'no doubt every proprietor will want to contribute to stop the Crown encroachment'.[109] This feeling of unity appears to have been a strong motivating feature and, as the examples above show, was a feeling that motivated even those who had a small extent of foreshore or could contribute only a small amount. There are a number of references to the proprietor offering his 'mite' in the cause: Sir Thomas Riddell of Ardnamurchan wrote that 'The subject is a very important one. I am sorry I cannot afford to subscribe to it as I would wish; I dare say, however, you will not refuse my mite so please put me down for £5.'[110] But it would be wrong to suggest that the feeling of unity was all pervading. There were some proprietors, albeit small in number, whose decision to join was motivated not by a feeling of unity with fellow proprietors but by a desire to see a decision in the courts which personally benefited them. Sir James Hall of Dunglas, for example, wrote, in a letter that contrasted strongly with the feelings

[106] DVGN 572/125, Letter Baikie to Macleod, 1 February 1865.
[107] DVGN 572/18, Letter Clarke to Macleod, 7 October 1861.
[108] DVGN 572/72, Letter Hill to Macleod, 15 December 1863.
[109] DVGN 572/1/3, Letter Macleod to Macleod, 10 November 1863.
[110] DVGN 572/99, Letter Riddell to Macleod, 26 December 1863.

of unity suggested by James Baikie who had no personal interest that needed protection:

> Thinking it possible that as holding from the Crown and paying heavy feu duties thereunto I might not be liable to the encroachments complained of by other proprietors whose terms might be different or whose Charters might be differently worded I resolved to defer communicating with you until I had spoken to my agent in Edinburgh. He tells me, however, that my case is precisely similar in effect . . . to make it worthwhile to subscribe for £25.[111]

The Earl of Zetland was a proprietor that the committee was keen should join the Association; Skene & Peacock considered he had 'perhaps as large a seaboard as any proprietor in Scotland and we think he should be asked for a subscription of £100 at least'.[112] At the end of 1863 the Earl explained that if the case selected for trial by the committee had applied to his estates, he would have joined for £100; but when the Association took up the case involving Maclean of Ardgour, he considered that it fulfilled his criteria and so he then joined. He was not, however, prepared to join simply to show a united front.[113] Nevertheless, these examples of pure self-interest are limited,[114] and the actions of the Office of Woods and the manner in which it had conducted itself were enough motivation, in themselves, for most of the proprietors to join the Association. Sir William Dalyell complained of the 'most arbitrary, scandalous act of tyranny in which [the Office of Woods] tried to frighten a single handed individual'.[115] David Napier of Kilmun in Argyll was 'pleased to see such a formidable array of names determined to oppose such a monstrous, injudicious and tyrannical exercise of a pretended prerogative of the Crown' and when Napier sent his first call on the subscription moneys in 1866, he referred to 'that most impolitic and injudicious interference of the Woods & Forests into the shores of the County . . . [their actions] . . . are ill judged and imprudent meddling'.[116] The actions

[111] DVGN 572/132/1/2, Letter Hall to Macleod, 25 January 1865.

[112] DVGN 570/4/30, Letter Skene & Peacock to Macleod, 23 November 1863.

[113] DVGN 570/1/3, Letter Zetland to Macleod, 28 December 1863.

[114] There are further examples of self-interest that are noted below of proprietors who decided not to join because they did not believe the Association would be of personal benefit to them.

[115] DVGN 572/116/1, Letter Dalyell to Macleod, 24 January 1865.

[116] DVGN 570/1/3, Letter Napier to Macleod, 20 September 1861; Letter Napier to Macleod, 1 January 1864. Napier's reference to the formidable array of names is to the list of those who had already subscribed when the 1861 circular was sent out and suggests that publication of the names was not as inadvisable as Loch had thought it might be.

of the Office of Woods were considered by a number of proprietors as being nothing less than theft: Lord Saltoun described their actions as 'robberies and usurpations by the Crown of the foreshore',[117] and David Dundas complained at the actions of James Howard, the Commissioner at the Office of Woods, in selling to him

> with cool effrontery scarcely credible a hundred acres on my father's estate . . . well knowing that my father holds ample charters for these lands which have descended to him for upwards of seven centuries . . . My father and I naturally feel very indignant at an attempted act of spoliation, aggravated by the endeavours to wrong us made by a public officer who should protect us and not injure our interests.[118]

The Duke of Argyll considered that the actions of the Office of Woods amounted to 'illegal encroachments of the Crown on the rights of the proprietors'.[119] Euan Baillie of Dochfour considered that it was the lawyers who were to blame: 'These attempts are got up against the rights of proprietors by the lawyers to take credit from the Government and to put money into their own pockets.'[120] We shall see in Chapter 4 that the actions of Donald Horne, the Solicitor in Scotland to the Office of Woods, were regarded with suspicion by the Duke of Argyll, and Euan Baillie's letter is an example of the suspicions held by other proprietors; indeed, a number of other proprietors referred specifically to Horne: Major Cumming Bruce referred to Horne as being 'grasping' and Captain Mackay considered that Horne had, in effect, misled him into conceding his foreshore to the Crown.[121] The Earl of Selkirk was concerned at the manner in which Horne had conducted proceedings that Selkirk had been concerned with and specifically referred to the suggestion that Horne had probably benefited from the foreshore question when Horne's business account was questioned in the House of Commons.[122] At least one proprietor saw the Association's victory in the Macleod of Ardgour case as being nothing less than a personal defeat of Donald Horne.[123] The injustice, as the proprietors saw it, of

[117] DVGN 570/1/3, Letter Saltoun to Macleod, 28 August 1864.

[118] DVGN 572/134, Letter Dundas to Macleod, 29 September 1865.

[119] DVGN 572/9, Letter Argyll to Macleod, 26 August 1861; see further in Chapter 4.

[120] DVGN 572/69, Letter Baillie to Macleod, 4 December 1863.

[121] DVGN 572/71/1, Letter Cumming Bruce to Macleod, 1 December 1863; DVGN 572/1/3, Mackay to Macleod, 6 February 1865.

[122] DVGN 572/36, Letter Selkirk to Macleod, 5 November 1861.

[123] DVGN 572/98/2, Letter Cowie to Macleod, 29 January 1866.

the claims of the Crown was an affront to them. The Duke of Hamilton considered the proceedings of the Crown to be 'very alarming' and he was prepared 'to oppose by every means in my power what I consider to be most unjust grounds'.[124]

The sense of injustice felt by proprietors at what were seen to be illegal demands being made by the Office of Woods is reflected in the second broad category of motivating factors, and this is the sense which a number of proprietors expressed in writing, that the rights of the proprietors amounted to nothing less than vested interests which the Crown should be protecting, not attacking. This plea that vested interests should be protected is exactly the same as the plea by the kelp proprietors in 1827 for the continuation of the fiscal protection the kelp estates had enjoyed.[125] In the letters from most, if not all, the proprietors who expressed their reasons for wanting to join the Association, there is a very clear sense that the rights of the proprietors were being violated by the actions of the Office of Woods, and references to proprietorial rights and the protection or defence of those rights are commonplace.[126] A number of proprietors expressed their proprietorial rights as being vested interests. For example, Duncan Davidson of Tulloch saw the claims of the Crown 'to be an encroachment on vested interests which in some cases have existed for centuries'.[127] So far as Davidson was concerned, however, it would hardly be fair to say that these interests had been vested in his family for centuries because his ancestors were West Indian merchants in London whose estates in Ross had been purchased with the fortunes earned from this business.[128] Hercules Scott of Craigo told Macleod: 'My ancestors and I have always for centuries enjoyed undisturbed the fruits of the shore and I look with great apprehension

[124] DVGN 572, Letter Hamilton to Macleod, 22 June 1861. A similar strength of feeling over the actions of the Office of Woods was evident in Wales; for example, one landowner protested against the alleged infringement of his rights by the Crown's 'asserting dormant claims shrouded in obscurity, and upheld by Prerogative – maxims, originating in a feudal age'; Pryce and Owen, 'Mid-Victorian foreshore', p. 176.

[125] J. MacAskill, 'The Highland kelp proprietors and their struggle over the salt and barilla duties, 1817–1831', *Journal of Scottish Historical Studies*, 26:1–2 (2006), pp. 64, 68.

[126] Examples of this may be seen in DVGN 572/38, Letter Blantyre to Macleod, 8 November 1861; DVGN 572/69, Letter Baillie to Macleod, 4 December 1863; DVGN 572/37, Letter Rainey to Macleod, 7 November 1861.

[127] DVGN 572/107, Letter Davidson to Macleod, 28 November 1863.

[128] See Rev. G. Henderson (ed.), *Memoirs of a Highland Gentleman, Being the Reminiscences of Evander Maciver of Scourie* (Edinburgh, 1905), pp. 109–10.

to the possible extinction of these rights.'[129] We see in these letters the distinct belief that something that proprietors had considered had been theirs for centuries should be protected and that the encroachments on these vested interests by the Crown were particularly difficult to accept. Linked to, and part of, this sense of the usurpation of proprietorial rights is the concern expressed by a number of proprietors that not only was it objectionable that the Crown should be challenging rather than protecting these rights, but it was particularly objectionable that the public should, through the Office of Woods, be asserting rights and, moreover, rights which damaged proprietorial interests, including the right of privacy. Captain Allan Macdonald of Waternish was concerned at 'the possibility of the public asserting rights and damaging the seaware which is of considerable importance'.[130] Macdonald's concern was over the economic interest in the foreshore being challenged by the public, but other proprietors expressed a concern over the privacy of their estates being invaded by the public if the claims of the Crown were to be vindicated.[131] We know that the Duke of Argyll was especially fond of the privacy which his estate at Rosneath provided him and his family, and it was the privacy of the shores which was of particular importance:

> Magnificent beeches drooped their branches over the very water at high tide, whilst true Scots fir trees and the two largest silver firs in Europe adorned the elevations which sloped gently into the sea. One great attraction of the place was its privacy. Being a peninsula, there were no public roads following the line of the coast, as is very usual in the Highlands. The shores were part of the estate.[132]

The enthusiasm for the building of gothic and picturesque mansion houses on Scottish estates in the 1830s and 1840s has been noted by

[129] DVGN 570/1/3, Letter Scott to Macleod, 26 January 1865.

[130] DVGN 570/1/3, Letter Macdonald to Macleod, 3 December 1864. A point that was, as we shall see in Chapter 7, to be made in relation to the proposed legislation in 1891 that aimed to give rights to seaware to crofters and the public.

[131] We should, however, note that Macdonald had, in 1863, purchased the Waternish foreshore from the Crown. Although he was the owner of the *ex adverso* land, he did not challenge the Crown's title to the foreshore and his acquisition of it was 'to employ the poor people of my property in the cutting and manufacturing of seaware into kelp as they are becoming every year more destitute and require that every measure should be tried, in order to improve their condition and raise them above the demoralising influence of public charity'; NRS, CR 11/374, Letter Macdonald to the Office of Woods, 27 June 1863.

[132] Argyll, The Dowager Duchess (ed.), *George Douglas, Eighth Duke of Argyll: Autobiography and Memoirs* (London, 1906), vol. I, p. 266.

Macinnes, a trend which was 'probably begun by Kirkman Finlay with his acquisition of his Castle Toward estate in . . . 1818 . . . [and reaching] its apogee with the mansion building of the Malcolms of Poltalloch'.[133] Devine has noted the wholesale transformation of the pattern of landownership in the western Highlands and islands by the 1850s, with the sale of Highland estates out of the hands of the hereditary proprietors to be replaced with a new breed of proprietors comprising, in the main, Lowland or English interests. The acquisition of Highland estates at this time by this new elite was often by men 'who could afford to indulge themselves because they were among the wealthiest in Britain';[134] it is no surprise, therefore, to find in the letters from members of the Association objections to the policies and actions of the Office of Woods based on concerns that the privacy afforded by these estates, and by implication the aesthetics of the mansions built, was threatened by these actions and policies. Indeed, the article in the *Edinburgh Evening Courant* had appealed directly to these concerns of proprietors by referring to the dreadful possibility of factories or fish curing establishments being erected under the drawing room windows if the Crown's claims to the foreshore were to be successful. But the surprise, perhaps, that we do find in examining these letters is that the most vociferous complaints of invasion of privacy come not, as we might have expected, from a member of the new elite, but from the Earl of Selkirk.[135]

Before the formation of the Association, the Earl of Selkirk had been negotiating with the Office of Woods for the purchase of stretches of the foreshore *ex adverso* his estate. As he said to Macleod, he had fallen in with the policies of the Office of Woods in relation to the foreshore because he supposed 'that such a claim [by the Crown] would not be put

[133] A. I. Macinnes, 'From clanship to clearance in Argyllshire', in T. M. Devine (ed.), *Scottish Elites* (Edinburgh, 1994), p. 19.

[134] T. M. Devine, 'The emergence of the new elite in the western Highlands and islands, 1800–60', in T. M. Devine (ed.), *Improvement and Enlightenment* (Edinburgh, 1989), pp. 109–42. This transformation took place throughout Europe; indeed, 'The middle-class purchase of landed estates from impoverished noble families was one of the most widespread social phenomena of the post-feudal period in nineteenth century Europe'; R. J. Evans, *The Pursuit of Power: Europe 1815–1914* (London, 2016), p. 286.

[135] Indeed, the three members of the new elite whose extravagance in acquiring Highland estates has been highlighted in Devine, 'Emergence of the new elite', pp. 129, 130 (James Morrison of Islay – through his son Charles – and Sir Alexander Matheson and his uncle Sir James Matheson) made no mention of this particular concern.

forward unless the right was really and substantially in the Crown'.[136] In his negotiations with James Howard at the Office of Woods, Selkirk had made clear the main reason why he wanted to secure his title to the foreshore:

> it would be very important to acquire the right of keeping people off the shore – for if they come round there it is impossible to prevent trespass upon the walks and the consequences you may imagine considering the peculiar habits of the people would be very intolerable – and the seafaring population are almost the worst in this respect . . . [and Selkirk wanted] . . . the power of excluding trespassers who might make the place intolerable to a family of females and children.[137]

Selkirk objected to the fact that the Crown was asserting ownership of the foreshore when, it now appeared, they had no right to it, and he also chose, on joining the Association, to complain bitterly about the general right of way that the public claimed over the foreshore. Not only did Selkirk want his own title to the foreshore confirmed, he also wanted to exclude the public from the foreshore entirely. In his letters to Macleod, Selkirk made clear his distaste at the public being allowed near his family residence. He believed that to concede to the public a right of way over the foreshore 'would destroy all comforts in this place' and, worse, that if the right of way was conceded, he would 'have all the blackguards in the town bathing on the shore of this place where the bathing house is situated' and 'the concession of this right would make it impossible to keep drunken sailors out of the place at all seasons: in short the place would have to be given up as a residence'.[138] Unsurprisingly, the Office of Woods refused to insert a clause in the transfer deed expressly conferring on the purchaser a right to exclude the public from the foreshore.[139] We should note that Selkirk's concern to deny the public any rights over the foreshore of his estate was not, in the main, shared by the Association. The opinion obtained by the Association's counsel

136 DVGN 570/1/3, Letter Selkirk to Macleod, 5 March 1861.

137 NRS, CR 11/393, Letters Selkirk to Howard, 14 April 1859, 1 March 1860.

138 DVGN 572/36, Letter Selkirk to Macleod, 16 July 1869.

139 See Hope v. Bennewith (1904) 6 F 1004 at p. 1007 – a case in which the court commented on the fact that the late Earl of Selkirk had acquired the foreshore to protect his privacy but nonetheless refused to grant an interdict preventing a member of the public from entering on the foreshore, and the Lord Justice-Clerk gave his opinion that the public had the right to shoot wildfowl on the foreshore, a decision and opinion that, had he still been alive, would have horrified Selkirk. The question whether Selkirk's desire to deny to the public access to the foreshore for bathing may have had a legal foundation is considered in Chapter 9.

in 1862 had, as we saw, made it clear that whoever owned the foreshore, the public had rights to use the foreshore for 'various purposes'; and, as we see in Chapter 5, the Bill proposed by the Association to settle the ownership question acknowledged some public rights over the foreshore. In addition to his concern to protect the ladies of his family from embarrassment while bathing, the Earl of Selkirk made two telling points. He told Macleod that 'were kelp ever to recover its value, the property in question would amount to a serious sum'.[140] We shall return to this point in a discussion of the comments from those members of the Association who made a similar point. Selkirk also expressed a concern that to be seen to be challenging the Crown by joining the Association could have unfortunate consequences, and he had some advice to give Macleod. While he was very happy to subscribe the substantial sum of £100,

> I should not like [my membership] to appear in any printed or circulated list – I have a strong idea that one is liable to heavy penalties for so doing, so for any sake be cautious and recollect that you have to deal with an adversary who has sharp eyes, long ears and no mercy.[141]

The third broad category of motivation was that the actions and policies of the Crown raised issues generally of great magnitude and importance that should be taken seriously by proprietors. Alexander Campbell of Auchindarroch hoped that, in applying for membership, 'the magnitude of the interests at stake may cause a powerful association to arise',[142] and Thomas Edmonstone felt 'a great interest in the question at issue and I beg to enclose my mite for the purpose . . . of determining this very important matter'.[143] Charles Forbes of Kingairloch believed that 'the question of the right of the use of foreshores is of so much importance to every proprietor'.[144]

In addition to the comments from members as to the reasons for their membership of the Association, the letters from members, and also from proprietors who decided not to join the Association, contain a number of other interesting issues. As we noted above, the Earl of Selkirk saw wider risks that might flow from involvement with the Association, and

[140] DVGN 572/36, Letter Selkirk to Macleod, 5 November 1861.

[141] DVGN 570/1/3, Letter Selkirk to Macleod, 16 December 1863. Macleod's friend William Brand had expressed, as we noted above, similar concerns on behalf of Macleod.

[142] DVGN 572/16, Letter Campbell to Macleod, 22 January 1861.

[143] DVGN 572/97, Letter Edmonstone to Macleod, 9 February 1864.

[144] DVGN 570/1/3, Letter Forbes to Macleod, 11 April 1861.

two other proprietors expressed similar concerns. Mr Carrick Moore wrote to Macleod rejecting membership, saying that he was not sufficiently satisfied with the claims being put forward 'as to wish to enter into litigation with such an adversary as the Crown'; and Mr Bruce of Kennet declined membership because he did not want to be a party to the promotion of a case against the Crown.[145] Some proprietors were not prepared to join before receiving information on the membership and management of the Association. David Balfour of Kirkwall, notwithstanding that he told Finlay that the aims of the Association had the support of the Commissioners for Supply in Zetland, asked for information as to membership in 1861 and did not, in fact, join until January 1865 after he had received it; and Colonel Carrick Buchanan of Drumphellin was only prepared to join after requesting and receiving information from Macleod as to membership.[146] Duncan Darroch wrote to Finlay in October 1861 saying that he was disposed to join but that, before doing so, he needed information on the management of the Association. On being told the composition of the committee, Darroch responded: 'I am glad to find your Committee so well selected and will give in my name to join.'[147] Sir J. M. Macleod of St Kilda wanted to meet with Norman Macleod because he did not 'at the moment have sufficient information for the purpose of judging what course of action interested proprietors should pursue'.[148] In addition to these requests for information and clarification, a larger number of proprietors expressed concern or confusion over the limits of their liability in joining the Association. We have examined this aspect of the proprietors' letters earlier in this chapter, but we should note here that the fact that a number of proprietors did raise the issue is indicative of a level of financial concern which might suggest that at least some of the proprietors were wary of taking on the Crown in the uncertain world of litigation. This is emphasised by the fact that there were a number of proprietors who wrote to Macleod and who gave as their reason for not joining the Association the uncertainties of cost and expense. Mr Campbell of Shirvan said that

145 DVGN 572/35, Letter Moore to Macleod, 1 November 1861; DVGN 570/1/3, Letter Bruce to Macleod, 11 December 1863.

146 DVGN 570/1/3, Letter Balfour to Finlay, 31 June 1861; DVGN 572/130, Letter Balfour to Macleod, January 1865; DVGN 572/88/1, Letter Buchanan to Macleod, 7 January 1864; DVGN 572/88/2, Letter Macleod to Buchanan, 12 January 1864; DVGN 572/88/3, Letter Buchanan to Macleod, 18 January 1864.

147 DVGN 572/21, Letter Darroch to Finlay, 7 October 1861; DVGN 572/26, Letter Darroch to Macleod, 17 October 1861.

148 DVGN 572/49, Letter Macleod to Macleod, 5 June 1862.

he feared 'great expense and I am unable and unwilling to forgo any uncertain measure of responsibility'.[149] Captain Campbell of Barbreck said: 'there being nothing along the foreshore of this property which the Crown could take to its advantage I do not feel inclined to incur any expense in the matter referred to in your circular'.[150] Patrick Royle of Sheralton made a similar point in declining membership:

> I should in any circumstances decline in joining any association, however laudable its object, without having some idea of what extent I should be expected to contribute. But in my own case, I do not anticipate any aggression on my rights for me to subscribe to the proposed object.[151]

These last two letters are, of course, examples of proprietors who were not disposed to join because they did not believe the Association would benefit them, and they fall to be classified with the letters from proprietors examined above who did decide to join because they believed the Association *would* personally benefit them. There are further examples of proprietors who decided not to join because they did not believe the Association would benefit them personally: Thomas Cameron of Zetland did not wish to join because 'Zetland is too distant and insignificant for our rights to be interfered with'[152] and Mr G. M. Henderson, having consulted his lawyers, considered that it 'would be unnecessary for me to join the Association', although he wished the Association well.[153] Sir Andrew Agnew of Lochnaw, whose estate was to be involved in the leading case on the issue in 1873 discussed in Chapter 5, originally declined membership in 1863, explaining that while he 'agreed as to the injustice, my relevant property is of small value and I would rather try to buy off all chance of annoyance for a mere trifle'.[154] These are all examples of proprietors who did not share the same feelings of unity that we saw expressed in the letters from proprietors who did join the Association. And there is a further, high-profile example of a proprietor who did not wish to join for his own personal reasons and did not see the need for proprietors to act in a united front: that of Sir James Matheson, the proprietor of Lewis. In his letter to Macleod,

149 DVGN 570/1/3, Letter Campbell to Macleod, 10 January 1861.

150 DVGN 570/1/3, Letter Campbell to Macleod, 21 December 1863.

151 DVGN 572/13, Letter Royle to Macleod, 28 August 1861.

152 DVGN 572/19, Letter Cameron to Macleod, 7 October 1861. He might also have added that as udal law applied, his case would have been different from the rest of Scotland.

153 DVGN 572/100, Letter Henderson to Macleod, 18 February 1864.

154 DVGN 570/1/3, Letter Agnew to Macleod, 28 November 1863.

Matheson explained his decision not to join: 'various circumstances of a peculiar nature affecting my interests in the Foreshores render it necessary for me to have the power of acting in my own behalf and independently of others'.[155] Matheson clearly had in mind the foreshore at Stornoway Bay where he wanted to establish a title so that proposals for the management of the quay could be finalised. He was not prepared to wait for what he saw as 'the slow and doubtful result' of litigation proposed by the Association and he had been advised to purchase the alleged interest of the Crown in the relevant piece of the foreshore.[156] Matheson petitioned the Treasury for a grant of the foreshore in July 1862 and the relevant piece of foreshore was transferred to him on 14 July 1863.[157] The Association would not have appreciated such a move by a high-profile proprietor such as Matheson. One of the complaints of the Association was that proprietors were, in effect, being bullied by the Office of Woods into purchasing pieces of foreshore from the Crown. Matheson could not be said to be a person who fell into the category of the oppressed private proprietor.[158]

We conclude this examination of the letters from proprietors as to membership of the Association by noting what was said about kelp. We might, perhaps, have expected that the implications for the kelp industry would have been a prominent feature of such correspondence but this is unlikely for three reasons. First, by the 1860s the kelp industry was, apart from one or two areas, still in a depressed state: it was not a source of huge profit as it had been or, indeed, profitable at all. Second, most of the leading kelp proprietors in the Western Isles had, by the 1860s, lost their estates through enforced sale or bankruptcy. So, Mackenzie of Seaforth had sold the island of Lewis in 1844 to Sir James Matheson; the bankrupt Alexander Norman Macleod of Harris had sold Harris to the Earl of Dunmore in 1834; Clanranald had sold significant amounts of

155 DVGN 572/53, Letter Matheson to Macleod, 22 July 1862.

156 Private statement in relation to the Report of Proceedings of Meeting held at Stornoway, 1 June 1863. (The author is grateful to Alexander Matheson of Stornoway for drawing his attention to, and providing him with a copy of, this document.)

157 PP, 1863, L, Copy of any Petition by Sir James Matheson, Baronet, to the Treasury, for a Grant of Foreshore in Stornaway [sic], in the Island of Lewis; of any Report by the Crown Agent in Scotland; and of any Disposition by the Crown of such Foreshore, in favour of Sir James Matheson; see also DVGN 552/1&3. Matheson also decided not to challenge the Crown over foreshore at Ullapool in 1868, preferring, again, to purchase the relevant piece for a nominal price; see TNA:PRO, MT 10/131.

158 He was one of the wealthiest men in the country.

his estates, in particular South Uist in 1839 to Lieutenant Colonel John Gordon of Cluny; MacNeil of Barra had sold the island of Barra in 1839 to James Menzies who sold it in 1840 to Gordon of Cluny; and Lord Macdonald had sold his North Uist estate in 1856 to Sir John Powlett Orde.[159] Third, the purchase price for the estates sold would not have included any significant sum for kelp rentals and, therefore, purchases of the estates would not have been made on the basis of a material income from the manufacture and sale of kelp.[160] The kelp proprietors who had led the campaigns against the abolition of the salt tax and the duty on barilla in the 1820s were, therefore, no longer involved. The old guard and many others of the Highlands and islands estate proprietors had been replaced by members of what Devine has termed the 'new elite': they were 'men who had made their money in trade, industry and the urban professions of banking and law'.[161] If the kelp industry had still been a profitable business, we would have expected the threat to these men's interest in the foreshores of their estates to have been a prominent reason for their membership of the Association. But, for the reasons we have explained, it was not. The continuum between the experiences of the kelp proprietors at the height of the industry and the owners of the kelp shores at the time of challenge to ownership of the foreshore by the Crown had been largely broken.[162] Nevertheless, the significance of the ownership of the foreshore in the context of kelp was raised by a number of members of the Association. We saw earlier that Sir Thomas Riddell of Ardnamurchan wrote, in 1861, to Alexander Finlay to thank him for his contribution to the debate in the House of Commons

[159] J. Barron, *The Northern Highlands in the Nineteenth Century* (Inverness, 1907), vol. 2, pp. 245, 291; J. Hunter, *The Islanders and the Orb* (Stornoway, 2001), p. 19; W. C. Mackenzie, *History of the Outer Hebrides* (Paisley, 1903), pp. 494–6.

[160] See PP, 1841, VI, First Report from the Select Committee on Condition of the population of the Islands and Highlands of Scotland, and Practicability of affording Relief by means of Emigration, Qs 160, 2091. There would, however, have been some estates (e.g. those where the British Seaweed Company had leases, i.e. North Uist), where the estate would have had some value from kelp leases; see British Seaweed Company (1866) 4 M 1139 and John Gordon of Cluny (1866) 4 M 1141 as to the value of the kelp shores of North and South Uist under the Lands Valuation (Scotland) Act 1854; see also Chapter 7.

[161] T. M. Devine, *Exploring the Scottish Past* (East Linton, 1995), p. 168.

[162] A point that was noted by the Rev. R. C. Macleod who commented, as we saw in Chapter 1, that it was as well the challenge to ownership from the Crown had not occurred 'during the palmy days of the kelp industry'; Macleod, *Book of Dunvegan*, vol. 2, p. 116.

> on the attacks made by the Crown on the rights of proprietors to the foreshores. It is really becoming a very serious question . . . what would have been the result if these claims had been asserted at the time when kelp was a great source of income to the Highland Proprietors? And even now seaware is extensively used for manure; to which I suppose we have no right![163]

Sir John Orde, the owner of North Uist, was aware of the significance of kelp because the kelp industry in North Uist was still marginally relevant to the economics of the estate in the context of the production of iodine. In his letter to Macleod requesting that his name be added to the list of members of the Association, Orde referred to the fact that he had just returned from a visit to North Uist with his wife where 'the Kelp making was in great force and I was interested in some experiments by our seaweed company tending to more profitable use of the weed'.[164] It is reasonable to assume that kelp was an important reason for Orde's membership of the Association. Hercules Scott of Craigo referred, as we saw earlier, to the fact that he and his ancestors had enjoyed undisturbed possession of the fruits of the shore and he was concerned that the Crown's actions would extinguish this possession.[165] Sir James Hall of Dunglas had decided to join the Association because he had 'sufficient interest in the possession of the shore arising from the ware'.[166] Sir John Forbes of Kincardineshire told Macleod that the interest proprietors had in the foreshore was for 'kelp, sand, ware etc.';[167] and, as we saw above, Captain Allan Macdonald, who had purchased Moidart from Macdonald of Clanranald in 1827 and Waternish in Skye from Charles Grant MP in 1831,[168] was 'concerned at the possibility of the public asserting rights and damaging the seaware which is of considerable importance'.[169] In discussing the letters from the Earl of Selkirk to Macleod, we drew attention to his telling comment that 'were kelp ever to recover its value, the property in question would amount to a serious sum'.[170]

[163] DVGN 570/1/3, Letter Riddell to Finlay, 20 April 1861, making the same point as the Rev. R. C. Macleod.

[164] DVGN 570/1/3, Letter Orde to Macleod, 12 March 1861.

[165] DVGN 570/1/3, Letter Scott to Macleod, 26 January 1865.

[166] DVGN 572/93, Letter Hall to Macleod, 25 January 1865.

[167] DVGN 572/93, Letter Forbes to Macleod, 2 May 1861.

[168] Devine, 'Emergence of the new elite', pp. 139–40.

[169] DVGN 570/1/3, Letter Macdonald to Macleod, 3 December 1864.

[170] DVGN 572/36, Letter Selkirk to Macleod, 5 November 1861.

## CONCLUSIONS

It was the increased interest on the part of the Crown in asserting its rights in the foreshore and the manner in which the Office of Woods had exercised its management responsibilities for the foreshore from the 1830s that had created such dissatisfaction, indeed anger, among the ranks of the private proprietors, and led to the confrontation between the Crown and private proprietors over the ownership of the foreshore and the formation of the Association. The formation of the Association in 1861 was a significant event in the history of landownership in Scotland. It showed a real determination on the part of private proprietors to use the law to defend what they saw as an unwarranted attack on private property and, even worse, an attack that came from the Crown. Proprietors had believed that it was an 'incontrovertible principle that protection was due to the landed interest of Great Britain'[171] and so this attack by the Crown on their perceived vested interests, the sacred right of property, came as a rude shock.

As to conclusions on what the Association achieved through its actions up to the end of 1866, we have seen that the Association fought and won two cases. But the main legal question – did every foreshore belong to the *ex adverso* proprietor whether expressly granted or not? – was still an open one and so, to that extent, the efforts of the Association were less than successful. The Crown's public position on the foreshore (that unless expressly granted by it or through possession, the foreshore belonged to the Crown) was not changed. But if the Association had not achieved success in relation to the main legal question, there can be little doubt that it had raised the issue of ownership of the foreshore to an important level and the Crown had been left in no doubt as to the feelings of the private proprietors. Furthermore, as we shall see in Chapter 3, the work and actions of the Association played a telling part in the decision to transfer the responsibility for the management of the foreshore from the Office of Woods to the Board of Trade in the Crown Lands Act 1866.

From 1867 onwards, the work of the Association would involve not just a series of confrontations with the Crown in a court of law, but also attempts to negotiate with the Board and, in particular, to persuade the Board to legislate in favour of the proprietors on the main legal question. This important aspect of the Association's work, together with its involvement in the crucial Agnew case, are examined in Chapter 5. The

[171] See MacAskill, 'Highland kelp proprietors', p. 68.

later work of the Association, in 1891, concerning legislation proposed by Charles Fraser Mackintosh MP that aimed to give rights to seaware to crofters and the public, and the winding up of the Association in 1952, are considered in Chapter 7.

# 3

# 'A strange piece of legislation' and 'a Jesuitical paper'

## INTRODUCTION

As we saw in Chapter 2, the responsibility for the management of Scotland's foreshore had been vested in the Office of Woods since 1833 and since 1862 the Board of Trade had assumed limited responsibilities for the foreshore relating to navigation. In 1866 the Crown Lands Act was passed, including provisions transferring the responsibility for the management of most of the foreshore from the Office of Woods to the Board. In the first part of this chapter we look at the reasons for the transfer and the passage of the Act through Parliament, with particular reference to the significant part played by the Association and its law agents Skene & Peacock. Shortly after the Act came into force, T. H. Farrer, the permanent secretary at the Board,[1] produced a memorandum explaining how the Board would deal with its new responsibilities for the foreshore and the bed of the sea, and in the second part of this chapter we examine this important memorandum. The reactions of the 8th Duke of Argyll and of the Association towards the memorandum are examined in, respectively, Chapters 4 and 5.

[1] Farrer was the first sole permanent secretary to the Board and 'as the architect of the nineteenth-century Board of Trade' he was 'one of the pillars of the mid-Victorian civil service'; J. Davis, 'Farrer, Thomas Henry, first Baron Farrer (1819–1899)', in *Oxford Dictionary of National Biography*, Oxford University Press, available at <http://www.oxforddnb.com/view/article/9194> (last accessed 25 October 2017).

## THE CROWN LANDS ACT 1866: 'A STRANGE PIECE OF LEGISLATION'

### *The reasons for the transfer of responsibilities for the management of the foreshore*

The received wisdom as to why the Crown Lands Act included provisions transferring responsibility for the management of the foreshore from the Office of Woods to the Board of Trade is based on correspondence between the Treasury and the Board at the end of 1865 and the beginning of 1866.[2] This correspondence suggests that the Board was proposing the transfer for administrative reasons. At the end of December 1865 Farrer had written to the secretary of the Treasury highlighting the division of responsibilities between the Office of Woods and the Board. He wrote that the Office of Woods, 'in whom the title to the soil is vested',[3] had the duty 'to deal with [the foreshore] as a matter of property and revenue' while the Board was charged 'under the Harbours Transfer Act 1862 . . . with the duty of protecting navigation, previously performed by the Admiralty'.[4] Farrer pointed out that the two departments could discharge their respective duties independently of one another and, at times, without consultation. So, for example, the Office of Woods might support a proposed project that the Board would wish to reject as a danger to navigation. Farrer wrote: 'It appears to the Board of Trade to deserve the consideration of the Treasury, whether this anomaly may not be put an end to.' He pointed to the several advantages which would result if the whole management of the Crown's rights and duties with respect to the foreshore was placed in the hands of the Board, but he noted, crucially, that if the Board was to take overall responsibility, it should do so on the basis of being empowered 'to deal with the foreshore with a view to public interests generally' and that therefore 'the revenue to be derived from it by them may be less than that derived from it by a department whose sole duty is to treat it as property'. Farrer suggested that the Treasury should consult with the Office of Woods over this

[2] Marston, *Marginal Seabed*, p. 24; PP, 1866, LX, Return of Correspondence between the Treasury and the Board of Trade as to the transfer of the Management of certain rights of the Crown in Tidal Lands.

[3] Farrer was incorrect: the Office of Woods had responsibility for management, but title to the foreshore remained vested in the Crown.

[4] Section 5 of the Harbours Transfer Act 1862 had provided that the responsibilities of the Admiralty under sections 12, 13, 16, 18 and 19 of the Harbours, Docks, and Piers Clauses Act 1847 should be transferred to the Board.

proposal.[5] But the Treasury files also show that the Office of Woods and the Treasury were already having discussions over a proposed transfer before Farrer's letter to the Treasury was written, and that the Treasury had already received a memorandum from the Office of Woods that had suggested 'a scheme for the settlement of the much vexed question of the Crown's interest in lands covered by Tidal waters, which . . . was long since before you in reference to a case in Scotland', and that the scheme suggested by this memorandum was directly linked to the actions of the Duke of Argyll that are discussed in Chapter 4 and the problems the Association had been causing.[6] While, no doubt, the reasons given in the 1866 Parliamentary Paper for the proposed transfer of responsibilities were correct in themselves, it is important to understand the forces and feelings which underlay these officially stated reasons and the effect the actions of the Association of Seaboard Proprietors of Scotland had had on the Office of Woods. It is possible that it was hoped that with the transfer from the embattled and heavily criticised Office of Woods (which had a duty to make a profit from its dealings with the foreshore) to the more neutral Board of Trade (which would not have such a duty but, rather, would be obliged to act in the public interest), there might exist the possibility for a more rational and less excitable debate between the Crown and the Association; and the Office of Woods believed that under the proposals, the system of dealing with the foreshore would be more favourable to proprietors and local communities. However, as we shall see in Chapter 5, that hope was not wholly realised; and one of the reasons for this was the form in which the provisions in the Crown Lands Act for transferring the responsibilities for the foreshore was finally approved by Parliament, to which we now turn.

[5] PP, 1866, LX, Return of Correspondence between the Treasury and the Board of Trade as to the transfer of the Management of certain rights of the Crown in Tidal Lands, Letter Farrer to the Treasury, 28 December 1865.

[6] TNA:PRO, T 250/2, Letter Gore to Gladstone, 22 November 1865; TNA:PRO, CRES 36/7, Draft Report with changes suggested by W. James Q.C., November 1865; TNA:PRO, CRES 36/7, Letter Gladstone to Gore, 25 November 1865; TNA:PRO, T 250/2, Letter Howard to Childers, 18 December 1865. Certainly Argyll believed that it was his 1865 correspondence with the Treasury that we discuss in Chapter 4 which had been decisive – see PD, Third Series, vol. 192, House of Lords 1868, col. 1816 (19 June 1868); although Richmond did not agree with this analysis – see column 1824.

## *The passage of the Crown Lands Bill through Parliament: the role of the Association and Skene & Peacock*

The Crown Lands Bill was presented to Parliament by the Chancellor of the Exchequer and read for the first time on 10 April 1866.[7] The part of the Bill relating to the foreshore was contained in clauses 6–26. The Association of Seaboard Proprietors of Scotland took a close interest in the Bill, and on 24 April George Loch wrote to Skene & Peacock sending them a copy of the Bill and asking them to consider the relevant provisions. In a letter to Loch, Skene & Peacock explained that their concern over the Bill centred on clauses 6, 7, 8, 9 and 10. Clause 7 provided that from 31 December 1866,

> all such Parts of and Rights and Interests in the Foreshore as then belong to Her Majesty in right of the Crown, except as in this Act provided, shall . . . be and the same are hereby transferred from the Management of the Commissioners of Woods to and thenceforth the same shall be under the Management of the Board of Trade.[8]

Clause 8 gave to the Board the power to sell or lease for such consideration or rent and on such conditions as the Board thought fit, parts of the foreshore to be used as sites for, or for the purposes connected with, harbours, docks or piers or other works of navigation, or public utility. Clause 9 gave to the Board the right to sell or to lease for such consideration or rent and on such conditions as the Board thought fit, any part of the foreshore not within the provisions of clause 8, provided such a sale or lease was expedient and would not be injurious to the interests of navigation or be inconsistent with the lawful or reasonable public use or enjoyment of any part of the foreshore. Clause 10 gave to the Board the power to grant licences to occupy the foreshore instead of sales or leases authorised by clauses 8 or 9, for such time, for such consideration or rent and on such conditions as the Board thought fit. These provisions were materially different from the existing powers of the Office of Woods contained in the Crown Lands Act 1829 and would not require, as the 1829 Act did, that sales and leases of the foreshore should be at full value. Farrer had believed it was critical that, if the Board was to be given responsibility for the foreshore, the Bill should empower the Board to deal with the foreshore 'with a view to public

[7] PD, Third Series, vol. 182, House of Commons, col. 1075 (10 April 1866).

[8] PP, 1866, Bills and Acts, Bill to amend Law relating to Woods, Forests and Land Revenues of Crown, Bill Number 98.

interests generally' and that the Board should not be required to make a profit out of its dealings. These clauses were drafted to give the Board the flexibility it needed and to free it from the constraints the Office of Woods had worked under. But this was not how Skene & Peacock saw it:

> We have gone over the Bill carefully. It happens to us a strange piece of legislation and we have felt a difficulty in getting at its real object and effect. It evidently means a lot more than a mere transference of management. A general enactment similar to Clause 7 should have been sufficient to transfer the management of the foreshore from one department to another on the assumption that it is the exclusive property of the Crown as contended by the Woods & Forests . . . and it is unusual to say the least to ask legislative authority to sell and lease what in their view partakes of the nature of exclusive property, as is proposed by Clauses 8 & 9.[9]

What, however, Skene & Peacock had missed was that there was already 'legislative authority to sell and lease' in the 1829 Act and that the existing powers of sale and lease had 'been purposely framed so as to prevent [the Office of Woods] parting with land at less than its value',[10] whether this was in the public interest or not. If the Board was to take a transfer of the management of the lands on the same basis as these existing legislative powers, the Board would be obliged to deal with the foreshore in the same manner as the Office of Woods. There was no question of the Bill giving to the Board powers of sale and lease over the foreshore, but simply to remove the requirement that any sale or lease should be at full value. Skene & Peacock was also concerned about the provisions of clause 24, which provided that the Crown was not to be liable to pay compensation for damage sustained by anyone in consequence of the exercise of any of the powers given by the Bill, by any lessee or other person claiming under the Crown. Skene & Peacock said that 'if the principle of the act were in other respects unobjectionable we should say that Clause 24 . . . is unjust and unfair towards the subject'. There was also, in clause 6, a provision that gave a definition of the foreshore that included any encroachment, embankment or enclosure of the foreshore. Skene & Peacock objected to this clause 'in so far as it is proposed to include any encroachment, embankment or enclosure on the foreshore without limitation. This would expose many proprietors who have enclosed large portions of shore at great expense to very

[9] DVGN 570/4/85, Copy letter Skene & Peacock to Loch, 1 May 1866.

[10] PP, 1867/68, LVII, Copy of Memorandum as to Board of Trade's Dealings with Foreshore and Bed of the Sea [hereafter Farrer Memorandum], p. 7.

serious questions.'[11] Skene & Peacock concluded its letter of advice to Loch by saying:

> Altogether this Bill appears to us to require very serious consideration and immediate steps should be taken to get Members of Parliament interested in the question. We cannot help thinking . . . the true effect of the Bill is to establish by implication the claims which in Scotland at least are disputed and to deal with the rights of proprietors and public as regards the foreshore in a very novel if not unconstitutional manner. Would it not be well to bring the matter under the notice of the Duke of Argyll and endeavour to extract from the Government some explanation as to the object and intent of the Bill?[12]

They wrote to Macleod enclosing a copy of this letter of advice, telling him:

> We consider [the Bill] contains many objectionable Clauses seriously affecting the interests of Proprietors in this Country. Hitherto the Woods & Forests have generally limited their grants of foreshores to the adjacent Proprietor. This Bill authorises the Board of Trade to lease or alienate the foreshore to third parties without limitation.
>
> We think no time should be lost in arranging with some Members of influence to take up the question in the House of Commons . . . Mr Baillie MP for Inverness might . . . be able to lend a material aid and he must already be interested in the matter. We shall be glad to receive your views and to send a set of papers to the MPs who may be disposed to take up the question.[13]

As to an explanation from the government on the object and intent of the Bill which Skene & Peacock had asked for, all that was forthcoming was a statement by the Attorney General when the Bill was considered in committee on 3 May that

> the Lord Advocate having brought to his knowledge the fact that some apprehension with regard to foreshores had been excited by the language of [clause 6] which was in reality an interpretation clause, to obviate any possible misunderstanding he proposed to omit it and to introduce corresponding provisions into clause 7.[14]

In an effort to soothe concerns, the Attorney General, however, continued to say:

> any question which might be in dispute as to the title to Crown lands . . . would have to be decided in the ordinary Courts of Law . . . The Bill only

11 DVGN 570/4/85, Copy letter Skene & Peacock to Loch, 1 May 1866.

12 DVGN 570/4/85, Copy letter Skene & Peacock to Loch, 1 May 1866.

13 DVGN 570/4/84, Letter Skene & Peacock to Macleod, 2 May 1866.

14 PD, Third Series, vol. 183, House of Commons, col. 426 (3 May 1866).

> transferred from one Governmental Department to another for the public interest such rights and interests as the Crown actually possessed.[15]

He also assured the House that the rights of persons other than the Crown 'would not be taken away or at all prejudiciously affected by anything contained in this Bill'.[16]

It was, however, Edward Pleydell-Bouverie, the Member of Parliament for Kilmarnock who had been Vice President of the Board in 1855, who articulated best what the Bill was all about. He said:

> For years a violent controversy had been going on between certain persons and the Commissioners of Woods and Forests. The latter had always considered themselves as trustees of the Crown, and had always acted with a view of making money out of the foreshores, instead of putting them to best use for the public advantage. The result had been that a vast amount of ill will had been created by this method of administering Crown lands, and many persons had had just cause for complaint. He apprehended that the transfer of the administration of the foreshores to the Board of Trade would be not for the pecuniary advantage of the Crown but for the public advantage. The public were greatly indebted to Her Majesty's Government for taking the matter up.[17]

In his speech on the third reading on 14 May the Chancellor of the Exchequer echoed this by referring to the long-vexed question of the foreshores, admitting that 'in Scotland at this moment it formed a subject of very serious controversy', but he went on to assure the House that the question 'of foreshores would be put in a train of settlement most satisfactory to the interests of the public by the provisions of this Bill'.[18] The Bill went to the House of Lords on 15 May 1866 and the only material change from the Bill first considered by the House of Commons was the deletion of the definition of foreshore in clause 6 and its inclusion within the body of clause 7 (which did not meet Skene & Peacock's concerns).

The battleground moved to the House of Lords. Finlay wrote to Macleod as to the vital importance of drumming up support in the Lords for the changes to the Bill recommended by Skene & Peacock:

> I suppose you have seen the Crown Lands Bill ... is to be read 2 times tonight. Loch has taken an opinion on it and this opinion is now with the Duke of Buccleuch. I have not seen it but Loch has told me that the Bill must

15 PD, Third Series, vol. 183, House of Commons, col. 426 (3 May 1866).
16 PD, Third Series, vol. 183, House of Commons, col. 426 (3 May 1866).
17 PD, Third Series, vol. 183, House of Commons, col. 427 (3 May 1866).
18 PD, Third Series, vol. 183, House of Commons, col. 926 (14 May 1866).

> not be allowed to pass in its present shape. We must therefore get it altered in Committee if possible. Could you get the most influential members of our Association who are Peers to oppose it and propose such amendments as may be desirable?[19]

On the second reading of the Bill in the House of Lords on 7 June 1866, two peers, neither of whom was, in fact, a member of the Association, spoke on the foreshore provisions of the Bill which Skene & Peacock had found problematic. They were Lord Chelmsford (who had been Attorney General in 1852 and Lord Chancellor in 1858 and was to become Lord Chancellor again in the Derby administration shortly to take power) and the Duke of Buccleuch who had been given a copy of Skene & Peacock's letter of advice. The Duke of Buccleuch said that far from the Crown Lands Bill being 'some matter-of-course measure . . . of no great importance',[20] the Bill

> did a great deal more than it purported to do . . . It was not a mere matter of the transfer of the foreshores from the Commissioners of the Woods to the Board of Trade but it proposed to take a power which it was doubtful that the Crown possessed at the moment, namely the power of selling, leasing and applying the foreshores. He believed that great evils would result from the proposed transfer of power from one Board to another. In Scotland the Crown had made various claims in reference to the foreshores, and the consequence was that landowners were obliged to combine to resist the encroachments of the Crown . . . He would add that almost every legal decision obtained had been against the Crown.[21]

Buccleuch, perhaps misled by Skene & Peacock's letter, had missed the point that there was no question of the Bill giving to the Crown powers of sale and lease over the foreshore that it did not already have, but it simply removed the requirement that any sale or lease should be at full value. Lord Chelmsford also said that the Bill conferred rights on the Crown that it did not currently have, and that his objection to the Bill 'had most force in relation to Scotland . . . [where] . . . the right of the Crown was altogether doubtful'. He gave notice that he would propose, in committee, the deletion of clauses 8, 9 and 10 and their replacement with a simple clause that would make it clear that the powers of the Board over the foreshore would be the same as they currently were under the Office of Woods.[22] The Lord Chancellor responded to the Duke of

[19] DVGN 570/4, Letter Finlay to Macleod, 31 May 1866.
[20] PD, Third Series, vol. 183, House of Lords, col. 2025 (7 June 1866).
[21] PD, Third Series, vol. 183, House of Lords, col. 2025 (7 June 1866).
[22] PD, Third Series, vol. 183, House of Lords, col. 2026 (7 June 1866).

Buccleuch's suggestion that the Bill 'under the pretence of making a mere transfer of powers from one Department to another clandestinely sought to give new powers to the Crown' by telling him 'with the most perfect Confidence that the proposed enactment . . . conferred on the Crown not one particle of power which it did not possess at present. On the contrary, the clause had been carefully worded so as to preclude all possible doubt on that head.'[23] Shortly after the second reading, William Peacock came to London for the purpose of having a meeting with Loch to discuss the Bill and Skene & Peacock's proposed amendments.[24]

The Bill was considered on 13 July by a committee of the whole House of Lords. The Dukes of Argyll, Buccleuch and Sutherland spoke to make clear their concern over the effect of the Bill,[25] and the Bill was duly amended.[26] Each of the principal amendments made to the Bill was in line with the recommendations made by Skene & Peacock in their letter of advice of 1 May to Loch. The offending words in the definition of the foreshore (now contained in clause 7 following the amendment proposed by the Attorney General) that brought within the definition any encroachments, embankments or enclosures were deleted. Clauses 8, 9 and 10 were deleted and replaced by a clause which simply provided that

> The Board of Trade shall have and may exercise all the Powers and Authorities, Rights and Privileges, whatsoever with regard to the Foreshore, which the Commissioners of Woods now have or are entitled to exercise with respect to the same.

Clause 24, which excluded the liability of the Crown to pay compensation and which Skene & Peacock had described as unjust and unfair, was deleted. The Bill received the Royal Assent on 6 August 1866. It is important to note that certain parts of the foreshore were excluded from the transfer, and so the conflicts created by the anomaly of dual responsibility that Farrer had highlighted in 1865 were not entirely dealt with. This was a matter that would be revisited in the future, as we see in Chapters 6 and 9.[27]

[23] PD, Third Series, vol. 183, House of Lords, col. 2026 (7 June 1866). This was, perhaps, economical with the truth – the power to sell and lease certainly did already exist but the Bill would release the Board from the 'full value' constraints on this power in the 1829 Act.

[24] DVGN 544/3/6, Business Account for 1866 for the Association for vindicating rights of Seaboard Proprietors of Foreshore in Scotland.

[25] See Farrer Memorandum, Appendix 4. The Duke of Argyll was in the Cabinet at the time as Lord Privy Seal.

[26] House of Lords Journals, 1866, vol. XCVIII, pp. 564–5.

[27] The exclusions from the transfer are set out in sections 17–20; these were the

While the Association of Seaboard Proprietors of Scotland may have been happy with the result it eventually obtained in the Crown Lands Act 1866 because it accorded exactly with the advice it had received from Skene & Peacock, the Board was very much less than happy. Farrer considered that the effect of the removal of clauses 8, 9 and 10 had been seriously to fetter the Board in its administration of the foreshore. Farrer asked F. S. Reilly, one of the counsel who had drafted the Bill,[28] for his opinion on the effect of the amendments made to the Bill in the House of Lords. Reilly agreed with Farrer's conclusions and gave Farrer advice that was to have an important bearing on the Board's future dealings with the Association of Seaboard Proprietors of Scotland:

> The only course open to the Board of Trade in order to relieve itself from the difficulties imposed on it by the Act in the administration of the foreshore, will be to obtain an amendment of the Act.
>
> With regard to England there would, I apprehend, be no difficulty in obtaining an Act containing provisions identical with those of the Bill as introduced.
>
> The only difficulty would be with regard to Scotland. It would be necessary for the Board of Trade either to come to terms with the Scotch proprietors, or to ascertain by legal proceedings the exact nature and extent of the Crown's rights to the foreshore in Scotland and then to prepare legislation on that basis.[29]

Before turning to an examination of the Farrer Memorandum, we should note the rather curious contribution to the debate on the Crown Lands Bill made by the antiquary and pamphleteer Mr James W. Pycroft. During the debate in the House of Lords on 7 June, Lord Redesdale presented a petition from Pycroft. Redesdale said:

foreshores of the Thames, Tees and the County Palatine of Durham; any part of the foreshore already dealt with by the Office of Woods in various ways; and foreshore in front of Crown or government property; under section 21 minerals were excluded from the transfer. The amount of compensation to be paid to the Land Revenues of the Crown in respect of the transfer was fixed by arbitration as £496,000, although no actual funds passed; TNA:PRO, BT 243/95, Foreshore and Seabed. Memorandum by Crown Estate Commissioners, 7 August 1958, p. 6.

28 Sir Francis Savage Reilly, QC, KCMG (1825–83). Reilly was paid 185 guineas for his work on the Crown Lands Bill. While Farrer conceded that this was a large sum, he defended it because, as he said, 'You cannot get the experience and ability required for drawing Government Bills without paying a high price'; TNA:PRO, BT 13/1/3, Letter Reilly to Farrer, 21 August 1866, enclosing his bill for the work done and Note by Farrer, 26 August 1866.

29 Farrer Memorandum, Appendix 4, Opinion of Mr Reilly on Powers of Letting and Selling Foreshore, 17 December 1866.

> Pycroft . . . was a gentleman who had paid a great deal of attention to the question as to how far the rights of the Crown over the foreshores extended; and he now complained that in the Bill there was an indirect assumption on the part of the Crown of a right to the foreshores. The matter was of considerable importance, and as there had been a recent decision against that assumed right, there ought not to be an attempt made to indirectly assume such a right in an Act of Parliament.[30]

When Lord Chelmsford spoke about the Bill he said that he wished to 'bear testimony to the importance of that gentleman's researches upon this important question'.[31] One might have expected that with such a fulsome tribute from a past Attorney General and Lord Chancellor, the contribution of Mr Pycroft would have been taken seriously. It appears, however, that he was something of an eccentric with a passion for pursuing, as he put it, great constitutional questions. The Crown Lands Act, Pycroft considered, was nothing less than a constitutional outrage. After the Act was passed, Pycroft continued his polemical crusade and published long and detailed critiques of the government's actions in passing the Act in a number of journals and newspapers.[32] He obviously saw the Association of Seaboard Proprietors of Scotland as a body that might help him in his mission. Pycroft had corresponded with Skene & Peacock at some length between August and December 1866, and at one stage Skene & Peacock had discussions with the editor of the *Edinburgh Evening Courant* as to a proposal for the publication of one of Pycroft's articles on the Act.[33] Pycroft also wanted Skene & Peacock to circulate his articles to the members of the Association. However, eventually Skene & Peacock came to the conclusion that Pycroft was too much of a maverick for the Association to be linked with: 'he has considerable talent, great pertinacity and much antiquarian knowledge of the subject, but is destitute of tact, and his knowledge of the law is inaccurate. We

30 PD, Third Series, vol. 183, House of Lords, col. 2022 (7 June 1866).

31 PD, Third Series, vol. 183, House of Lords, col. 2022 (7 June 1866); House of Lords Journals, 1866, vol. XCVIII, p. 378.

32 A taste of these may be had from *The Caernarvon and Denbigh Herald* and *North and South Wales Independent* of January 1867, *City Press* of March 1867, *The Western Daily Mercury* of 18 January and 1 February 1867 and the *Daily Telegraph* of 30 June 1868, copies of which may be found in TNA:PRO, MT 10/35. For a further taste of Pycroft's writings on the foreshore, see J. W. Pycroft, *Arena Cornubiae* (London, 1856).

33 DVGN 544/3/6, Business Account for 1866 for the Association for vindicating rights of Seaboard Proprietors of Foreshore in Scotland. The editor was not prepared to publish Pycroft's article unless a response was published at the same time.

doubt if the Association can safely make any use of him.'[34] George Loch was less restrained in his views: 'I return Mr Pycroft's communications. I have seen others from him and I fancy he is as mad as a march hare.'[35]

Pycroft became a thorn in the Board's flesh and he bombarded the Board with a series of letters during March and April 1867, commencing with a letter in which he warned the Board: 'I have now to state that if any action is taken by your Board of Trade in reference to foreshore will [sic] under the public law lead immediately to an impeachment by those attacked.'[36] C. Cecil Trevor, the assistant secretary to the Board, was not unduly concerned by this. His file note drily recorded: 'We are threatened with impeachment! It is fortunate that by section 9 of the Crown Lands Act 1866 Mr Farrer and I are absolved from the consequences.'[37] The Board initially responded to Pycroft's letters, one of which included a draft Bill for the repeal of the Crown Lands Act 1866, in a polite, but dismissive, manner. But by the middle of March, Farrer's patience was wearing thin. In a note to Trevor, Farrer wrote: 'This man is absolutely mad. He has written 5 times and we have acknowledged them. I think we had better take no more notice of him.' The Duke of Richmond, who was then the President of the Board, appended his concurrence to this note with a simple 'I quite agree.'[38] By the beginning of April, Trevor agreed a standard response to Pycroft's letters which 'may be sent to this gentleman not oftener than once a month – we cannot waste time which ought to be devoted to more important subjects''[39] At the conclusion of the correspondence Trevor directed that the standard letter should 'omit the F.S.A. [Fellow of the Society of Antiquaries] as I understand that the Society are no longer honoured by the fellowship of Mr Pycroft'.[40]

## THE FARRER MEMORANDUM: 'A JESUITICAL PAPER'

The Board probably considered the transfer to it of the responsibility for the foreshore under the Crown Lands Act 1866 as something of a poisoned chalice. While it is true that the Board had recommended to the Treasury that the transfer should happen, we have seen that the

[34] DVGN 570/1–9, Letter Skene & Peacock to Macleod, 26 August 1868.

[35] DVGN 572/148/1, Letter Loch to Macleod, 20 March 1867.

[36] TNA:PRO, MT 10/35, Letter Pycroft to Board of Trade, 7 March 1867.

[37] TNA:PRO, MT 10/35, Note Trevor, 8 March 1867.

[38] TNA:PRO, MT 10/35, Note by Farrer, 23 March 1867; Note Richmond, 25 March 1867.

[39] TNA:PRO, MT 10/35, Note by Trevor, 4 April 1867.

[40] TNA:PRO, MT 10/35, Note by Trevor, 13 April 1867.

real inspiration for the transfer may well have come from the Office of Woods who could not wait to be rid, in particular, of the problems the Scottish foreshore proprietors were causing them in the shape of the Association. If the Board was at all keen to assume the responsibility for the foreshore, it will only have been on the basis that it had all the necessary powers to deal with the foreshore in the public interest; and Skene & Peacock and the Association had made sure that the Crown Lands Act 1866 was, in this respect, emasculated. So Farrer had to consider carefully how the Board was to manage its new responsibilities in the circumstances of a defective Act, and he laid out his conclusions in the Farrer Memorandum. The main problem which Farrer identified was that the Office of Woods had considered itself obliged under the Crown Lands Acts 1829 to treat the foreshore as, in effect, a profit centre, whereas it was intended that the role of the Board would be different. In a significant note to the President and Vice President of the Board, Farrer said:

> It is obvious that [the Office of Woods] have acted on the principle that [the foreshore] is property, out of which they are to make as much as they can. We shall be obliged to take a wider view – e.g. to consider whether if an undertaking is to be of considerable public advantage we should not forgo a portion of the proportion of profit properly belonging to the Soil rather than ask such a price as will stop the undertaking – to consider whether there are not rights or customs of landing, boating, walking, bathing, which, though incapable of pecuniary measurement and perhaps not legal, ought to be carefully preserved to the general public.[41]

The Vice President of the Board, Stephen Cave, responded to Farrer's note with his own very important note:

> We must be careful that we appear what in fact we are; not promoters of Crown claims against the rights of individuals, but the protector of Public rights against the encroachments of individuals. Our object is not to make money out of the public but to preserve rights in trust for the public.[42]

Farrer considered that the Board had four duties in relation to the foreshore. The first was to ascertain in what parts of the coast the Crown had parted with its rights, in what part those rights were undoubted and in what part the title was doubtful. The detail of the extent of the foreshore remaining in Crown hands would not, Farrer said, be easy to come by. In words that have resonance for the present state of the

[41] TNA:PRO, MT 10/35, Note by Farrer, 15 November 1867.
[42] TNA:PRO, MT 10/35, Note by Cave, 28 November 1867.

assessment of the extent of Crown ownership of the foreshore referred to in Chapter 1, Farrer described the problem:

> The Office of Woods will give us as complete a statement as can be furnished of the present state of the title all round the coast; but this must necessarily be very imperfect. They can give us those cases in which the Crown has undoubtedly conveyed away its rights, but their knowledge must be very imperfect of the titles set up by innumerable claimants, especially as regards the claims which virtually rest upon user.[43]

As to this duty, Farrer believed that 'in the end we shall have to do something to ascertain or define these rights, but with the present prejudice against the Crown, it would be unwise to stir the question now'. This is a reference to the dispute with the Association of Seaboard Proprietors of Scotland. Farrer believed that if the Board could, in the course of its dealings, make it clear that its main concern was the public interest, the protection of the public property of the nation, 'we shall be able to raise the question of title in a much less invidious way and with much greater prospects of success than would at present be possible'.[44] But Farrer was also well aware that delay in undertaking this task of verifying title was likely to mean that the Crown's title to the foreshore was threatened through acts of possession. As to public rights over the foreshore, Farrer, guided by the principles that he and Stephen Cave espoused, was clear as to what the policy of the Board should be:

> Whatever may have been the principles which the Office of Woods, guided by their statutes, have been compelled to pursue, there can be no doubt that it should be the policy of the Board of Trade, so far as the law will permit, to admit and even encourage, and perhaps in some cases to enforce, such [public] rights, whether over the soil which still remains in the Crown, or over those parts of it which have been granted away to private persons. Indeed, it is with a view to the protection of such rights rather than with a view to revenue that it is desirable to maintain the title of the Crown.[45]

The second duty was to prevent encroachments on the foreshore. The examples Farrer gave were the construction of piers and walls; taking gravel and other material from the foreshore; the exclusion of the public from walking, bathing, landing and fishing; and other acts of ownership inconsistent with the rights of the Crown and the public.[46] It was

[43] Farrer Memorandum, p. 1.
[44] Farrer Memorandum, p. 1.
[45] Farrer Memorandum, p. 2.
[46] For the existence under the common law of the public rights Farrer mentioned, see Chapter 9.

important that the Board should put in place procedures for the notification of all such encroachments because, without such notice, the Board would not be able to act to prevent them.[47] However, Farrer believed that the Board should be guided in any decision as to what action should be taken by a careful consideration as to whether the encroachment was 'injurious to the rights hitherto enjoyed by the public'. If it was not, 'We shall have no public support in protecting a mere title which does not appear to be of any immediate public advantage.'[48] But the level of injury could not be definitive: there may be encroachments which were not injurious

> but the pecuniary value, present or future, of the title affected by it, may be such as to make it important on this ground to assert the rights of the Crown. These are the cases of which I am most afraid. We cannot give way, and we shall fight at great disadvantage.[49]

Then Farrer made the statement, which gave rise to the copy of the Farrer Memorandum in the possession of the Association being marked in manuscript with the comment 'What a Jesuitical paper'.[50] He said:

> Lastly, in cases where the Crown's title is doubtful we must act in the same way as if it were good, except that we must do so with greater caution, and be more ready to compromise the question on the principle of reserving to the public their rights and easements over the soil.[51]

What had caused Lord Blantyre who wrote the comment to believe that Farrer was being deceitful was the suggestion that the Crown should, even if it had doubts over its title, act as if its title to the foreshore was undoubted. As Moore put it in his 1888 book on the history of the foreshore, the Board would act 'just as vigorously when the Crown doubts its right as when it is confident in the justice of its claim'.[52]

The third duty was that the Board should watch for Bills that contained enactments affecting the title to the foreshore. Farrer understood this as being a very laborious, but necessary, task but in deciding how enactments might affect the Crown's rights in the foreshore, the Board

[47] It is interesting to note that Farrer also suggested that the gathering of seaware was a public right when the Scottish courts had held, as we have noted in Chapter 2, that it was not; Farrer Memorandum, p. 2.

[48] Farrer Memorandum, pp. 2, 3.

[49] Farrer Memorandum, p. 3.

[50] See DVGN 560/3, Copy of The Farrer Memorandum marked as received by Lord Blantyre on 10 June 1868.

[51] Farrer Memorandum, p. 3.

[52] Moore, *History of the Foreshore*, p. 596.

should 'endeavour ... not to reserve questionable legal privileges, but ... endeavour to get courts and juries to see that we are protecting the public, and to give us fair measure accordingly'.[53]

The fourth duty, that of selling, leasing or licensing the use of the foreshore, was the duty most affected by the amendments made to the Crown Lands Bill in the House of Lords, and because of this it was the duty that most troubled Farrer. There was a conflict between balancing the duty to administer the foreshore in the public interest with the perceived legal requirement not to part with property at less than full value. Farrer broke the duty down into three parts. The first related to disposals of the foreshore where it was required for some purpose of public utility. In such a case, there could, Farrer considered, 'be no question as to the propriety of the Crown parting with its rights'[54] because a disposal would, by definition, be in the public interest. The second and third parts were more difficult because the relevant class of cases involved those where applications to purchase were made and where encroachments were being made on the foreshore, and the persons making the encroachments were stopped and only allowed to proceed on condition that they purchased or acknowledged the Crown's title. It was, of course, this kind of situation which had caused the dispute between the Association of Seaboard Proprietors of Scotland and the Office of Woods to arise. Farrer said that it would be the duty of the Board to institute enquiries as to the encroachment and the extent to which the rights of the public were interfered with. Farrer believed that it would be important for the Board to put forward prominently the fact that the Board in these cases sought the protection of the public. However, Farrer acknowledged that the *ex adverso* proprietor, while he may have no legal title to the foreshore, 'has certainly a considerable interest in the foreshore, and we must take care that he is heard, and that we do not hastily or wantonly authorise works on the foreshore which will be detrimental to him'.[55] The terms of the sale or lease proved a particular difficulty because, as Farrer said:

> A great deal of the prejudice which exists upon this subject has arisen from the fact that the Office of Woods has been bound to get the best possible price; and it is not unnaturally alleged that they have been ready to sacrifice important public rights if they could only get high prices.[56]

53 Farrer Memorandum, p. 4.
54 Farrer Memorandum, p. 5.
55 Farrer Memorandum, p. 6.
56 Farrer Memorandum, p. 6.

Farrer recognised it could be argued that the Board had a duty to protect the foreshore as an asset of the Crown and that a disposal of it should achieve the highest price for the benefit of the public purse. But he did not believe the issue was as simple as this. Such a view, he thought, proceeded on 'the assumption, [which] is fatally erroneous, that the pecuniary interest of the public in the foreshore is its most important interest'.[57] It was Farrer's belief that it was the clear duty of the Board to protect the foreshore in the interests of the public, and that 'To sell [the foreshore] to private persons because a high price is offered, without reference to these interests would be ... absurd', and so Farrer said that 'we must be prepared to forego in many cases the prices which, if we were private landowners, we might insist on demanding'.[58] But the manner in which a disposal of the foreshores, if approved, could then take place posed real difficulties because the original provisions in the Crown Lands Bill giving the Board unrestricted powers of sale, leasing and granting of licences had been deleted in the House of Lords. The Board was restricted to the powers which the Office of Woods had under the Crown Lands Act 1829, which required 'a sufficient consideration' for a sale and a 'reasonable rent or consideration' for a lease. Of these provisions Farrer said that the legislation had 'been purposely framed so as to prevent [the Office of Woods] parting with land at less than its value'. He went on: 'it is obvious that according to the spirit of [the legislation] this rent or consideration ought to represent the full value'.[59] The Board had no power to grant a licence to use the foreshore. Furthermore, no sale or lease could be made without a survey or valuation 'except in cases where the value cannot be ascertained by survey, or when the value is known to be so inconsiderable as not to be worth the expense of survey'.[60] Farrer believed that these requirements would mean it would not be possible for the Board to act on the principles contained in his memorandum. He gave as an example the construction of a pier by an *ex adverso* proprietor. So far as the Board was concerned, the foreshore required for the pier would probably be of 'small importance in point of money to the Crown, the work is in itself useful, but [the construction of the pier] will certainly be used hereafter as an evidence of title against the Crown'. The Board would want simply to grant the proprietor a licence

[57] Farrer Memorandum, p. 6.

[58] Farrer Memorandum, pp. 6–7.

[59] Crown Lands Act 1829, sections 34 and 28 (the marginal note to section 28 said that leases were to be at a Rack Rent); Farrer Memorandum, pp. 7–8.

[60] Crown Lands Act 1829, sections 61 and 62; Farrer Memorandum, p. 8.

or lease for a nominal sum and take an acknowledgement of the Crown's title from the proprietor and 'the difficulty would probably be at an end'. But the Board would be forced, by the legislation, to ask for a survey and valuation at the expense of the proprietor, the proprietor would resist this and the issue would end up in court 'with a prejudice against us. Our alternative would be to let the matter entirely alone, and allow the title of the Crown and the future rights of the public to be silently, but not less effectually, defeated.'[61] Farrer did, however, make the significant concession in his memorandum that, with a liberal construction of the legislation, it might be possible to

> enable the Board of Trade to escape from these difficulties in some cases. But the whole scope and purport of the Acts concerning the Crown property is to prevent sales and leases at less than the real value; and if we are to act on a different principle it is desirable, if not necessary, to have the distinct sanction of Parliament.[62]

There is a suggestion that Farrer was prepared to act on a different principle and without the sanction of Parliament in the case of a member of the committee of the Association of Seaboard Proprietors of Scotland, Henry Baillie MP. Rather oddly for a member of the committee, Baillie had been trying in 1867 to negotiate with the Board a transfer to him of part of the foreshore opposite a low-lying farm on his Beauly Firth estate. The main issue was the Board's insistence on, and Baillie's reluctance to concede, the standard survey and valuation of the land. Farrer had told Trevor that he did not believe the law permitted the Board to dispense with a survey and valuation in such a case,[63] but notwithstanding this, Farrer was disposed to make a concession to Baillie because 'it is bad policy to irritate the Scottish proprietors'[64] and he recommended in 1869 that the Board should accept Baillie's offer to purchase the foreshore without asking for the survey and valuation. The Board wrote to the Treasury to justify its decision in the following terms:

> having regard to the open question as to the claims of seaboard proprietors in Scotland to the foreshore adjacent to their property, to the alleged difference of the law of Scotland and the law of England upon the subject, and to all the circumstances of the case they would be disposed to dispense with a survey . . . and advise the Treasury to accept the sum of £3 per acre.[65]

[61] Farrer Memorandum, p. 8.
[62] Farrer Memorandum, p. 8.
[63] TNA:PRO, MT 10/88, Note by Farrer, 17 June 1867.
[64] TNA:PRO, MT 10/88, Notes by Trevor and Farrer, 19 February 1869.
[65] TNA:PRO, MT 10/88, Letter Farrer to the Treasury, 24 June 1869.

The Treasury accepted this advice and the foreshore was duly transferred to Baillie at the agreed price without a survey and valuation. The Duke of Richmond was annoyed with Baillie's actions in his dealings with the Board and told Macleod: 'I think it was very foolish of Baillie taking a lease [sic] from the Crown.'[66] While Baillie may have behaved foolishly, the way in which the Board dealt with his application might suggest that he was given preferential treatment because of his position. Perhaps, however, it was not preferential treatment after all, but rather Farrer putting into practice his hope that a liberal construction of the legislation might permit the Board to pursue its public interest policy, because it appears that this approach was indeed to prove the way forward over the following years. A 1958 memorandum was to say that 'no rigorous policy of getting the best return' had been pursued by the Board and its successors, even after 1927 when, as we see in Chapter 9, the requirement to obtain full value on a sale or lease of the foreshore (a requirement that Farrer had said was implied by the spirit if not the letter of the legislation) was made explicit.[67] However, the 'inherent conflict between the broad public interest and a rigorous policy of getting the best revenue'[68] that had so troubled Farrer was to raise its head again in the middle of the twentieth century, as we see in Chapter 9.

## CONCLUSIONS

The passing of the Crown Lands Act 1866 and the publication of the Farrer Memorandum were significant moments in the history of the foreshore. The Office of Woods had reached the end of its tether over its dealings with the Scottish proprietors and the Association of Seaboard Proprietors of Scotland. The Office of Woods did not believe that its continuing responsibility for the foreshore was sustainable in the light of the campaign by the Association and in the light of the constraints the Office of Woods perceived it was under in its dealings with the foreshore – that it was obliged to obtain full value on any dealing with the foreshore. It is, therefore, ironic that, as a result of the efforts of Skene & Peacock, the Association of Seaboard Proprietors of Scotland and individual Scottish proprietors in the House of Lords, the foreshore

[66] DVGN 571/10/6, Letter Richmond to Macleod, 5 July 1869.

[67] TNA:PRO, BT 243/95, Memorandum by Ports Division, Ministry of Transport – Foreshores and Seabed and the Crown Estate, 10 April 1958.

[68] TNA:PRO, BT 243/95, Agreed note between Ministries of Transport Power etc., Foreshores and Seabed and the Crown Estate, March 1959.

provisions of the Crown Lands Act 1866 were passed in a form which preserved for the Board the very difficulties under which the Office of Woods had laboured.

So far as the Farrer Memorandum is concerned, it is clear that a document that was written not for publication but for the internal guidance of the Board became, once published as a Parliamentary Paper on 29 November 1867,[69] the subject of vilification. Moore reproduced the Farrer Memorandum in his 1888 history of the foreshore to 'help to guide owners of foreshore either in approaching the Board with a view of making a compromise for the Crown's claim or in resisting the Board's attack'.[70] Moore's book was written to reassert the claims of private proprietors to the foreshore in the face of what Moore thought was an unwarranted attack on private ownership. He believed that the Farrer Memorandum showed that the Board had a policy of treating every claimant of the foreshore against the Crown as a usurper, and he had strong views as to the Board's intentions:

> King Charles I put pressure on the judges to warp the law; the Board of Trade would seem, if we are to judge them by their own Memorandum, desirous of misleading Courts and juries by a doctrine of expediency for the benefit of the public in order to get decision against the rights of the subject. If these be the principles which commend themselves to the official mind, I ask, in conclusion whether they are the best custodian of the public right.[71]

A reasoned consideration of the Farrer Memorandum and the departmental minutes and letters shows, however, that while Farrer and the Board's officials were clearly motivated in their administration of the foreshore by a desire to protect the interests of the public, this was not to be at the expense of individual proprietors if this was at all possible. This assessment is shared by the anonymous reviewer in 1889 of Moore's book who said:

> a careful reading of [the Farrer Memorandum] has failed to convince us that it is, after all such a very nefarious document. The impression is to be cultivated that the Board is acting in the interests of the public and that these interests will be better served by the ownership of the Crown than that of individuals. In these directions what is there so heinous?[72]

[69] PD, Third Series, vol. 192, House of Lords, col. 1825 (19 June 1868); PD, Third Series, vol. 190, House of Commons, col. 419 (29 November 1867).

[70] Moore, *History of the Foreshore*, p. 596.

[71] Moore, *History of the Foreshore*, pp. liii–liv. The copy of the Farrer Memorandum in Moore's book did not include the Appendices.

[72] Anon., *The Solicitor's Journal*, 33 (1888–9), pp. 313–14.

It was not, Stephen Cave, the Vice President of the Board, had said, the policy of the Board to promote Crown claims against the rights of individuals, but rather to protect public rights against the encroachments of individuals. The subtlety of this difference may not have been properly appreciated by proprietors or those advising them, particularly the Scottish proprietors who did not, in any event, accept that the Crown had any title at all to the foreshore, and as we see in Chapters 4 and 5 the 8th Duke of Argyll and the Association believed that the Farrer Memorandum evinced an animus against private proprietors.

The issue that had so bothered Farrer – that of balancing the duty to administer the foreshore in the public interest with the perceived legal requirement not to part with property at less than full value – was not addressed in any of the Crown Lands Acts passed after 1866 and was, as we shall see in Chapter 9, to raise its head again in the middle of the twentieth century and, indeed, in the context of the 2017 devolution of Scotland's Crown foreshore to the Scottish Parliament. The amendments to the Crown Lands Bill 1866 secured by the efforts of Skene & Peacock, the Association and individual proprietors in the House of Lords would leave a long-lasting legacy.

# 4

# 'One of the most prominent and assertive members'

## INTRODUCTION

George Douglas Campbell, the 8th Duke of Argyll, believed in the merits of private ownership of land and, moreover, a system of private property ownership which was justified on economic grounds. He believed that any attack on, and interference with, private ownership of land could lead to an attack on other forms of private property ownership. He was 'a forthright defender of the inalienable right of the landlord to control his estates without interference'.[1] As a member of every Liberal Cabinet from the 1850s until he finally resigned in 1881 and with his position as one of the leading landowners in Scotland, the large Scottish landowners accepted him as their spokesman on the Highland land issue in the 1880s.[2] His title and estates made him 'the dominant personality in the western highlands'.[3] Lord Napier saw the duke as being a very influential figure:

> I would, however, far rather win the support of the Duke than resist his aggression, not only because he is a dangerous adversary, but because by personal gifts, inherited station and political position, he has a peculiar faculty of usefulness in this emergency. He speaks with authority to the whole proprietary body.[4]

[1] E. A. Cameron, *Land for the People?: The British Government and the Scottish Highlands, c. 1880–1925* (Edinburgh, 1996), p. 26.

[2] J. W. Mason, 'The Duke of Argyll and the land question in late nineteenth century Britain', *Victorian Studies*, 21:2 (1978), pp. 159, 168.

[3] He owned about 175,000 acres; H. C. J. Matthew, 'Campbell, George Douglas, eighth Duke of Argyll in the peerage of Scotland, and first Duke of Argyll in the peerage of the United Kingdom (1823–1900)', in *Oxford Dictionary of National Biography*, Oxford University Press, available at <http://www.oxforddnb.com/view/article/4500> (last accessed 25 October 2017).

[4] Lord Napier, 'The Highland crofters: a vindication of the report of the Crofters' Commission', *The Nineteenth Century*, 17 (1885), p. 462.

We have, therefore, the picture of a man who was a leading member of government, a substantial private landowner, a man who spoke for the large landowners and whose writings on the subject made it very clear that possession of land and the private ownership of it were legitimised by the land being managed with economic efficiency; that this economic efficiency could only be achieved by the large landowners; and that it must not be upset, restricted or interfered with by legislative, executive or judicial actions. So far as the foreshore debate was concerned, the Board of Trade thought that Argyll was 'one of the most prominent and assertive members of the Association of Seaboard Proprietors of Scotland',[5] and, as one of the 'most vocal and respected political debaters of his day',[6] we might expect to find (as indeed we do in this chapter) that Argyll's contribution was significant. While Argyll is best known in the context of the Scottish land question as the 'arch-opponent' of land reform in the 1880s,[7] his contribution to the foreshore debate has been largely ignored in the historiography even though it is an important example of Argyll's belief that the government should not interfere with the business of private proprietors, a belief that would eventually result in Argyll's resignation from the Cabinet in 1881 in protest against government's increasing interference in the rights of private proprietors.[8]

## THE DISPUTE OVER THE FORESHORE TO THE DUKE OF ARGYLL'S ESTATE AT ROSNEATH

In the three years 1847, 1848 and 1849, Argyll had proposed erecting piers on the shores of his estate at Rosneath. The plans for the piers had been submitted to the Admiralty, being the department with responsibility for public rights of navigation.[9] The plans were approved and the piers erected. In 1857 Argyll proposed the erection of another pier on the same estate and, again, submitted the plans to the Admiralty. However, as we saw in Chapter 2, the Office of Woods during this period was beginning to assert the Crown's rights to Scotland's foreshore and the Office had arranged with the Admiralty that it should be notified of proposals such as the erection of piers that might affect the Crown's rights.

[5] TNA:PRO, MT 10/1813, Minute of the Harbour Department, 8 November 1881; see Chapter 8.

[6] K. M. Mulhern, 'The intellectual duke – George Douglas Campbell, 8th Duke of Argyll' (PhD thesis, University of Edinburgh, 2006), p. 7.

[7] Mulhern, 'Intellectual duke', p. 2.

[8] Mulhern, 'Intellectual duke', p. 59.

[9] Until the Board of Trade took over responsibility in 1862.

In June 1857 James Howard, the Commissioner of the Office of Woods, offered to grant a conveyance of the foreshore for the relevant part of Argyll's Rosneath estate. Argyll agreed to this proposal, mainly because the sums involved were small. As he put it: 'I was induced, as many others have been induced under similar circumstances, to acquiesce in the proposed arrangement as one which it was hardly worth while to dispute.'[10] However, Howard also made a similar proposal in relation to the piers built nine years earlier, thus reopening a matter Argyll had believed was closed. Argyll instructed his lawyer to 'remonstrate against this demand which appeared to me to be vexatious and unjust'.[11] But Howard persisted and this caused Argyll

> to look more closely, than I had done before, into the legal aspect of those claims, both generally and specially as effected by my own titles. I had no difficulty in arriving at the conclusion that the claim made by Mr Howard, was, as respected my own case at least, wholly illegal.[12]

In August 1857 Argyll's lawyer wrote to Howard saying that the charters under which Argyll held the land allowed the erection of piers without the consent of the Crown. Howard took the advice of Donald Horne, the Solicitor in Scotland to the Office of Woods, and responded in September saying that he was advised the charters contained no such rights.[13] The duke took his own counsel's advice, and in February 1860 Howard was told that the duke's advice was directly opposed to the advice given to the Office of Woods.

If the claim of the Crown was to be pursued, it appeared that this would now have to be by way of legal action against Argyll. It was at this stage that the opinion of the Law Officers was taken and, as we shall see later, this was one of the points that Argyll sought to complain about. A conference at the chambers of James Moncrieff, the Lord Advocate,[14] was held on 10 April 1860 and it is clear that the oral advice given by the Lord Advocate at this conference was not favourable to the Crown. But the Solicitor General had been unable to be present at the conference and the Lord Advocate was, apparently, called away

[10] PP, 1866, LVIII, Copies of the Correspondence which took place in the course of last Year between His Grace the Duke of Argyll and the Lords Commissioners of Her Majesty's Treasury [hereafter Argyll–Treasury Correspondence], p. 4.

[11] Argyll–Treasury Correspondence, p. 4.

[12] Argyll–Treasury Correspondence, p. 4.

[13] Argyll–Treasury Correspondence, p. 4.

[14] Later Lord Justice-Clerk from 1869 to 1888 and one of the judges in the Agnew case.

to London shortly after the conference and so further consideration of the matter, including the formal written opinion, was deferred. Argyll was not told of the consultation and, indeed, heard nothing more from the Office of Woods about its claim to the foreshore. It appears that the subsequent, unfortunate, events flowed from the incompetence of Donald Horne and a surprising administrative failure on the part of the Office of Woods. Horne did not report the oral advice of the Lord Advocate to James Howard. If he had, it is quite likely that the Office of Woods would have informed the duke that it would not contest his claim and thus the Association of Seaboard Proprietors would not have taken the duke's claim as the first test case. But the Office of Woods was not told of the views of the Lord Advocate, and the matter was allowed to lie, with no further communication being made to the duke. Horne's explanation of his failure to tell the Office of Woods what the Lord Advocate had said and his subsequent failure to chase the Lord Advocate for his written opinion were formally reported to James Howard on 3 March 1865. As to the former, Horne said that as he was expecting to receive a joint opinion, 'I did not feel at liberty before [he obtained such a joint opinion] to communicate what was verbally stated by the Lord Advocate at the consultation . . . I was led to believe that another meeting of Crown Counsel would be required.'[15] But he had no explanation for his failure to arrange such a further consultation. And there is no explanation of the failure of the Office of Woods to chase Horne to follow up the matter.

Had the issue not involved Argyll, it is possible that the proprietor concerned would not have taken the matter further. But Argyll had, by now, joined the Association whose expressed aim was to fight a case against the Office of Woods to test the issue of the ownership of the foreshore, and it is clear that the Association was keen to find a case which involved Argyll; indeed, Argyll had mentioned the possibility of the Association taking the case when he had a meeting with Macleod in November 1863, a meeting at which he confirmed that his guaranteed subscription to the Association was £100.[16] He was clearly angry at the way he had been treated by the Office of Woods. In a letter to Macleod, written on the official notepaper of the Office of the Lord Privy Seal, he said:

> I have often thought however, that I ought to resume the correspondence with the Woods and Forests challenging them either to abandon or to assert

[15] NRS, CR 11/284, Letter Horne to Howard, 3 March 1865.
[16] DVGN 570/1–9, Letter Macleod to Skene & Peacock, 1 December 1863.

> the claim that they have made ... Because they have no right to assert a claim, to threaten proceedings and then let the whole thing fall into abeyance.[17]

Skene & Peacock believed that the Rosneath case offered a good chance of success for the Association although interestingly Argyll's own lawyer, Mr Dalgleish, was not confident that the Rosneath case was all that strong. Dalgleish thought it would be advisable to find a case where the charter of the lands contained a description of the land such as 'bounded by the sea'. However, Argyll recognised that a case decided on such facts would not help to decide the main question of principle which it was the object of the Association to do and so he was 'disposed to abide by the advice of the Counsel of the Committee ... the Committee may therefore proceed as advised'.[18] The Association's lawyers proceeded to draft a summons of declarator against the Lord Advocate that the Rosneath foreshore was Argyll's property, and the first plea in law was that the shore was his property as part and pertinent of the adjoining land subject only to the right of the Crown as trustee for the public use.[19] The summons was served on 8 September 1864 and Horne consulted the Lord Advocate on 9 November. Not surprisingly, the Lord Advocate expressed the same opinion he had given four years earlier and directed that the case should not be defended. The Lord Advocate was clearly very unhappy at the turn of events and that the Crown was being forced to back down against such a high-profile litigant as Argyll:

> I adhere to the opinion which I expressed at consultation on the 10th April 1860 that the Crown had no claim against the Duke of Argyll in regard to this matter and I think it right to express my regret that, after the opinion so indicated, so long a period should have been allowed to elapse without some intimation to this effect being given to his Grace. It is not right for the public service that questions of this kind which have been substantially decided by Crown Counsel should be allowed to hang over the heads of the parties interested for so long a period.[20]

[17] DVGN 555/3/1, Letter Argyll to Macleod, 6 March 1864.

[18] DVGN 555/3/3, Letter Argyll to Macleod, 6 May 1864.

[19] DVGN 555/1, Summons of Declarator, His Grace the Duke of Argyll against James Moncreiff, July 1864.

[20] NRS, CR 11/283, Opinion J Moncreiff, Edinburgh, 24 November 1864. Howard was clearly embarrassed by the Lord Advocate's criticism and asked Horne to explain why it was that he had not communicated the Lord Advocate's 1860 opinion to anyone at the Office of Woods; NRS, CR 11/283, Letter Office of Woods to Horne, 2 December 1864.

The Crown, in the face of this advice from the Lord Advocate, did not defend the claim and a decree in absence was granted in favour of the duke on 22 November 1864 finding that the Rosneath foreshore 'is the property of [the duke] being part and pertinent of the adjoining lands, but subject always to any rights possessed by Her Majesty as trustee for public uses'.[21] Argyll's reaction was blunt. Writing to Macleod, he said:

> I heard on Saturday of the Woods and Forests leaving my conclusion as to Rosneath to pass by default. They have behaved so ill in this matter that I contemplate making a row about it. They threatened me with an action. When I defied them, they allowed 4 years to pass without taking any step. And when I take the initiative, they allow the case to go by default. I hold this to have been nothing short of an attempt to extort money under false pretences.[22]

Skene & Peacock were very surprised at the actions of the Crown. But it was their understanding that the Crown had decided not to contest the action because 'as a matter of policy they thought it expedient to avoid a conflict with his Grace' – something which they thought was in keeping with the previous tactics of the Office of Woods in these matters and which they believed was a policy towards the public and proprietors 'scarcely becoming any department of Government'.[23] William Peacock told Maclean of Ardgour that the decision not to contest the action was taken 'no doubt thereby expecting to propitiate his Grace'.[24]

The Lord Advocate's written opinion was dated 24 November 1864, but the decree in absence was granted two days earlier: this time Horne did not wait for the written opinion before taking steps to abandon the action. He was obviously sensitive to the delays that had previously occurred and the criticism that the Lord Advocate had made, and he reported on the case to the Office of Woods on 25 November, just after the Lord Advocate's written opinion was received. He wanted Howard to know that this time the delay between the conference with the Lord Advocate and the written opinion was not Horne's fault: 'Although repeatedly urged since the date of the consultation for his written opinion to be communicated to you it was only last night that I was able to obtain it from the Lord Advocate.'[25]

21 Duke of Argyll v. Lord Advocate (1864), Argyll–Treasury Correspondence, p. 34.

22 DVGN 555/3/4, Letter Argyll to Macleod, 28 November 1864.

23 DVGN 570/1–9, Letters Skene & Peacock to Macleod, 24 November 1864, 13 January 1865.

24 NRAS, 3583/Bundle 10, Letter Peacock to Ardgour, 21 December 1864.

25 NRS, CR 11/283, Letter Horne to Howard, 25 November 1864.

As foreshadowed by his letter of 28 November 1864 to Macleod, Argyll now decided to 'make a row' about the matter.[26] He wrote to the Treasury, as being 'the only authority to whom such a complaint can be addressed', on 7 January 1865 to complain at the behaviour of Howard and the Office of Woods over the Rosneath affair and the manner in which the Office of Woods was acting in relation to foreshore disputes.[27] He explained that

> It was with a view to check this system of procedure on the part of the Office of Woods and Forests, that I lately joined cordially in an association formed to bring these questions to the test of a legal decision, so that the law of Scotland should be settled and determined.
>
> The association decided, in the first instance, to take up the case of the shores of my estate in Rosneath, a case in which the Commissioners had held the most confident and peremptory language, and in which they had nevertheless shrunk from defending their claim before the courts of law.[28]

The purpose of the Association as explained by Argyll was to test the issue of ownership. But we should note that Argyll, somewhat surprisingly, had also suggested in this letter that it was not the main question of ownership of land as between the Crown and the private proprietor which concerned him but more the way in which the Office of Woods was asserting claims:

> What the legal rights of the Crown may be will probably soon be decided through the actions of the society which the Woods and Forests has called into existence. It matters little what those rights may be, if they are administered on some more intelligible principle than now, and free from the influences to which I have referred.[29]

It was, it seems, the system he objected to more, perhaps, than questions of underlying ownership. And it was the system and the tactics which Argyll had joined the Association with a view to changing.

The duke had two questions to put to the Treasury: first, how long had the Office of Woods known they had no case against him? He surmised that it was in May 1860 (in fact, it was April) that the Crown's

26 DVGN 555/3/4, Letter Argyll to Macleod, 28 November 1864.

27 Argyll–Treasury Correspondence, Letter Argyll to the Treasury, 7 January 1865, p. 3.

28 Argyll–Treasury Correspondence, Letter Argyll to the Treasury, 7 January 1865, p. 6.

29 Argyll–Treasury Correspondence, Letter Argyll to the Treasury, 7 January 1865, pp. 7–8.

case was being considered by Crown Counsel; the opinion, he thought, must have been given soon after that. Had, Argyll wondered,

> the law officers of the Crown advised Mr Howard that the claim was bad, and had he concealed this fact from me, lest even the admission that he had been wrong in my case should affect the claims of his office against others?[30]

Second, whose 'advice' was it that Mr Howard had so confidently relied on and stated in his letter of 7 September 1857; was it the opinion of the Lord Advocate or of a subordinate agent of the Crown?[31] Argyll also made some rather serious allegations that because the Solicitor in Scotland to the Office of Woods, Mr Horne, was paid, not by a fixed salary, but by the amount of business he transacted, this encouraged him to put forward what were, in effect, spurious claims on behalf of the Office of Woods because this increased what Horne would receive by way of remuneration. As we saw in Chapter 2, this was an issue that had also concerned the Earl of Selkirk and other proprietors. While not making a personal accusation against Horne, Argyll nevertheless asserted that the fact that Horne was remunerated by fees led to 'a direct and powerful inducement to an expensive and vexatious management for the sake of extending business'.[32] Argyll had, in making this allegation, probably touched on a raw nerve: the point had already been the subject of some discussion between the Treasury and the Office of Woods, but had not been resolved. The evidence given to the 1847 select committee of enquiry into the Office of Woods had strongly expressed the view that the Solicitor should be paid by way of salary but nothing had come of this; and in 1851 the Office of Woods made a formal recommendation that the Solicitor should be paid by salary, be required to give his whole time to the public service, and that he should be precluded from being in any manner connected with private practice.[33] The Treasury and the Office of Woods must have wished that this recommendation had been acted on so far as Donald Horne was concerned.

The Treasury obtained Howard's explanations as to what had hap-

30 Argyll–Treasury Correspondence, Letter Argyll to the Treasury, 7 January 1865, p. 6.

31 Argyll–Treasury Correspondence, Letter Argyll to the Treasury, 7 January 1865, p. 6.

32 Argyll–Treasury Correspondence, Letter Argyll to the Treasury, 7 January 1865, p. 6.

33 PP, 1852, XXVI, Twenty-ninth report of the Commissioners of Her Majesty's Woods, Forests and Land Revenues, Appendix, Letter to the Treasury, 25 March 1851.

pened between June 1857 and November 1864 and responded to Argyll, with a copy of Howard's letter of explanation, on 4 April 1865.[34] While Argyll was satisfied with the detailed explanation as to what had happened in relation to Rosneath, he was far from satisfied with what he took to be Howard's overall attitude to the way in which the Office of Woods should proceed in relation to the foreshore. It was this, of course, which the Commissioners of Argyll had complained about in their 1860 Memorial and it was this question of approach and tactics that had driven the duke to open the correspondence with the Treasury. Argyll detected no change of approach and he was concerned that the approach affected an important question of public administration. He believed that what the Office of Woods was doing was playing

> a game of tactics, and unless it is played with perfect fairness and candour towards individuals, it must tend to unjust and oppressive dealing. It then becomes a policy not merely for establishing the just claims of the Crown, but for breaking down and usurping both public and private rights.[35]

Further explanations from the Treasury did not mollify Argyll and he would not give up the point that the dropping of the Rosneath case by the Office of Woods after the threats Argyll felt he had received could not be called mere delay, as the Treasury had described it, but involved 'a principle of administration ... of the highest moment'.[36] He had taken up the issue with the Treasury, he explained, not through any hope of private aggrandisement or satisfaction. Argyll said he was one of the public, complaining of the conduct of a public department in a public matter:

> I attach no importance whatever to my own case, except in its connection with the general principle of administration which I conceive to be involved. It is my wish, therefore, to lay the whole of this correspondence before the Association which has been organised to resist what is held to be an invasion of both public and private rights by the Department of Woods and Forests.[37]

We may, perhaps, wonder at the actions and motives of a member of the Cabinet wanting to make public this correspondence, in particular

[34] Argyll–Treasury Correspondence, Letter Peel to Argyll with enclosures, 4 April 1865, pp. 9–14.

[35] Argyll–Treasury Correspondence, Letter Argyll to Treasury, 3 May 1865, pp. 15–16.

[36] Argyll–Treasury Correspondence, Letter Argyll to Treasury, 5 June 1865, p. 31.

[37] Argyll–Treasury Correspondence, Letter Argyll to Treasury, 5 June 1865, p. 32.

because of the very serious allegations which had been made in it about the policies and actions of another Crown department and the policies and actions of the senior permanent official at the department and its Solicitor in Scotland. In any event, it was at this stage that the Treasury decided that enough was enough. The Treasury's response to Argyll's statement that he would be giving copies of the correspondence to the Association left no doubt that the Treasury considered Argyll had gone too far, and that his membership of the Association was particularly significant:

> their Lordships have directed me to acquaint your Grace, that they are of opinion that it will be hardly consistent with what is due to the Crown and to the public (by which term my Lords mean the general public of the United Kingdom), to continue a correspondence with the representative of an association leagued together for the purpose of contesting the rights of the Crown regarding the conduct of a Department charged with the duty of maintaining those rights.[38]

The Treasury had corresponded with Argyll principally because it considered that his complaint was a matter in which he was personally concerned and that 'although you alluded to the establishment of the association in question, [the Treasury] did not understand that the explanations sought were for the use of a body which may be engaged hereafter in litigation with the Crown'.[39] The Treasury rounded off its letter in blunt terms:

> Their Lordships have only to add, that in the judgment of this Board, your Grace has failed to substantiate the general charge which you brought against the Department of Woods and Forests, and that they dissent entirely from the opinions which you now reiterate.[40]

Argyll was clearly stung by this letter and his response was an attempt to explain the motives of the Association. He denied that the Association was, as the Treasury had alleged, formed to contest the rights of the Crown but, rather, for the purpose of testing the pretensions of the Office of Woods. He agreed that while the Crown and the Office of Woods were not always to be considered as two different entities, he denied that they were always identical. But he was being disingenuous. As we saw in Chapter 2, the circulars of the Association to its members were full of references to the Crown and of the Association being formed

[38] Argyll–Treasury Correspondence, Letter Peel to Argyll, 15 June 1865, p. 33.
[39] Argyll–Treasury Correspondence, Letter Peel to Argyll, 15 June 1865, p. 33.
[40] Argyll–Treasury Correspondence, Letter Peel to Argyll, 15 June 1865, p. 33.

to try the question between the Crown and the sea coast proprietors, and the article in the *Edinburgh Evening Courant*, written as we know by the junior counsel for the Association and approved by the Association's committee and Argyll, was crystal clear that the Association had been formed to 'bring the Crown to book'.[41] So far as the Association was concerned, the Crown and the Office of Woods were synonymous. He also denied that he was a representative of the Association: 'I have had no previous communication with that body, and I have no authority to express their opinions. I have written as an individual.'[42] But, as we saw above, Argyll had corresponded with Macleod, the secretary of the Association, about the Association taking on the Rosneath case and he had also told Macleod that he was going to 'make a row' about his treatment by the Office of Woods. He and George Loch had also been in frequent correspondence and contact over Association matters[43] and the duke had corresponded on a number of occasions during the first six months of 1865 with Skene & Peacock on Association matters other than the Rosneath case. Furthermore, Skene & Peacock had received a copy of the duke's correspondence with the Treasury at the end of May 1865 – in other words, before the correspondence had terminated on 17 June 1865 and before Argyll told the Treasury that he would give copies of the correspondence to the Association.[44] The Association was certainly very willing to make use of the correspondence in its campaign. While there is no direct evidence that Argyll liaised with the Association over the correspondence, the facts simply do not support his contention that he had had no previous communication with the Association, unless we are to interpret his words as being limited solely to communications over the contents of the correspondence.

The correspondence ended with Argyll's letter of 17 June although Argyll, writing to Skene & Peacock on 19 June 1865, said that he was not sure, at that date, that it had ended[45] and he arranged for copies of the correspondence to be circulated to all the members of the Association. Skene & Peacock thought that the correspondence

41 'The foreshore', *Edinburgh Evening Courant*, 9 January 1865, p. 4; also found at DVGN 543/10.

42 Argyll–Treasury Correspondence, Letter Argyll to Treasury, 17 June 1865, p. 33.

43 DVGN 570/2/17, Letter Loch to Macleod, 29 November 1863.

44 DVGN 544/3–5, Business Account of Skene & Peacock with the Association for General Business, 1865.

45 DVGN 570/1–9, Copy correspondence between His Grace the Duke of Argyll and Messrs Skene & Peacock.

provided 'a most powerful and masterly exposition of the unfair policy of the department of Woods and Forests and of the true character and tendency of their proceedings'.[46] Argyll told them that 'Several persons to whom I have shown my correspondence . . . desire to see it printed and more or less circulated.'[47] It was sent to Association members on 29 September 1865 and the Board had it published as a Parliamentary Paper on 6 August 1866, the day that the Crown Lands Act 1866 received the Royal Assent.[48] A summary was published in the *Pall Mall Gazette* with a reprint of the article in *The Scottish Law Magazine* at the end of 1866. The article referred to the Parliamentary Paper which contained the correspondence between the duke and the Treasury and said that the Paper 'contains the details of as pretty a quarrel as we recollect to have assisted at, and affords a comforting proof that whenever officials fall out the public are likely to come by their own'.[49] Argyll was characterised in the article as representing the public. It appears that the article was written as an attempt to persuade the Board of Trade not to pursue the same policies as the Office of Woods so far as the foreshore was concerned. It is not clear who wrote the article, but Loch thought it might have been Macleod: 'Did you write the article in the *Pall Mall Gazette* of Monday last?' he asked. 'Very well done.'[50] Skene & Peacock's opinion of the article was rather more cautious: 'We read the Article . . . which we thought very good as far as it went, and ought to put the Board of Trade on their guard.'[51] The publication of the correspondence was well received by the proprietorial body. There were a number of letters of appreciation sent by members of the Association who had received copies of the correspondence, typical of which was one which said: 'I consider the Landed Proprietors of Scotland are much indebted to his Grace'[52] and another which said: 'we are delighted at the masterly and convincing arguments with which the Duke defends

[46] DVGN 570/1–9, Letter Skene & Peacock to Argyll, 29 June 1865.

[47] DVGN 570/1–9, Letter Argyll to Skene & Peacock, 28 June 1865.

[48] See an article in the *City Press*, 'The right to foreshore', contained in DVGN 573/1. In fact, the House of Commons had ordered it to be printed on 24 July 1866 and the delay before publication was thought by some to have been contrived so that it took place after the Crown Lands Act 1866 received the Royal Assent.

[49] 'The defeat of the foreshores', *Pall Mall Gazette*, 19 November 1866; Anon., 'The right of the Crown to foreshores', *The Scottish Law Magazine*, 5:12 (1866), p. 82.

[50] DVGN 572/143, Letter Loch to Macleod, 21 November 1866.

[51] DVGN 570/4/92, Letter Skene & Peacock to Macleod, 26 November 1866.

[52] DVGN 570/1–9, Letter Sir G. Grant Sutton to Macleod, 13 December 1865.

his position, and we feel that in doing so he is our champion in the same cause'.[53] Skene & Peacock said that the publication of his correspondence had 'caused a considerable sensation [in Edinburgh]'[54] and that in February 1866 'copies of the Correspondence are still eagerly sought after'.[55] Argyll himself commented in relation to the Maclean of Ardgour case that his correspondence 'had some effect in opening the eyes of the Judges in Scotland to the extent of the principles involved in the bit-by-bit operations of Mr Howard'.[56] It also had an effect on individuals at the Office of Woods. A letter from Argyll to Macleod in July 1865 suggests that there was some consternation within the Office of Woods as a result of Argyll's correspondence with the Treasury and, in particular, amongst the lawyers of whom Argyll had been so critical. Argyll wrote: 'I am happy to see we are giving such room for thought and reflection to the legal advisers of the Woods and Forests. I hope we shall yet live them down.'[57]

The foreshores of Argyll's Rosneath estate were again the subject of a dispute between Argyll and the Crown, now represented by the Board of Trade, in 1868, a dispute that led, indirectly, to Argyll's next attack on Crown policy over the foreshore. Towards the end of 1867 Argyll had applied for an interdict against a Mr Campbell, who had a feu from Argyll, to prevent him taking gravel and other material from the shores of the estate. Argyll was granted an interdict by the sheriff substitute on 28 January 1868 and Campbell appealed to the sheriff principal. During the course of this appeal, Campbell produced a licence issued to him by the Board, dated 10 February 1868, giving him permission to take gravel and other material from the Rosneath foreshores. The sheriff principal decided the licence was irrelevant to the issue being tried and upheld the interdict granted by the sheriff substitute. But the existence of the licence issued by the Board was brought to Argyll's attention who saw this as another example of the way in which the Crown was interfering in property which the court had decided, in the decree in absence granted on 22 November 1864, belonged to him.

By this stage, Russell's Liberal government had fallen and Argyll was no longer in office. The President of the Board was the Duke

[53] DVGN 572/134, Letter George Dundas to Macleod, 29 October 1865 (emphasis in original).

[54] DVGN 570/1–9, Letter Skene & Peacock to Macleod, 21 October 1865.

[55] DVGN 570/4/81, Letter Skene & Peacock to Macleod, 21 February 1866.

[56] DVGN 572/9, Letter Argyll to Macleod, 12 January 1866.

[57] DVGN 555/3/6, Letter Argyll to Macleod, 26 July 1865.

of Richmond in Disraeli's Conservative government. Argyll wrote to Richmond on 27 April 1868 protesting at the conduct of the Board. It was, he said, 'a matter which seriously affects the principles on which the assumed right of the Crown are to be administered in respect of the interests of Proprietors and of the public in the Foreshores of Scotland'.[58] He wanted an explanation as to how it was that the Board could grant a licence to someone to take gravel and other material from the foreshore without making any enquiries as to the ownership of the foreshore, and how, in particular, it was that such a licence could be granted after the sheriff substitute had granted an interdict to prevent the encroachment.

Richmond asked Farrer, the permanent secretary of the Board, and C. Cecil Trevor, the assistant secretary, for an explanation and was told that when the licence was granted Campbell had not disclosed the interdict proceedings and that from the maps he had provided it was not clear that the shores in respect of which he wanted the licence formed part of the Rosneath estate. But the Board acted quickly to withdraw the licence and Trevor drafted a careful letter of explanation and apology for Richmond to write to Argyll. As will be seen from Chapter 5, this incident took place while the Crown and the Association were waiting for the Law Officers to pronounce on the question of ownership of the foreshores as between the Crown and proprietors and, no doubt, the Board would have had no wish to allow this incident to inflame the position between the Crown and the Association. Farrer was impressed with the draft letter prepared by Trevor: 'You have settled this with care for the approval of the President. It will I think do us no harm if the Duke of Argyll publishes it.'[59] Farrer would have been very aware, given what had happened in 1865, that any correspondence between Argyll and the Board might well end up being published.[60] The letter explained how it was that the licence came to be granted and confirmed that the Board had no knowledge of the facts set out in Argyll's letter. As to the issue of the ownership of the foreshore, the letter told Argyll of the case which had gone to the Law Officers. As to the principles followed by the Board in respect of the grant of licences, there was enclosed with the

[58] TNA:PRO, MT 10/68, Letter Argyll to Richmond, 27 April 1868.

[59] TNA:PRO, MT 10/68, Draft letter Richmond to Argyll with manuscript note by THF. The letter was approved by Richmond on 1 May 1868. He made a small alteration: 'It is obvious that it is desirable to avoid any step which shall give rise to unnecessary litigation.'

[60] The letter was made public when Richmond read from it in his response to Argyll's criticism of the Farrer Memorandum discussed below; PD, Third Series, vol. 192, House of Lords, col. 1828 (19 June 1868).

letter a copy of the Farrer Memorandum.[61] In fact, Argyll will almost certainly already have been aware of, and may well have seen, the Farrer Memorandum; it had been published, as we noted in Chapter 3, as a Parliamentary Paper on 29 November 1867 and the Association appears to have had copies of it before it was published.

## THE DUKE OF ARGYLL'S CRITICISM OF THE FARRER MEMORANDUM

The Farrer Memorandum and the circumstances in which it was written were examined in Chapter 3. We look here at Argyll's criticism of it, which he made in the House of Lords on 19 June 1868. When the Duke of Richmond had sent a copy to Argyll in May, he could, perhaps, have hardly expected the attack Argyll was to mount on it just a month later.

Argyll began his remarks to the House by saying that he believed no one doubted that the Crown had certain rights over the foreshore, 'whether claims of ownership or as trustee for the public', but that these rights were subject to the rights not just of the public, but also of private individuals – rights which depended on the common law, on the terms of individual charters and 'rights acquired by individuals or public bodies in consequence of use and prescription, which was the foundation of a very great deal of the property held by Members of [this] House as well as by the public at large'.[62] This is fascinating because we see here Argyll appearing to accept the possibility that the Crown did have valid claims of ownership of the foreshore, as we also saw in relation to his correspondence with the Treasury over Rosneath, and stressing the importance of use and prescription as the foundation of much of the property rights of private proprietors.[63] This was not something the

[61] TNA:PRO, MT 10/68, Draft letter Richmond to Argyll, 2 May 1868.

[62] PD, Third Series, vol. 192, House of Lords, col. 1815 (19 June 1868).

[63] The concept of prescription as the foundation of property rights has been and continues to be, in the context of land ownership in Scotland, controversial: Cosmo Innes criticised the way in which common lands, and in particular the foreshore, had been appropriated; C. Innes, *Lectures on Scotch Legal Antiquities* (Edinburgh, 1872), pp. 154–8. J. Ramsay Macdonald drew attention to the unsatisfactory way in which the principle had allowed landowners in Scotland to acquire 'their broad acres'; T. Johnston, *Our Scots Noble Families* (Glasgow, 1909), p. xxx. And the land reform campaigner Andy Wightman has criticised the extent to which the principle has effected the transformation of common property into private property; Wightman, *Poor Had No Lawyers*, pp. 24–7. The generally accepted justification for the principle of prescription is that it serves the public interest; D. Johnston, *Prescription and Limitation* (Edinburgh, 1999), p. 17. However, the controversy

Association, on behalf of the proprietors, had conceded and, indeed, the draft legislation that the Association had proposed to the Board, as described in Chapter 5, aimed to make it clear that ownership of the foreshore lay, as a matter of law, with the *ex adverso* owner, not with the Crown and that the Crown's rights were limited to the rights of the public for navigation and commerce. As we shall see in Chapter 5, the Law Officers of Scotland and England were about to give a very important opinion on the question of the ownership of the foreshores. The opinion was dated 13 June 1868 – six days before Argyll was speaking in the Lords – but the Board did not officially receive it until 1 July. Although, as we shall see in Chapter 5, the Duke of Richmond did not know what the opinion said until 1 July, it is not inconceivable that Argyll may nevertheless have been aware of which way the opinion of the Law Officers was going. If so, he may have been attempting, in his remarks to the Lords, to stress the importance of prescriptive possession (which the Law Officers were to accept as a way in which private proprietors might prove their title to the foreshore) and to prepare for continued pressure on the Board based, not on the fundamental question of ownership, but on the way in which the Board attacked the private proprietor. While the main question as to ownership was not settled until the decision in the Agnew case and the Association was still arguing that proprietors did not require an express grant of the foreshore from the Crown, but that they had title by implication as part and pertinent of the *ex adverso* land, it is possible that the opinion of the Law Officers would have persuaded much of the proprietorial body that, in future, the battle against the Crown over the foreshore was to be fought over proof of possession, and indeed this is what the Association recommended in its 1869 Report to the members discussed in Chapter 5. Argyll returned, at the end of his and other Lords' remarks and as his final observation, to the importance of the rights of use and prescription and to the antipathy that the Farrer Memorandum showed towards these rights: 'Among the objections which he had urged against the Memorandum was that it throughout evinced the greatest antipathy to those rights of usage and prescription on which a large portion of the rights of property in this

over the claim by John Macleod of Macleod to the Black Cuillins in Skye, a claim which Crown Counsel (J. E. Drummond Young QC) confirmed was justified through proof of immemorial use and possession, suggests that this justification may not be universally accepted; Opinion of Crown Counsel for The Crown Estate Commissioners relative to the Cuillins, 2 July 2000; Wightman, *Poor Had No Lawyers*, pp. 125–37.

country depended.'[64] Argyll outlined the circumstances of his disputes with the Board over Rosneath, both the earlier dispute that had led to the Court case, and the later dispute over the licence, and drew attention to his correspondence with the Treasury published as a Parliamentary Paper. All of this, he said, left the impression that a

> systematic attempt was being made in Scotland, and he thought in England also, to convert the limited ownership of the Crown into a claim of absolute and unrestricted ownership over the bed of the sea and the foreshore and that . . . it was intended that this alleged absolute property of the Crown should be made a source of revenue.[65]

It also left the impression that the Office of Woods had been enforcing its claims in 'a very oppressive spirit, and . . . a very insidious and oppressive manner as regard[s] the interests and rights of private individuals'.[66] It was, Argyll believed and as we saw in Chapter 3, as a result of his correspondence with the Treasury that the responsibility for the management of the foreshore had been transferred in 1866 to the Board:

> Immediately after the correspondence, and, as he had reason to believe, in consequence of the facts brought under the notice of the Government . . . a Bill was introduced to transfer the management of the claims of the Crown from the Woods and Forests to the Board of Trade.[67]

One of his complaints against the Office of Woods had been that there had been no person who took direct parliamentary responsibility for that department and he had hoped that with the Board now responsible, this would be different. But the first action of the Board had been to publish the Farrer Memorandum, a publication which was signed by the secretary to the Board. Why, the duke asked, had not a document of such great importance been signed by the President? Argyll's concerns over the Farrer Memorandum went further: 'In looking over the document the first thing which struck him was the animus which pervaded it as regards the rights of private individuals' and he returned to his point about use and possession: 'He need hardly remind their Lordships that the rights of individuals and of public bodies over

[64] PD, Third Series, vol. 192, House of Lords, col. 1834 (19 June 1868).

[65] PD, Third Series, vol. 192, House of Lords, col. 1815 (19 June 1868).

[66] PD, Third Series, vol. 192, House of Lords, col. 1815 (19 June 1868).

[67] PD, Third Series, vol. 192, House of Lords, col. 1816 (19 June 1868). Richmond did not agree with this; see col. 1824. It was in any event hardly 'immediately after' – the Bill was not, in fact, introduced until April 1866.

foreshores depended to a great extent on user and wont.'[68] Argyll was critical of Farrer's attitude to the claims of private owners through acts of possession and he concluded that the Board was acting with the same animus as had the Office of Woods. It was, he said, a policy of getting individuals to acknowledge the right of the Crown rather than confront the issue at large, of driving proprietors into a corner and making them submit to a compromise. Argyll referred in his observations to the Association, formed, he said, 'for the defence of the right of individuals' and he thought that it was the successes of the Association that had contributed to the tone of the Farrer Memorandum.[69] Argyll also took issue with the Appendix to the Farrer Memorandum written, as we saw in Chapter 3, by a lawyer, F. S. Reilly, who had been very critical of the actions of the Dukes of Argyll, Buccleuch and Sutherland during the passage of the Crown Lands Bill of 1866 through the House. Their actions had, in Reilly's opinion, resulted in a piece of legislation which seriously fettered the Board in its task of administering the foreshore; an opinion that the duke thought 'was entirely at variance with the understanding which he had had with his Colleagues in Lord Palmerston's Government'. Argyll thought that it was quite wrong of Reilly to 'designate certain individual members of their Lordships' House who were represented as taking in their own interest a course contrary to the law and to the declared opinion of Parliament'.[70] Argyll believed the Farrer Memorandum was 'a most improper document' that 'ought at once to be withdrawn'.[71]

The Duke of Richmond as the President of the Board of Trade responded to Argyll. Richmond was, of course, also a member of the Association and he was quick to point this out to the House.[72] He had not, he said, been in office when the Farrer Memorandum was written but he nonetheless strongly defended it. He rejected Argyll's criticism over the alleged animus of the Farrer Memorandum in attacking the rights of individuals. On the contrary, he read out to the House extracts from the Memorandum that, he said, showed that the object of the Board was to protect the rights of the public.[73] He could not resist,

[68] PD, Third Series, vol. 192, House of Lords, col. 1817 (19 June 1868).

[69] PD, Third Series, vol. 192, House of Lords, col. 1819 (19 June 1868).

[70] PD, Third Series, vol. 192, House of Lords, cols 1821–2 (19 June 1868).

[71] PD, Third Series, vol. 192, House of Lords, col. 1822 (19 June 1868).

[72] PD, Third Series, vol. 192, House of Lords, col. 1826 (19 June 1868). The potential for a conflict of interest that Richmond had as President of the Board, as a private proprietor and as a member of the Association is examined in Chapter 5.

[73] See, for example, the extracts at PD, Third Series, vol. 192, House of Lords,

with some sense of irony, contrasting the present conduct of the Board under his leadership with that of the Office of Woods during the period when Argyll had been a member of the government and hoped that Argyll would allow Richmond 'to condole with him upon the manner in which he had been treated by his Colleagues when they were in Office'.[74] The Lord Chancellor, Lord Cairns, added some important remarks at the end of the debate. He was in no doubt as to the duty of the Board or the law. He had, he said, 'long experience and knowledge of what foreshore cases were'[75] and said:

> It might be a very bad law or a very good law; but beyond all doubt it was the law in this country that the whole foreshore of the kingdom *prima facie* belonged to the Crown; and the Crown had the right to say 'The foreshores of the Kingdom belong to us, unless you show either a grant or prescriptive right taking away that which otherwise belongs to the Crown.'[76]

It was the duty of the Crown, the Lord Chancellor said, to take care that encroachments were not made on the rights of the Crown, and until Parliament said that should not be the duty, 'he would be guilty of a dereliction of duty if he did not take care that encroachments were not made on the rights of the Crown'.[77] The Lord Chancellor had obviously thought that Argyll's remarks were motivated by self-interest and a concern for the rights of private individuals, as opposed to a concern for the public and he ended his remarks with something of an implicit criticism of Argyll's contribution, suggesting that it might be seen as special pleading:

> For [the Lord Chancellor's] part he was only anxious that nothing should fall from their Lordships to lead the public Department, which was intrusted with the care of this public property, to suppose that it would be acting rightly in neglecting the duty confided to it, or to cause any persons out-of-doors to fancy that Members of their Lordship's House, whose private

col. 1827 (19 June 1868) and, as we saw in Chapter 3, there can be little doubt that the Board *did* believe its prime duty was to act in the interests of the public.

[74] PD, Third Series, vol. 192, House of Lords, col. 1829 (19 June 1868).

[75] PD, Third Series, vol. 192, House of Lords, col. 1832 (19 June 1868).

[76] PD, Third Series, vol. 192, House of Lords, col. 1832 (19 June 1868). This, of course, foreshadowed the Law Officers' opinion which was dated 13 June 1868 and which we discuss in Chapter 5. Although the Duke of Richmond did not know what was in this opinion until it was received by the Board on 1 July, it is not an unreasonable assumption that the Lord Chancellor did know what the opinion said when he spoke in the Lords on 19 June.

[77] PD, Third Series, vol. 192, House of Lords, col. 1833 (19 June 1868).

> interests ought most properly to be protected, were desirous to place these private interests in opposition to the just rights of the public.[78]

In a leader published the day after Argyll's remarks in the House, *The Times* took up the comments of the Lord Chancellor. While Argyll may have thought he was defending the rights of the public, the private rights of individual proprietors, *The Times* thought, influenced him more heavily:

> He holds that the maintenance of the property of the Crown in Foreshores is adverse to public rights and public interests; and it is necessary 'to protect the public from the strained assertion of the rights of the Crown'. So easily can the most liberal of men misunderstand a question when they can indulge in general phrases! If we translate the Duke's language with exact reference to facts, we must read for 'public' 'private owners', and for 'rights of the Crown' 'rights of the public', and his object is 'to protect private owners from the strained assertions of the rights of the public'. Put in this way, the complaint has a very different look and it is impossible not to believe that when the case is really understood there will be no more room for the indignation the Duke expressed.[79]

*The Times* did nothing to encourage proprietors that Parliament might be asked to relinquish to them the ownership of the foreshore. 'As to the law itself, it is simply impossible to alter it', said *The Times*.[80] There was a response to this leader through the letters column of the *Daily Telegraph* from James Pycroft who, as we saw in Chapter 3, had been highly critical of the way in which the Crown Lands Act 1866 had been put through Parliament. He was offended by the stance of *The Times* on this issue and roundly condemned it in a letter published on 23 June 1868. He thought that the comments of *The Times* were vituperative and that the Lord Chancellor was wrong in law. It was his view that 'the landed proprietors of the United Kingdom are deeply indebted [to the Duke of Argyll] for having adopted the very spirited course he has done in these transactions'.[81]

## CONCLUSIONS

While Argyll's defence of the rights of private proprietors in the Scottish foreshore may not have had the degree of publicity or attention in the

78 PD, Third Series, vol. 192, House of Lords, col. 1834 (19 June 1868).
79 *The Times*, 20 June 1868, p. 9.
80 *The Times*, 20 June 1868, p. 9.
81 *Daily Telegraph*, 30 June 1868.

historiography which his contributions in other areas concerning land ownership and occupation in Scotland have had, we should not doubt the importance of the contribution he made to the nineteenth-century debate on the ownership of Scotland's foreshore and the role of the Office of Woods and the Board of Trade.

Argyll believed that he caused, or at the very least, contributed to, the transfer of responsibilities for the management of the foreshore to the Board in 1866,[82] and there is little doubt that his contribution affected the climate of opinion over the foreshore dispute, and certainly boosted the morale of the private proprietors. He also contributed to the demise of Donald Horne, the Solicitor in Scotland to the Office of Woods who was replaced during 1865 by Andrew Murray. Skene & Peacock told Macleod that they had it on good authority that this was a result of Argyll's correspondence.[83] And Argyll's criticism of the method of remunerating the Solicitor in Scotland to the Office of Woods almost certainly contributed to Horne's replacement being remunerated by a fixed salary, as had been recommended so many years earlier.[84]

[82] And, as we saw in Chapter 3, he certainly contributed to the amendments to the Crown Lands Bill in 1866 that left a legacy that would be relevant to the issue of how, and by whom, Scotland's foreshore should be managed, into the twentieth and twenty-first centuries.

[83] DVGN 570/1–9, Letter Skene & Peacock to Macleod, 21 February 1866.

[84] Skene & Peacock were informed that the new holder of the office would be remunerated by a salary and not by fees; see DVGN 570/4/82, Letter Skene & Peacock to Macleod, 28 February 1866; TNA:PRO, MT 10/32, Letter Office of Woods to the Board of Trade, 27 November 1866.

# 5

# 'A more favourable case to adopt could scarcely be obtained'

## INTRODUCTION

DURING THE FIRST FIVE years after the formation of the Association it was still the Office of Woods that had responsibility for the foreshore and which, as we saw in Chapters 2 and 4, had been involved in the cases brought by the Association. With the passing of the Crown Lands Act in 1866 discussed in Chapter 3 the Board of Trade became responsible for the management of the foreshore. We look, in this chapter, at the activities of the Association from the beginning of 1867 up to the Agnew case in 1873. It was a time when the attitudes and actions of the Board towards the Association will have been conditioned by the fact that the Board believed its powers of administering the foreshore had been seriously fettered by the last-minute changes to the Crown Lands Act 1866 discussed in Chapter 3; would have wanted the 1866 Act to be amended to remove these fetters; and would have been aware of the advice that this could only happen if either the Board settled the foreshore question with the Association or the court finally decided the question. The dispute between the Crown and the Scottish proprietors needed to be brought to a conclusion.

## THE ASSOCIATION'S 1867 PROPOSALS FOR LEGISLATION

The Association may, initially, have hoped that the transfer of responsibilities for the foreshore from the Office of Woods to the Board would bring with it a change of attitude to the Scottish proprietors as to the title to the foreshore. However, the publication of the Farrer Memorandum and the passing of the Oyster and Mussel Fisheries Act during 1866 and, in particular, the publication of the Board's regulations under that Act appeared to confirm for the proprietors that the situation was not going to change. We have seen in Chapters 3 and 4 how the Association and the Duke of Argyll had reacted to the publication of the Farrer Memorandum, and the Oyster and Mussel Fisheries Act raised further concerns. Skene & Peacock had been watching the passage of the Bill with interest.[1] They believed the question of title to the foreshore would arise at the first stage of every application under the Act for a grant to establish an oyster and mussel fishery. They wrote to Macleod:

> we fear that the practical result will be that proprietors applying for orders must either admit the Crown's claims [to the foreshore] or have their application rejected . . . We hope it may turn out otherwise, but we cannot help thinking that the Foreshore question is about to acquire a new and more serious aspect under the administration of the Board of Trade. Their future policy is chiefly foreshadowed by the last paragraph of page 1 of the Regulations.[2]

It is ironic that it was this paragraph of the regulations that most concerned Skene & Peacock, because it was also the one that bothered the Board. Farrer at the Board recognised that the Office of Woods had

> got into great trouble in consequence of asking an extreme price [for the foreshore] – On the other hand I do not see how we can give up asking any price at all . . . Perhaps we may leave the ultimate decision of these questions till the cases arise. I have put a paragraph into the Regulations with this in view.[3]

The Vice President of the Board, Stephen Cave, had made some amendments to Farrer's paragraph in an effort to show that the Board would act in accordance with what it understood its legal duty to be, but also as fairly as possible.[4]

The Association was anxious to discuss the foreshore question with the Board, and a meeting between the Board and representatives of the Association took place on 19 March 1867. The Duke of Richmond, who was now the President of the Board, was present and George Loch and Henry Baillie MP represented the Association.[5] Loch and Baillie

[1] DVGN 544/3/6, Business Account for 1866 for Association for vindicating rights of Seaboard Proprietors of Foreshore in Scotland.

[2] DVGN 572/146/2, Copy letter Skene & Peacock to Macleod, 12 December 1866.

[3] TNA:PRO, MT 10/32, Note by Farrer, 22 November 1866.

[4] Manuscript amendments to draft Board of Trade Regulations.

[5] It is surely no coincidence that what appears to have been the first meeting at such a level between members of the committee and the Board took place just days after the appointment of the Duke of Richmond as the President of the Board on 8 March. Macleod was, in fact, told on 14 March that the duke would 'be happy to receive a delegation on the subject of "foreshores" on the 19 March'; see DVGN 572/147, Letter Charles Peel to Macleod, 14 March 1867.

drew the attention of the Board to the memorial and opinion that the Association had obtained in 1862 that had referred to the 1860 Statement on behalf of the Argyll Commissioners, and the response and statement from James Howard, the Commissioner at the Office of Woods, in June 1860.[6] So that the Board should fully understand the views of the Office of Woods on the 1860 Statement, Howard was asked by C. Cecil Trevor, the assistant secretary with responsibility for harbours at the Board, to let the Board have a copy of Howard's response and statement, and to provide the Board with any general comments Howard might have on the general question of the Crown's rights to the foreshore in Scotland.[7] Howard told Trevor that

> The question really at issue seems to be whether a charter of lands abutting upon the sea . . . but containing no express grant of the foreshore confers on the grantee or vassal any right of property in the foreshore . . . in Scotland . . . This question has never I believe been judicially determined.[8]

He was, however, concerned at the fact that the decision in the Maclean of Ardgour case was being relied on as the latest authority on the subject.[9]

It was agreed at the meeting that the Association would prepare and submit their proposals as to how a settlement of the questions between the Board and the Association might be reached. This they did and in April 1867 Loch wrote to Richmond enclosing

> such a proposition [which] has been prepared with much care in order that it may at the same time meet jointly the legal rights of Proprietors, and of the public, represented by the Crown, respectively – it has been thought best to frame it in the shape of a Bill, as it is admitted that the difficulty is one that can only be removed by the authority of Parliament.[10]

Loch also sent, at Richmond's request, a statement explaining the proprietors' views of the past and present position on the problem. This statement summarised the origins of the Association and the actions of the Association to date, including the two cases so far fought on behalf

[6] DVGN 551/3, 1862 Memorial and Opinion; NRS, CR 11/95, 1860 Statement; both are discussed in Chapter 2.

[7] TNA:PRO, MT 10/139, Copy letter Trevor to Howard, 20 March 1867.

[8] TNA:PRO, MT 10/139, Letter Howard to Trevor, 30 March 1867.

[9] Lord Advocate v. Maclean of Ardgour (1866) 38 Scot. Jur. 584 and 2 Scottish Law Reporter 25. The case is discussed in Chapter 2.

[10] TNA:PRO, MT 10/139, Letter Loch to Duke of Richmond, 2 April 1867. Loch delivered this letter by hand and met with Richmond, Farrer and Cave, a meeting he described as 'useful'.

of the Association. It concluded that as the Board now had responsibility for the management of the foreshore, it was

> a suitable time for an adjustment of the Foreshore controversy in order to obviate further litigation and expense and with a view to removing the impediment it now presents to the application of the shore to the beneficial uses to which it is capable of being turned.[11]

The statement also made the highly significant point that there was no

> valuable pecuniary interest in the Crown which should retard such a Settlement, for it may be taken as certain that almost every part of the shore of Scotland capable of possession may be proved to have been possessed by the adjacent proprietors in the same way as the shores of the Estate of Ardgour have been possessed; and if there is any portion of the shores of Scotland unpossessed it can only be where from its physical character acts of possession are impossible or unprofitable.[12]

The Association's proposals to 'declare and settle the law relating to the Foreshore of Scotland' took, as Loch said, the form of a draft Bill prepared by Skene & Peacock. The Bill made it crystal clear that the Association wanted nothing less than a statutory acknowledgement of the *ex adverso* proprietor's ownership of the foreshore irrespective of grant or possession. The preamble to the draft Bill stated:

> Whereas doubts have been entertained as to the true state of Law relating to the Foreshore in Scotland, and in consequence disputes and litigation have arisen, and are likely further to arise: And whereas it is expedient that the Law relating to the Foreshore should be declared and settled.[13]

Clause 1 stated:

> The proprietors of all lands adjoining the sea or any tidal waters shall be held to be proprietors of the Foreshore *ex adverso* of such lands as part and pertinent thereof: Provided that such proprietors shall hold the Foreshore subject to all the lawful rights and interests of the public which are vested in the Crown, as Trustee for the public uses of navigation and commerce.[14]

[11] TNA:PRO, MT 10/139, Statement by the Committee of the Association of Seaboard proprietors as to the ownership of the Foreshores of Scotland, pp. 4–5. The statement was drafted by William Peacock.

[12] TNA:PRO, MT 10/139, Statement by the Committee of the Association of Seaboard proprietors as to the ownership of the Foreshores of Scotland, p. 5.

[13] TNA:PRO, MT 10/139, A Bill to declare and settle the Law relating to Foreshore in Scotland.

[14] TNA:PRO, MT 10/139, A Bill to declare and settle the Law relating to Foreshore in Scotland. The public uses conceded by the clause were rather more

The draft went on in clauses 2 and 3 to give the Board a right to apply for an interdict to prevent the sinking of mines, making of embankments, erecting of piers or houses on the foreshore or executing any other operations on the foreshore, which would cause a material change in the natural state of the foreshore. The first draft of the Bill did not contain such a right but the Association thought that without it the Board would be very unlikely even to consider the Bill. Skene & Peacock had, at first, not wanted to include the clause but Loch had had a strong indication from Farrer that if it was not included, 'the whole affair might suffer shipwreck'.[15] Loch was quite open as to what the Association wanted:

> What we seek is, stated shortly, on the one hand to obtain recognition of what we believe the real right of Proprietors – on the other, to arm the Board of Trade with summary means of protecting the public interests connected with the Foreshore under their protection.[16]

## THE BOARD'S RESPONSE

Before considering the response we turn, briefly, to consider the Duke of Richmond's rather delicate position as President of the Board. Richmond was aware of the potential for a conflict of interest by virtue of his membership of the Association and his position as President of the Board, and he was to acknowledge the difficulty his appointment as President had caused, in the exchanges he had with the Duke of Argyll in the House of Lords in June 1868 over the Farrer Memorandum discussed in Chapter 4:

> when he became President of the Board of Trade he found himself in a somewhat invidious position, because, as a Scotch proprietor, he had subscribed to an association the views of which, to say the least, did not exactly coincide with those of the Department.[17]

His position was, however, a little more than invidious. He was responsible for a department whose policy over the foreshore was likely to be in direct contradiction to his own interests as a private landowner. This, of course, might not have been a particularly unusual state of affairs, but what made the conflict stark was Richmond's membership

restricted than as described by Lord Hope in Officers of State v. Smith (1846) 8 D 711 at p. 719 and by Lord Kinloch in Nicol v. Blaikie (1859) 22 D 335 at p. 340; see further in Chapter 9.

[15] DVGN 570/2/33, Letter Loch to Macleod, 8 April 1867.

[16] TNA:PRO, MT 10/139, Letter Loch to Farrer, 5 April 1867.

[17] PD, Third Series, vol. 192, House of Lords, col. 1826 (19 June 1868).

of, and subscription of funds to, an association which was, as we saw in Chapter 4, described by the Treasury as 'an association leagued together for the purpose of contesting the rights of the Crown regarding the conduct of a Department charged with the duty of maintaining those rights'.[18] When Richmond joined the Association, his letter to Macleod made clear his feelings as to the actions of the Crown: 'I shall have much pleasure in joining the Association to restrain the Crown from its encroachment on the liberty of the subject.'[19] There is no suggestion that Richmond resigned his membership of the Association or withdrew the funds he had subscribed while he held office. After he left office in December 1868 he joined the committee of the Association, and he was present at the meeting of the committee which took place in June 1869 to discuss the letter to be sent to members of the Association reporting on progress thus far and giving the committee's decision as to further action, a letter that commented critically on the Farrer Memorandum, as discussed later in this chapter.

Trevor believed that the main argument of the Office of Woods had been that, insofar as land (including the foreshore) in Scotland was originally vested in the Crown, all land that had not been expressly granted by the Crown remained with the Crown. The proprietors, on the other hand, believed that the foreshore was part and pertinent of their land, irrespective of Crown grant, or at least that evidence of possession for forty years raised the presumption that the foreshore was included in a grant or charter of the *ex adverso* land. Trevor believed that 'from a pecuniary point of view the "property" of the foreshore in Scotland is now for the Crown little better than a *damnosa hereditas*'.[20] Trevor had been convinced by the argument of Loch and Baillie at the March meeting that it would not be possible to select a case to go to the House of Lords 'for a decision on the question of law unencumbered with the question of user . . . as no proprietor would be willing to leave out of consideration what he considered the strongest point in his favour'.[21] This was probably a point of view both Loch and Baillie would certainly wish to have encouraged because it might be thought to make their proposal of legislation rather than judicial action more acceptable. Trevor concluded that

> provided we can do so without unfairly shirking our responsibility which has been put upon us, we should receive a proposition of this sort [i.e. the

[18] Argyll–Treasury Correspondence, Letter Peel to Argyll, 15 June 1865, p. 33.
[19] DVGN 572/6, Letter Richmond to Macleod, 3 July 1861.
[20] An inheritance that is more of a burden than a benefit.
[21] TNA:PRO, MT 10/139, Minute, 3 April 1867, CCT.

> draft Bill] favourably and endeavour to have a question, which is certain to be continually raised, settled if possible once and for all. But before doing anything we ought to have the joint opinion of the Law Officers of Scotland and England upon the general question.[22]

He suggested that Andrew Murray, the newly appointed Solicitor in Scotland to the Office of Woods, should be asked to prepare a very detailed case and that he should be told

> that provided we can legally do so we should be willing – with the consent of the Treasury – to join in any reasonable arrangement whereby this vexed question may be settled, and that with such consent we should be ready to relinquish the claim to property, of course retaining our jurisdiction for the protection of public use and enjoyment.[23]

As we have seen in previous chapters, the fundamental fact that the Crown did have a property interest in the foreshore had never been conceded. The Farrer Memorandum had expressed the very clear view that it was important to maintain the title of the Crown if the rights of the public were properly to be protected.[24] So this minute by Trevor is an important moment in the dispute over foreshore between proprietors and the Crown because it appears to be the first instance of officials being prepared to consider relinquishing the Crown's claim to a property interest in the foreshore. Farrer said that he generally agreed with Trevor's minute and, in particular, he took no issue with Trevor's suggestion of relinquishing the property right in the foreshore. He, too, thought it was premature to discuss the draft Bill submitted by the Association although he did not think, at first sight, that it provided sufficiently for public rights. However he took no issue with the principles of clause 1 of the draft Bill. He agreed that Murray should be asked to prepare a case that should be as full and as complete as possible and that Murray should, in preparing the case, 'avail himself of the best legal assistance'.[25] Richmond agreed that the papers should be referred to the Law Officers and supported what Trevor and Farrer had said:

> It is of the greatest consequence that some amicable arrangements should be come to if possible. If the rights of the public are preserved, it appears to me this is all the Board of Trade should have to care for.[26]

22 TNA:PRO, MT 10/139, Minute, 3 April 1867, CCT.
23 TNA:PRO, MT 10/139, Minute, 3 April 1867, CCT.
24 See Farrer Memorandum, p. 2.
25 TNA:PRO, MT 10/139, Minute, 4 April 1867, THF.
26 TNA:PRO, MT 10/139, Minute, 4 April 1867, R.

The conclusions of the Board were communicated by Trevor to Loch who was told 'the questions raised [in Loch's letter of 2 April and enclosures] are in the opinion of this Board of considerable importance and it appears to them desirable that before coming to any decision upon the subject the Law Officers of the Crown should be consulted'. Farrer asked Trevor to include in the letter the words 'no pains will be spared on the part of the Board of Trade to bring this question to an amicable and satisfactory conclusion'.[27]

## THE LAW OFFICERS OF SCOTLAND AND ENGLAND ARE CONSULTED

Murray was instructed, as agreed, and in particular was told that

> the object of the Board of Trade in entering on this matter is, while determined to preserve and protect the rights of the public in the use and enjoyment of the shore to endeavour to settle – if possible in an amicable manner a dispute which has been for so long a cause of irritation to proprietors but of little advantage to the Crown.[28]

He was also told that 'the case should be drawn so as if possible to exhaust the dispute'.[29] That the Lord Advocate and Solicitor General for Scotland and the Attorney General and the Solicitor General for England were all to be instructed gives a measure of the importance with which the Board considered the issue.[30] In addition to the Law Officers, W. M. James[31] was also instructed and, at a later stage, Thomas Ivory was added at the request of the Lord Advocate.[32]

[27] TNA:PRO, MT 10/139, Letter Trevor to Loch, 6 April 1867. Loch regarded this response from the Board as 'not unsatisfactory'.

[28] TNA:PRO, MT 10/139, Letter Farrer to Murray, 6 April 1867.

[29] TNA:PRO, MT 10/139, Letter Farrer to Murray, 6 April 1867.

[30] TNA:PRO, TS 25/1581, Letter Board of Trade to Treasury, 18 December 1867.

[31] James had advised the Office of Woods in the Maclean of Ardgour case; see Chapter 2.

[32] TNA:PRO, MT 10/139, Letter Murray to Trevor, 17 December 1867. The Law Officers comprised: Sir John B. Karslake, the Attorney General; William Balliol Brett, the Solicitor General for England and Master of the Rolls in 1883; Edward Gordon, the Lord Advocate who was a Lord of Appeal in Ordinary from 1876 to 1879; and John Millar, the Solicitor General for Scotland. Millar had, of course, been instructed on behalf of the Association in 1863 and had represented the Association in 1866 in the Maclean of Ardgour case. Ivory had represented the Crown in the Maclean of Ardgour case; see Chapter 2.

The case when printed ran to fifty-eight pages and set out comprehensively the judicial authorities and institutional writings both for and against each of the contending propositions, commenting in detail on the authorities and the writings. It is a fascinating document. At the outset the case noted, following the mindset of Richmond, Farrer and Trevor as revealed in their minutes, and indeed echoing what the Farrer Memorandum said, that

> the pecuniary interest of the public in the fore-shore . . . is a secondary one, and the primary object of a Government Department charged with the functions now committed to the Board of Trade, should be to protect the public in the due enjoyment of the rights of navigation, fishing, boating, bathing, walking etc. But in the present state of the law, the Board of Trade are bound to deal with the fore-shore, if belonging to the Crown as *property*, whilst the rights of the public over it, as well as the title to it, are constantly matters of dispute.[33]

If the Law Officers were able to advise that the Crown's property interest in the foreshore was doubtful, it seems that a compromise solution with the proprietors may readily have been achieved, even to the extent of the draft Bill. The case set out the two differing views as to the law:

> The seaboard proprietors maintain that the shore between high and low water mark must be regarded as the private property of the owners of the coterminous ground and . . . they deny that the sovereign has any right of property in the soil of the shores of Scotland . . . On the other hand the [Office of Woods] have thought it their duty to assert a right of property, which they believe to be vested in the Crown, both for the benefit of the public, and for the protection of the interests of the sovereign.[34]

The case said that the decisions in the Argyll and Maclean of Ardgour cases had not resulted in a final and authoritative judgment and that 'the original nature of the Crown right, the extent to which it may be alienated, and the titles which will import such alienation, are points still open to discussion'.[35] After reviewing all the judicial authorities and the works of the institutional writers, the case put thirteen questions for the opinion of the Law Officers and counsel. It seems to have been the intention of the Board that the case should present as even-handed a view as was possible, and to this end the Association had been invited to

33 TNA:PRO, MT 10/139, Case for the opinion of the Law Officers and Counsel in reference to the Foreshores of Scotland [hereafter 1867 Case], p. 1 (emphasis in original).

34 TNA:PRO, MT 10/139, 1867 Case, p. 2.

35 TNA:PRO, MT 10/139, 1867 Case, p. 3.

give its views on the case. When Loch sent the views of the Association's counsel to the Board, he commented that

> The case has been drawn up with great ability and with much impartiality – perhaps the arguments of the Crown side are a little more prominently produced than on the other and it is the purpose of the paper which I send, to point out where this seems to be the case.[36]

Loch had asked Farrer to consider how best these views could be presented in the context of the case and Farrer had replied that the case would have the views attached to it when it was submitted to the Law Officers, explaining how they had arisen. But Farrer's letter of response to Loch on this matter is interesting more because of the suggestion in it that the question of who owned the property in the foreshore should not be the main issue:

> The more I see of this controversy the more deeply do I regret that the issue has been ever taken on the question of property. It is altogether a false issue both for the Proprietors and the Public. The real question for the public is – what use they shall have of the Foreshore? The real question for the proprietors is – How to get the greatest benefit for their Estates out of the Foreshore consistently with the uses of the public.
>
> The interest both of the Public and the Proprietors goes to the wall in this unhappy dispute concerning the Title of the Crown.
>
> On both sides – at any rate on that of the Crown – and I think on the other side also – there is an assumption that the Foreshore is not a Common – but private property – an assumption as it seems to me very fateful to the real interests of everyone.[37]

Loch sensed from this letter a weakening of Farrer's resolve and his reply is instructive. He blamed the unhappy position which had been reached, not on the proprietors but on the actions of 'a not very scrupulous Edinburgh solicitor' (a reference to the unfortunate Donald Horne whose actions had so incensed other proprietors and, in particular, the Duke of Argyll as we saw in Chapter 4) who he said had led the Office of Woods in a course of action aimed at establishing a beneficial interest in the foreshore with a view to turning it into money. This, said Loch, was entirely opposed to the public interest. There was, thought Loch, no doubting the Crown's fiduciary duties in relation to the foreshore, duties which the proprietors entirely accepted and which Loch thought under the present law were amply protected. With a recognition of

[36] TNA:PRO, MT 10/139, Letter Loch to Farrer, 29 November 1867.
[37] TNA:PRO, MT 10/139, Letter Farrer to Loch, 30 November 1867.

these fiduciary duties and of the right of property in the foreshore in the *ex adverso* proprietor, Loch thought, 'a better state of things could hardly be supposed – for it may be taken for granted that in the long run, owners of property will employ it in the manner most profitable to themselves and most useful to the public'. And there would be the added protection, Loch believed, that the Crown could prevent, in exercise of their fiduciary responsibilities 'any selfish application of the foreshores by which the Crown interest would suffer'.[38] Loch reiterated that this was exactly what the draft Bill produced by the Association was seeking to achieve and, indeed, that the provisions of the Bill as to the means by which the Crown could protect the public interest would give the Crown greater powers than it held at present. Loch was clearly arguing that the Crown really did not need to have a property interest in the foreshore. All that the Crown was concerned with could be achieved without such an interest. Loch ended his letter with a warning:

> My opinion is that some such legislation is desirable on public grounds – and that it would rather be an embarrassment than otherwise for a Department such as the Board of Trade, to be advised by Counsel that some trifling, valueless, disputable title may exist in the Crown, alike unimportant to affirm and difficult to resign.[39]

Loch's concluding words are prophetic. If, as seems to have been the case, the Board was, in principle, prepared to concede the right of property to the proprietors, it would find it difficult, if not impossible, to do so if the Law Officers advised the Board that the Crown did, in fact, own the foreshore, albeit that it could alienate it. The Board, if it received that advice, would be duty bound to enforce the rights of the Crown that it was advised it had, and it would not, as a practical matter, be open to the Board to propose legislation to give those rights away. *The Times* agreed; its leader that discussed the exchanges between the Dukes of Argyll and Richmond (described in Chapter 4) said: 'As to the law itself, it is simply impossible to alter it. Parliament cannot relinquish to the proprietors of the littoral lands of the Kingdom the property in the Foreshore . . . such valuable rights cannot be abandoned without compensation.'[40]

The case was submitted at the end of December 1867, but it was not until 13 June 1868 that the opinion was signed by all the Law Officers

[38] TNA:PRO, MT 10/139, Letter Loch to Farrer, 1 December 1867.
[39] TNA:PRO, MT 10/139, Letter Loch to Farrer, 1 December 1867.
[40] *The Times*, 20 June 1868, p. 9.

and counsel, and the Board received it on 1 July.[41] The opinion gave answers to each of the thirteen questions. The opinion said that the original right of the Crown in the foreshore included both a right of property and a trust for the public rights of the community; that the right of property could be conveyed to a subject but only by express grant, except in the case of a barony title or possibly of lands bounded by the sea followed by prescriptive possession evidencing the extent of the grant; the Crown could not divest itself of its position as trustee for the public rights of the community, and on any grant of property in the foreshore the Crown had to retain control of the foreshore to protect these rights; the property in the foreshore was not carried by a grant by the Crown of lands *de facto* bounded by the sea, with parts and pertinents and in which the boundary was expressed as 'the sea shore', 'the beach' or 'the flood mark' or where no sea boundary was expressed (the opinion was less certain on the effect of the words 'the sea'); an express grant of the privilege of 'wreck and ware' or any similar privilege had no effect directly or indirectly in transferring the property of the foreshore but was limited in its operation to the conveyance of the specified privilege; the grant of a barony title adjacent to the sea did not, of itself and without prescriptive possession, imply a right to the property of the foreshore; the foreshore could be acquired in property by prescriptive possession but a barony title was required as a basis of prescription except in the case of a grant of land bounded by the sea; and the possession necessary to evidence a prescriptive right of property had to be by acts which only a proprietor would be entitled to do and which would therefore infer adverse possession (such acts as may be considered as having been done in the exercise of rights of servitude and not in the exercise of a right of property would not be sufficient to show a prescriptive right of property). The opinion also said that the public uses of the foreshore vested in the Crown as trustee were those which were required for the purposes of protecting navigation and the general right of fishing, and for the defence of the realm. The Law Officers said

[41] Richmond was most anxious to know what the Law Officers were going to say. He had told the House of Lords on 19 June 1868 in his response to the Duke of Argyll's observations in the House, discussed in Chapter 4, that 'he had not yet received it; but he was told it would shortly be ready'; PD, Third Series, vol. 192, House of Lords, col. 1826 (19 June 1868). Ten days later he wrote an impatient minute to Trevor: 'What I want to know is when I shall receive the answer to the case submitted to the Law Officers . . . Perhaps Mr Trevor will take the necessary steps for obtaining this information'; TNA:PRO, MT 10/139, Minute, 30 June 1868, R. Trevor promised the matter would be expedited.

that the question of the extent of the foreshore was an open one but they thought it not improbable that the English limit of the average of the medium high tides between spring and neap would be adopted in the Scottish courts as being the most equitable in all the circumstances, citing two cases;[42] and in giving their opinion that the right of property in the foreshore could be transferred to a subject, the opinion cited just one authority;[43] these were the only authorities cited in the opinion.[44]

The opinion had, therefore, given no support at all to the main proposition of the proprietors. To some extent the opinion had vindicated the actions of the Office of Woods and the policy behind the Farrer Memorandum. If the Crown had the property right in the foreshore, unless expressly granted to a private proprietor or unless a private proprietor could show a suitable title and prescriptive possession, there must be a duty on the Crown to ascertain the extent of its property and to protect the property right. But the opinion would now make any concession by the Crown to give up its claim to the property right extremely difficult, if not impossible. Certainly any prospect of legislation in which the Crown acknowledged that the right of property in the foreshore was held, not by it, but by the proprietors, was most unlikely. Skene & Peacock were not impressed with the opinion, believing it to be 'probably an explanation of the Law of England and not of Scotland'.[45]

If the minutes exchanged between Richmond, Farrer and Trevor before the opinion was given had shown a willingness to concede the title to the proprietors, Farrer's reaction to the opinion indicated a hardening of his position. The opinion was, perhaps surprisingly, what Farrer said he had expected and he said that 'the foundations of any future arrangements must be the present state of the law'.[46] It is taken by this that he meant that in any discussions with the Association, the proprietors would have to accept the opinion as to the Crown's fundamental right of property in the foreshore; in a subsequent minute

[42] Berry v. Holden (1840) 3 D 205; and the English case of Attorney General v. Chambers (1854) 4 De G. M. & G. 206 (this citation perhaps suggesting the influence of the English Law Officers). The Scottish courts have not, of course, adopted this interpretation.

[43] Sutherland (Duchess of) v. Watson (1868) 6 M 199.

[44] TNA:PRO, MT 10/139, Foreshores (Scotland). Opinion of the Law Officers, W. J. James and Thomas Ivory, 13 June 1868. As to the rights of the public, the Law Officers' opinion was rather more constrained than the view expressed by Lord Hope in Officers of State v. Smith (1846) 8 D 711 at p. 719.

[45] DVGN 570/4/110, Letter Skene & Peacock to Macleod, 27 July 1868.

[46] TNA:PRO, MT 10/139 Minute, 1 July 1868, THF.

Farrer made clear his understanding that the opinion 'was taken . . . in order that it might form the basis of an arrangement'.[47] Farrer thought that the case together with the opinion should be printed and published as a Parliamentary Paper and it seems likely that his desire for this was as much motivated by his expressed concern that the Board wished 'to do nothing in secret', as by the thought that it may be easier publicly to justify future actions of the Board if the underlying legal position was clear for all, and not just the proprietors, to see. Richmond, initially, concurred with Farrer's views on publication.[48] But at the last minute the publication of the case and the opinion was cancelled as a result of advice from Lord Cairns, the Lord Chancellor, that it was unusual for the opinion of the Law Officers to be published to the House. This annoyed Farrer; he thought that letting the Association have a copy was equivalent to publishing it and if this was so, why not publish it to Parliament? The Lord Chancellor was, however, adamant and Richmond had by now changed his mind and was of the view that the case and opinion should not be published.[49]

## THE ASSOCIATION'S 1869 REPORT TO ITS MEMBERS

Hopes for an amicable settlement between the Board and the Association based on the Association's draft Bill seemed to have been dashed by the opinion, and so the committee of the Association resolved that there was no alternative but to find further cases, to bring them to court and hope that the Board's resolve would be turned. But what was the policy of choosing cases to be? Loch was firmly of the view that 'the Association would not be justified in going to Court to try a case founded only on possession, or depending mainly on it – for that is a step that any landowner would obviously take for himself'.[50] Skene & Peacock, however, anticipated great difficulty in finding any case in which the question of possession was not more or less involved and advised Macleod that the Association's policy should be to select cases with a barony title and strong possession on the basis that the Crown would wish to compromise and agree the legislation in favour of the

[47] TNA:PRO, MT 10/139, Minute, 7 July 1868, THF.

[48] TNA:PRO, MT 10/139, Minutes, 1 July 1868; 3 July 1868, R.

[49] TNA:PRO, MT 10/139, Minutes, 7 July, CCT; 7 July, THF; 9 July 1868, R. On the confidentiality of the Law Officers' opinions, see J. Ll. J. Edwards, *The Law Officers of the Crown* (London, 1964), pp. 256–61; J. Ll. J. Edwards, *The Attorney General, Politics and the Public Interest* (London, 1984), pp. 207–27.

[50] DVGN 570/2/35, Letter Loch to Macleod, 7 June 1868.

proprietors discussed above; indeed, they thought that if it had not been for the delay in proceedings due to the transfer of the responsibility for the foreshore in 1866, this policy would already have been put into effect.[51] The committee was persuaded by this advice even though it was given before the Law Officers had given their opinion, and the policy of the Association changed to take account of the advice.

Skene & Peacock also believed that in the aftermath of the Law Officers' opinion, the time was right to report to the members on the position the Association had reached and, in particular, to tell the members 'what treatment they may expect under the system of administration recommended by Mr Farrer in his remarkable memorandum'. There would also be a call for a further one-quarter of the guaranteed subscriptions to pay for more cases.[52] Skene & Peacock drafted a report to be sent but it was not until June 1869 that the draft was considered and approved by the committee and sent to members, and that the members were told that if the new policy was adopted, then the Crown, if

> thus made aware of the real state of title and possession by *proper legal evidence*, . . . might ultimately be disposed to have the matter adjusted on reasonable terms by legislation instead of prolonging an expensive contest for a right which can be of little pecuniary value to the Crown, and which, even if in some cases established, could scarcely be justified.[53]

It seemed that the committee of the Association did not believe that, after all, the opinion of the Law Officers had removed the prospect of legislation on the basis of the Association's draft Bill.

We now look at what was included, and what was omitted, from the 1869 Report in the context of what has been discussed in the preceding pages of this chapter. We should first of all note the names of those present at the meeting of the committee of the Association on 7 June 1869 which considered and approved the 1869 Report; they were the Duke of Richmond (who by now was out of government office), George Loch, Henry Baillie and Macleod.

The agenda for the meeting shows that the committee had reported to it an explanation of the actions taken by the Association since it was formed in July 1861, and certain key events. These were the formation

[51] DVGN 570/4, Letter Skene & Peacock to Macleod, 15 June 1868.

[52] DVGN 570/4, Letter Skene & Peacock to Macleod, 26 August 1868.

[53] DVGN 565/3, Report by the Committee of the Scottish Foreshore Association and the Present Position of the Foreshore Question and the Proposed Future Procedure, June 1869 [hereafter 1869 Report], p. 3 (emphasis in original).

of the committee, the appointment of Skene & Peacock as law agents, the search for suitable cases to test the main question, the decisions in the Association's favour of the cases involving the Duke of Argyll and Maclean of Ardgour, the circulation in July 1865 of the Duke of Argyll's correspondence with the Treasury, the transfer of responsibility for the foreshore from the Office of Woods to the Board under the Crown Lands Act 1866, the Farrer Memorandum, the exchanges in the House of Lords between the Dukes of Argyll and Richmond over the Farrer Memorandum, the draft Bill prepared by the Association, and the 1868 case to, and opinion of, the Law Officers. This was a comprehensive list of the key events over the preceding eight years. The minutes of the meeting are very brief and simply record that the committee ordered that the 1869 Report be printed and circulated, and that the committee considered that the Association should take up a further case against the Crown.[54]

A comparison between the agenda, the minutes and the 1869 Report as published, however, reveals some interesting discrepancies. The 1869 Report makes no mention of the Association's draft Bill or of the case to, and opinion of, the Law Officers. Nor does it refer to the exchanges which took place in the House of Lords in June 1868 between the Dukes of Argyll and Richmond over the Farrer Memorandum. As to the former, the omission is really very strange. The expressed purpose of the 1869 Report was twofold. It was, first, to ensure that the members should be 'fully informed' of the 'present position of the foreshore question and the proposed future procedure'.[55] Second, it was to request a payment from the members of a further one-quarter of the amount guaranteed by each member on joining the Association for the purposes of fighting further legal cases against the Crown. The 1869 Report made it clear that it was the policy of the Board as indicated by the Farrer Memorandum (extracts of which were included in the 1869 Report) which had persuaded the committee that further action against the Crown was required and that further cases should be selected 'to bring them into Court with a view to settle the position of title, and thus anticipate and defeat the policy of the Board of Trade'.[56] The 1869 Report mentioned the success of the Association in the Maclean of Ardgour case and suggested that many other proprietors ought similarly to be

[54] DVGN 543/15, Agenda. Meeting of Committee on Monday 7 June 1869 and Minutes.

[55] DVGN 565, 1869 Report, p. 1.

[56] DVGN 565, 1869 Report, p. 3.

able to succeed against the Crown: 'most, if not all, of the Proprietors of Seaboard Estates in Scotland have exercised acts of possession similar to those which were held sufficient to establish the title of Mr MacLean to the shores of Ardgour'.[57]

On the basis of this explanation in the 1869 Report as to 'the present position of the foreshore question', the members of the Association were asked to provide further funds to allow the Association to bring further court cases. The members were not, however, told about the draft Bill proposed by the Association that had led to a joint case being put to the Law Officers of Scotland and England on 'the foreshore question'; that the opinion, so far as the main argument of the Association was concerned, had been unfavourable to the proprietors; and that this meant, so far as the Board was concerned, that the prospect of legislation favourable to the proprietors was unlikely. The handwritten agenda and minutes of the meeting of the committee and correspondence suggest that the members of the committee did discuss whether a reference to the case and the opinion could be made in the 1869 Report. Skene & Peacock had been concerned at the issue of confidentiality but Loch had thought it important that the 1869 Report should make reference to the case and the opinion and, indeed, in an early draft of the 1869 Report, Skene & Peacock had reluctantly included a reference to it. Loch, although he accepted there was something in Skene & Peacock's concerns, thought that it was very important that the public should be made aware of the practical effect of the opinion. He thought that Richmond would, given that he was President of the Board of Trade when the opinion was obtained, be 'peculiarly able to advise on the point'.[58] It appears, however, that the committee came to the conclusion that the case and opinion were confidential and so could not be disclosed; a conclusion that Skene & Peacock said was 'judicious in the circumstances'.[59] This is a surprising conclusion. Richmond would have been fully aware that although the Lord Chancellor had said that the case and opinion should not be published as a Parliamentary Paper, he had not said anything about passing it to members of the Association, and Richmond himself had appreciated there was a distinction to be drawn between publishing as a Parliamentary Paper and supplying Loch with a copy. He would also have known that the officials at the Board

[57] DVGN 565, 1869 Report, p. 3.

[58] DVGN 570/2/36, Letter Loch to Macleod, 6 May 1869; DVGN 570/4/120, Letter Skene & Peacock to Macleod, 11 June 1869.

[59] DVGN 570/4/120, Letter Skene & Peacock to Macleod, 11 June 1869.

fully expected the case and opinion to receive wide publicity within the Association; the duke's own minute on the matter had been clear: 'We may give it privately to any person who is interested in the matter.'[60] On any reasonable view the persons interested must have included the members of the Association. And Farrer's minute, which Richmond had seen, had been unequivocal on the point; there was, he said, 'a distinct understanding with Mr Loch on behalf of the Scotch proprietors that they should be made acquainted with the opinion given' and 'if the Scotch proprietors are to have [the opinion] and have it they must'.[61] Furthermore, there could be no question that the fact that the whole issue was being considered by the Law Officers was itself confidential. Richmond had expressly referred to it in his exchange with the Duke of Argyll in the House of Lords in June 1868.[62] The Board had sent copies of the case and opinion to Loch, the Dukes of Argyll and Buccleuch, Lord Blantyre, Baillie, Macleod and Skene & Peacock, and the minute that directed this said that a copy should also be provided to 'any other Scottish proprietors who apply for it'.[63] While the recipients were told that 'it is the desire of the Board that the document should not be made public as it is unusual to publish the opinion of the Law Officers of the Crown',[64] there was no suggestion that the other members of the Association should not be told about it. Indeed, it must have been assumed they would be told, and should be provided with copies of it, otherwise Farrer's minute of 22 July was meaningless.[65] The publication of the 1869 Report without any reference to the case or the opinion has to be regarded as an omission of a material fact and one not really justified on grounds of confidentiality.

The omission of any reference to the June 1868 exchange in the

[60] TNA:PRO, MT 10/139, Minute, 9 July 1868, R (emphasis in original).

[61] TNA:PRO, MT 10/139, Minute, 7 July 1868, THF (emphasis in original).

[62] PD, Third Series, vol. 192, House of Lords, col. 1826 (19 June 1868).

[63] TNA:PRO, MT 10/139, Minute, 22 July 1868, THF.

[64] TNA:PRO, MT 10/139, Draft letter, 23 July 1868. It was Richmond who had asked for the letter to be phrased in this way; see TNA:PRO, MT 10/139, Minute, [n.d.], R, accompanying the draft. Farrer's note on the draft makes it clear that, notwithstanding the Lord Chancellor's ruling, he was still keen to see the case and opinion published: 'I should like to lay the case before Parliament in spite of Lord Cairns.' He expressed this view, again, in 1872; see below in this chapter.

[65] And, indeed, in October 1870, Sir R. Anstruther, Bart (who was not a member of the Association) wrote to the Board asking for a copy, which was sent to him on the same terms as to publishing; see TNA:PRO, MT 10/139, Letter Anstruther to Board of Trade, 9 October 1870; draft letter Board of Trade to Anstruther, 12 October 1870.

House of Lords between the Dukes of Argyll and Richmond over the Farrer Memorandum might be regarded as less serious than the omission of the case and opinion, but it is, nonetheless, surprising. The 1869 Report made considerable play of the Farrer Memorandum, quoting selectively from it to suggest that the policy of the Board in relation to the foreshore as explained in it was motivated by an animus against the proprietors – in much the same way as Argyll had attacked the Farrer Memorandum in the House of Lords. However, to have referred to the views of Argyll on the Farrer Memorandum as expressed in the House would, if the full facts were to be disclosed, also have required the Report to quote from the response by Richmond and, of course, Richmond's response had made it very clear that Argyll had misunderstood the purposes of the Farrer Memorandum and that Richmond had defended it in strong terms. But what is perhaps more surprising is that Richmond was prepared to see published in the 1869 Report what was, in effect, a similar criticism of the Farrer Memorandum based on selected extracts and, in particular, a criticism which said that 'the main feature . . . [of the Board's policy as laid down in the Farrer Memorandum] seems to be an attempt to alarm individuals into concessions on which they will afterwards found as precedents in support of their pretensions in other cases'.[66] It is surprising that Richmond allowed the 1869 Report to be published with such criticisms, because this was exactly the misrepresentation of the Farrer Memorandum for which Richmond had castigated Argyll in the House of Lords in June 1868: that Argyll had selected passages 'with a view to show that the object was to drive the proprietors into a corner and make them submit to a compromise'.[67]

## THE ASSOCIATION TAKES FURTHER CASES

Skene & Peacock found two cases soon after the 1869 Report was sent to members; one concerning the estate of an Association member, Stuart Munro of Teaninich, and the other at Cardross. The Association's counsel considered that the Teaninich case was favourable to be taken to trial,[68] but the Board was reluctant to become involved, hoping that they

[66] DVGN 565, 1869 Report, p. 3.

[67] PD, Third Series, vol. 192, House of Lords, cols 1826–8 (19 June 1868).

[68] DVGN 570/4, Letter Skene & Peacock to Macleod, 20 July 1869; Memorial for the Committee of the Association of Foreshore Proprietors of Scotland for the opinion of Counsel, and opinion, 13 April 1870.

could avoid a conflict by getting the Association's lawyers to agree to restrict the conclusions in the summons so as to save the Crown's rights in the foreshore. Not surprisingly, this was not agreed and the Crown decided not to put in an appearance, allowing a decree in absence. Skene & Peacock believed that the Crown was afraid to go to trial.[69] The Association also had success in a case involving Mr Scott of Brotherton where the Board had threatened to indict Scott from quarrying stones on the foreshore of his estate but again declined to proceed to trial. By the end of 1870 Skene & Peacock reported to Macleod that they were without a representative case and presumed that one or more others should be found to further the committee's policy as reported to members in June 1869. But they wondered if the Board could be made to appear in court; the Board, they said, 'has evidently resolved to evade joining issue with us if possible'.[70] In fact, it was not to be long before the Association took up the landmark case of the foreshore on Sir Andrew Agnew's Wigtownshire estates.

## THE AGNEW CASE

During 1871 Sir Andrew Agnew issued a summons of declarator against the Crown to have it decided that the foreshore *ex adverso* his estate belonged exclusively to him. The opinion of the Law Officers as to this claim was sought and they were supplied with a number of precognitions as to possession that Agnew's agent had obtained. The Law Officers gave their opinion that Agnew's barony title to the estate was a good foundation on which to acquire a right to the foreshore by prescriptive possession, that the precognitions supplied showed that Agnew had possessed the foreshore for the full prescriptive period and that, accordingly, Agnew's claim should not be contested.[71] On the face of it, then, this was not a case that we would have expected the Crown to fight or, indeed, one that would, in time, be regarded as the leading case on the issue. In the early stages when the initial evidence had been

[69] DVGN 570/4/135, Copy correspondence between Beith and Skene & Peacock November 1870; DVGN 570/4, Letter Skene & Peacock to Macleod, 21 December 1870.

[70] DVGN 570/4, Letter Skene & Peacock to Macleod, 21 December 1870.

[71] TNA:PRO, MT 10/130, Memorial for the Commissioners of Her Majesty's Woods, Forests etc and the Board of Trade for the opinion of counsel, and opinion, 31 August 1871. The Law Officers were George Young, the Lord Advocate, and Andrew R. Clark, the Solicitor General. Both of these men had, as we saw in Chapter 2, written the 1862 Opinion for the Association.

seen there was, in fact, a certain amount of hesitation on the part of the Board's officials over defending the case. Trevor said:

> the case, in itself, does not appear at all favourable to the Crown and I should be very unwilling at present to stir up the whole subject and have the Scottish landlords about our ears. The Office of Woods in Maclean of Ardgour's case decided not to appeal – and why should we stir the matter again?[72]

Nor did Farrer at first believe the case a good one for the Crown. However, as we shall see, neither Farrer nor the Board's solicitor, Donald Beith, was prepared, for different reasons, simply to concede Agnew's claim without further consideration.[73]

Beith wrote a long letter to Trevor in October 1871 about the case. While he said it was not for him to differ from the opinion of the Law Officers, he told Trevor that, at the consultation with the Law Officers before the opinion was written, it had seemed to him that the Law Officers had been heavily influenced by the fact that the Crown had acquiesced in the judgment in the Maclean of Ardgour case and that he had always regretted that the Crown had not appealed that decision to the Inner House of the Court of Session. And he warned the Board that,

> in my humble opinion, if such acts of possession as Sir Andrew Agnew proposed to prove, of the foreshore *ex adverso* of his land, be sufficient to secure him a right to the foreshores independently of the Crown, there are few proprietors in Scotland . . . who will not be able to establish a right to the foreshore of their estates.[74]

Trevor was not impressed with Beith's concern and was inclined to follow the Law Officers' advice. Farrer, however, was not so certain and thought the matter should be taken further.[75] After he wrote to Trevor, Beith received an offer from Agnew's lawyers to drop a claim Agnew was making to some oyster beds and salmon fishings if the Crown would accept Agnew's claim to the foreshore. Beith spoke to the Crown's junior counsel, Ivory, on this offer and Ivory suggested that the offer should be accepted because the case was not a favourable one to try the main question between the proprietors and the Crown as to the foreshore. Beith asked the Board for a decision as to whether or not the offer should be accepted.[76] Trevor was inclined to accept the offer, but

[72] TNA:PRO, MT 10/139, Minute, 3 July 1871, CCT.
[73] TNA:PRO, MT 10/139, Minute, 3 July 1871, THF.
[74] TNA:PRO, MT 10/130, Letter Beith to Trevor, 20 October 1871.
[75] TNA:PRO, MT 10/130, Minute, 24 October 1871, CCT and THF.
[76] TNA:PRO, MT 10/130, Letter Beith to Trevor, 24 November 1871.

Farrer was, again, not so sure. He believed that Beith was telling him that Agnew's evidence as to possession could be defeated, but 'what weighs most with me is the fear that if we do not fight in this case we shall have all the Scotch proprietors starting similar proceedings. I believe the best policy will be to let [Agnew] prove his case.'[77]

Farrer wrote a long minute in which one can sense his increasing frustration with the whole issue. We saw that Farrer had wished that some form of compromise could be reached. But his duties to defend the interests of the public seemed to be irredeemably opposed to the wishes of the private proprietors and one senses that he did not believe the law, or the lawyers, and in particular the enthusiasm of the private proprietors (encouraged by the Association) to indulge in litigation, were making this problem any easier to solve. Farrer returned to what, as we saw in Chapter 3, he believed was the root of the problem. He blamed the Office of Woods for creating the problem because he believed they had not acted pursuant to any obvious public interests but simply 'as a matter of £. s. d.'. They had exacerbated the problem through acquiescing in the Maclean of Ardgour judgment, a decision that cast a long shadow over the claim of the Crown to title in other instances. He did not believe that the Crown could entertain such a compromise as was put forward by Agnew's lawyers because the Board had no right to abandon the Crown's right without proof of Agnew's title. But there was another reason not to accept the offer of a settlement:

> principally because if we show that we are ready to compromise and give up except on the most distinct proof of title we shall encourage Scotch proprietors to bring similar actions. At present we avoid litigation as much as possible in the hope that we may establish a good character for protecting public rights and get the question ultimately settled by appeal, or compromise and legislation on terms favourable to the real interests of the public. If we show the white feather when we are attacked we should encourage litigation and destroy our hope of a more favourable settlement.[78]

So the Board resolved to fight the Agnew case, but without any real degree of enthusiasm. There is a clear sense that Farrer considered that he had no real option but to carry on and he must have been reinforced in this view when he heard in December 1871 that the Association had taken up the case as an Association test case. Members of the committee of the Association, Macleod, Loch, the Duke of Richmond and Colonel Malcolm of Poltalloch all expressed their enthusiasm for the

77 TNA:PRO, MT 10/130, Minute, 26 November 1871, THF.
78 TNA:PRO, MT 10/130, Minute, 27 November 1871, THF.

Association becoming involved, and the Association's counsel thought that 'a more favourable case to adopt could scarcely be obtained'.[79] Loch thought that the case was favourable but was concerned that the Crown appeared ready to fight, in contrast to earlier cases. Had, he wondered, the Crown found some circumstance favourable to it and decided, therefore, to make a stand when it had declined to do so in other cases?[80]

Shortly after the Association decided to adopt the case, Macleod met with Farrer on other business but they both took advantage of the opportunity to discuss the dispute between the Crown and the proprietors. Farrer spoke to Macleod of his unhappiness over the matter and gave Macleod to understand that he still wanted a compromise over the main question, and it seems that Farrer understood from his conversation with Macleod that the Association had similar views. Farrer's minute recorded: 'I have had some conversation with Macleod which leads me to think we might effect a compromise on some footing which would secure public rights, and give pecuniary value to the proprietors. This will require thought and care.'[81] Farrer followed up this meeting with a letter to Macleod in which he said it appeared that the Agnew case was not to be settled and that the Crown would have no choice but to fight it. He said he considered the whole prospect with dismay because 'it will not give us exactly what we want for the public; it will, if we succeed, take from the proprietors what they want; and will in short probably do nobody any good but the lawyers'. He proposed to Macleod that, to give time for a compromise to be worked out, the proceedings in the Agnew case should be suspended and the status quo maintained for the time being. He dreaded litigation 'not so much for the expenses as for the angry feelings it excites and which will make a fair settlement so difficult'. Farrer wrote that he needed time for a compromise to be worked out and 'possibly, which is worse, the consent of the Treasury; just at this moment we really have neither time nor power to grapple fairly with

[79] DVGN 570/4, Letter Skene & Peacock to Macleod, 27 December 1871; DVGN 570/12/2, Letter Macleod to Skene & Peacock, 27 December 1871; DVGN 571/12/3, Letter Richmond to Macleod, 29 December 1871; DVGN 570/2/39, Letter Malcolm to Macleod, 4 January 1872. The Association's counsel were John Millar and Donald Crawford.

[80] DVGN 570/2/39, Letter Loch to Macleod, 28 December 1871.

[81] DVGN 570/4/137, Letter Macleod to Skene & Peacock, 12 January 1872; TNA:PRO, MT 10/130, Minute, 29 January 1872, THF (emphasis in original).

the subject'.[82] Macleod discussed Farrer's letter with other committee members. Loch responded that he did not doubt Farrer's sincerity in wishing to find a solution. But he thought that Farrer, in writing to Macleod, had overlooked all that had passed between the Association and the Board in 1867 and, in particular, the solution then suggested by the Association of the draft Bill to settle the issue. There was, Loch said, 'no authority competent to dispose of the question, except Parliament by legislation – or the Court of Law, by judicial decision' and as the Board had rejected the legislative proposal in 1867, there was now no option but a court action.[83] Loch did not share Farrer's apprehension about the effect of litigation; indeed, he was not aware of any angry feelings raised

> by the course or by the results of the actions we have hitherto tried. It would be much more true to say that angry feelings are raised by the objectionable manner in which the alleged rights of the Crown are often asserted by the [Crown] . . . these proceedings have really created angry feelings.[84]

Macleod responded to Farrer sending him a copy of Loch's letter and suggested going back to the draft Bill prepared by the Association in 1867: 'Why should that not be the foundation of a renewed negotiation, if the Board of Trade really wish to settle the matter on terms of mutual concern?'[85] Macleod discussed Farrer's letter with Skene & Peacock who, not surprisingly, thought that it would be very desirable for the legislative proposals prepared by them in 1867 to be resurrected. But they felt it was for the Board now to take the initiative.[86] But of course legislation was not really a practical possibility. Ever since the 1868 opinion of the Law Officers that it was the Crown who had the underlying right of property in the foreshore, not the *ex adverso* proprietors, there was no realistic hope of the Treasury approving legislation which deemed the *ex adverso* proprietor to have the title; not, at least, without financial compensation for the Crown which private proprietors would not have been willing to consider. The Association was not prepared to delay the Agnew case and it went ahead.

It was now recognised by everyone that the outcome of the Agnew case would be highly significant. Skene Webster & Peacock wrote that

[82] DVGN 571/13/5, Letter Farrer to Macleod, 29 January 1872.

[83] TNA:PRO, MT 10/130, Letter Loch to Macleod, 5 February 1872.

[84] TNA:PRO, MT 10/130, Letter Loch to Macleod, 5 February 1872 (emphasis in original).

[85] TNA:PRO, MT 10/130, Letter Macleod to Farrer, 5 February 1872.

[86] DVGN 570/4/138, Letter Skene & Peacock to Macleod, 8 February 1872.

> The case we now have on hand may, as Mr Loch observes, become one of the highest importance and certainly deserves the greatest care and consideration. Mr Peacock has accordingly personally inspected the Foreshore of Sir Andrew Agnew's estate and seen and examined about 30 witnesses who can speak to possession beyond the prescriptive period and the opinion we have formed is that if we do not succeed in this case it will be hopeless to try any other – the acts of possession being of a peculiarly marked character.[87]

They wrote that the Crown was also taking the case very seriously as witnessed by the fact, they said, that the Lord Advocate and the Solicitor General were personally present when the evidence was examined by the Lord Ordinary.[88]

The judgment of the Lord Ordinary, Lord Ormidale, given on 31 July 1872, was adverse to the Crown. The Lord Ordinary's interlocutor said that the foreshore *ex adverso* of Agnew's lands belonged to Agnew by virtue of his titles to the land and more than forty years' possession of the foreshore, subject to the rights of the Crown for public uses. The immediate reaction of the Crown's junior counsel was that the judgment was erroneous, and the officials at the Board were also disappointed. Trevor thought it was a replica of the Maclean of Ardgour case and Farrer had a strong view that the judgment should be appealed against. He was, again, worried about what would happen if the Board was seen to be weak: 'The Scottish Foreshore Association have forced this litigation upon us against our will and if we give way in the least we shall have actions of the same kind brought against us by all the Scotch proprietors.'[89] Farrer also stressed that the Board's actions were driven by the public interest, not by antipathy towards the private proprietors:

> whilst we can give up willingly to those who attack us it is to be remembered that our real object is not to divest the proprietors of property which is valuable to them, or to make money for the Exchequer. Our object has throughout been and is to assert the rights of the Crown for the purpose of protecting the public in the enjoyment of the Foreshore and preventing those encroachments and inclosures which all proprietors and Scotch proprietors especially are ready to make.[90]

Farrer again raised the issue of a compromise:

[87] DVGN 570/4, Letter Skene Webster & Peacock to Macleod, 16 April 1872. Skene & Peacock was now named Skene Webster & Peacock.

[88] DVGN 570/4, Letter Skene Webster & Peacock to Macleod, 25 May 1872.

[89] TNA:PRO, MT 10/130, Minute, 7 August 1872, THF.

[90] TNA:PRO, MT 10/130, Minute, 7 August 1872, THF.

> If a compromise could be come to by which the proprietors should have all the pecuniary benefit to be derived from the shore (when it can be turned to use without injuring the public) and by which the Board of Trade should be invested with full powers for preventing proprietors from excluding the public from reasonable enjoyment of the shores, it would be a good thing for all parties – I wish this could be made public: but I fear the first step on our part must be to show that we can fight.[91]

The Law Officers now believed that this was as favourable a case as was ever likely to occur for the Crown and so the Board decided, on their advice, to appeal against the decision of the Lord Ordinary.[92] In the appeal the judges in the Inner House took an intermediate position between the two contending views being put forward. The court held that while the foreshore originally belonged to the Crown in the same way as all other land, it was not as *inter regalia minora*; there was, therefore, no requirement for there to have been an express grant of the foreshore to the proprietor claiming it. But neither did the court agree with the principal contention of the Association that the foreshore passed to the *ex adverso* proprietor by implication as part and pertinent of his land. Lord Benholme was crystal clear on this:

> Where an estate is on the sea-shore held by titles that do not, by express grant or specific boundary, extend the right of the proprietor beyond the high water mark, there is no presumption that the foreshore is a pertinent of the land . . . This is a very important principle and I am glad that we all agree, as I understand we do, in the assertion of it.[93]

As to requirements for proving a transfer of the foreshore, where there was no specific description of the land conveyed and no specific boundary expressed, the extent of the lands conveyed (in other words, whether the lands conveyed included the foreshore) could be explained by the state of the possession of the foreshore; the foreshore could also be acquired by prescriptive possession founded on an appropriate title.[94] As to the public rights over the foreshore for navigation and other public

[91] TNA:PRO, MT 10/130, Minute, 7 August 1872, THF. Farrer also indicated in this minute that he still wanted to lay the 1868 case and opinion before Parliament.

[92] TNA:PRO, MT 10/130, Memorandum for the Board of Trade in case of Sir Andrew Agnew v. Lord Advocate for Opinion of Crown Counsel, and opinion, 16 August 1872; TNA:PRO, MT 10/130, Letter Beith to Trevor, 16 September 1872.

[93] Agnew v. Lord Advocate (1873) 11 M 309, Lord Benholme at p. 330.

[94] The distinction between these two examples of the significance of possession is helpfully explained by Lord Maxwell in Luss Estates Co. v. B. P. Oil Grangemouth Ltd (1982) SLT 97 at p. 100.

purposes, the court held that these were *inter regalia* and could not be alienated.[95]

An appeal to the House of Lords was considered. The Scottish Law Officers advised:

> We are of the opinion that this is a very proper case for settling what is the Law of Scotland with respect to the rights of the Crown and Seaboard Proprietors in the foreshores and that if the Board of Trade considers that the question itself is of sufficient importance to submit the views of the Crown upon it for the consideration of the House of Lords the present affords a fitting opportunity. The authorities and the judicial *dicta* are so conflicting that we cannot usefully say any more than that we think an appeal in this case is altogether reasonable and proper assuming the Board of Trade think that the pretensions hitherto maintained by the Crown with respect to foreshores are not too insignificant in point of value to be any longer insisted on.[96]

The English Law Officers confined themselves to the brief advice that 'upon a consideration of the case . . . it would be expedient to appeal to the House of Lords against the judgment of the Court below'.[97] This advice was hardly optimistic as to the prospects for success and really left it to the Board to decide if an appeal should be made. A petition for the appeal was drafted and a letter was sent to the Treasury justifying the costs of such a petition on the ground that the Board could not give up public property without all the possible remedies being pursued.[98] In

[95] Agnew v. Lord Advocate (1873) 11 M 309; and see Reid, *Law of Property in Scotland*, paras 314–15; Robbie, *Private Water Rights*, para. 3.39; Ferguson, *Law of Water*, pp. 48–9; G. J. Bell, *Principles of the Law of Scotland* (10th edn, Edinburgh, 1899), paras 641–5; J. Craigie, *Principles of Conveyancing: Heritable Rights* (3rd edn, Edinburgh, 1899), pp. 117–21. The part of the decision relating to the principal contention of the Association was *obiter dictum*. The decision of the court was remarkably similar to the conclusions reached by the Scottish and English Law Officers in their 1868 opinion, as Loch pointed out to the Duke of Richmond; DGVN 570/2/42, Letter Loch to Richmond, 14 June 1874.

[96] NRS, CR 11/546, Case for the Board of Trade for the opinion of Crown Counsel, February 1873: George Young, the Lord Advocate, A. R. Clark, the Solicitor General, Sir John Coleridge, the Attorney General and George Jessel, the Solicitor General for England.

[97] NRS, CR 11/546, Case for the Board of Trade for the opinion of Crown Counsel, February 1873: George Young, the Lord Advocate, A. R. Clark, the Solicitor General, Sir John Coleridge, the Attorney General and George Jessel, the Solicitor General for England.

[98] See TNA:PRO, MT 10/158, Letter Beith to Trevor, 17 July 1873. Petition to House of Lords and draft letter to Treasury, July 1873.

June 1874 George Loch wrote a long letter to the Duke of Richmond (who had been appointed to Disraeli's Cabinet in February 1874 as Lord President of the Council) outlining all that had gone before in the discussions between the Association and the Board in 1867, and the 1868 opinion of the Law Officers. As to the draft Bill proposed by the Association in 1867, Loch now believed that this would not be practicable and so the only solution lay in the courts. He proposed to the duke that the decision of the Inner House in the Agnew case should be agreed as deciding, finally, the law on the foreshore question. It was by now clear to the Association that the private proprietors had all they wanted on the basis of prescriptive possession. Loch said:

> It seems therefore deserving of consideration whether this judgement of the Court of Session may not be accepted as settling the principle involved in the question, in accordance as it is with the law laid down by the Crown Law Officers in 1868. No decision can carry the matter further.[99]

On 29 June 1874 Skene Webster & Peacock wrote to Macleod that they had been told the Crown's appeal to the House of Lords was to be withdrawn; they did not understand the policy behind this decision and wondered if it might be because the Crown preferred to leave the law on the basis of a Court of Session judgment which might allow the Board to continue asserting its rights because the main question had not been settled by the court of last resort.[100] In fact, the decision not to proceed with the appeal to the House of Lords appears to have been taken because it was feared that the result of the appeal could actually make the situation worse for the Crown and also affect the situation in England. After the petition for the appeal was drafted, there was a change of government and Disraeli's administration decided to consult the new Law Officers who would, after all, have to conduct the appeal on behalf of the Crown.[101] The instructions to the Law Officers questioned whether it was expedient in the general interest of the Crown to go on with the case:

> As the case at present stands the mischief is confined to Scotland but there is an apprehension that the decision of the House of Lords may be adverse to the Crown, i.e. that the Judgement of the Court of Session may be affirmed,

[99] DVGN 570/2/42, Letter Loch to Richmond, 14 June 1874.

[100] DVGN 570/4/145, Letter Skene Webster & Peacock to Macleod, 29 June 1874.

[101] This decision is explained in NRS, CR 11/546, Letter Board of Trade to Commissioners of Crown Lands, 23 February 1928.

> and if so that it might not improbably have the effect of unsettling the Crown's title to the foreshores of England. This would be so very serious a matter that some hesitation is felt by the Board of Trade as to the expediency of proceeding further.[102]

The Law Officers agreed and advised:

> We are of the opinion that the decision of the Court of Session both upon the law and the facts was right and we see no reasonable chance of the present appeal being successful. The House of Lords might indeed upon appeal put a construction upon grants of land running up to the sea shore more favourable to the Respondent than that adopted by the Court of Session and if this were done the result of the appeal would be very disadvantageous to the Crown. This is of course an additional reason why the proceedings should be abandoned.[103]

## THE ASSOCIATION'S MEMBERS TAKE FURTHER CASES

Given Loch's comment on the Agnew case that 'no decision can carry the matter further', it is something of a surprise to find that Skene Webster & Peacock returned to the fray after the Agnew case on behalf of two of the Association's members: Lord Blantyre and Colonel Andrew Buchanan, whose estates bordered the navigable part of the river Clyde.[104] When the Blantyre summons was served against the Lord Advocate, Donald Beith commented: 'I infer that the present action is really an action of the Foreshore Association and its importance therefore is not little.'[105] In fact, the Association had not adopted the case as Beith had assumed: George Loch had refused to allow the Association to do so as he thought that the 'case would not raise the question in a simple form [and] that it was complicated by all the special legislation of the Clyde Trustees'.[106]

In both cases the first plea in law of the Association's member was still that by virtue of his title alone the foreshore belonged to him

[102] NRS, CR 11/546, Case for and Opinion of Law Officers, 13 June 1874.

[103] NRS, CR 11/546, Case for and Opinion of Law Officers, 13 June 1874. The Law Officers who signed the opinion were Sir Richard Baggallay, the Attorney General, Edward Gordon, the Lord Advocate, and John Holker, the Solicitor General for England.

[104] Lord Advocate v. Blantyre (1879) 6 R (HL) 72; Buchanan and Geils v. Lord Advocate (1882) 9 R 1218.

[105] NRS, CR11/263, Letter Beith to Asst. Sec. Harbours Dept. Board of Trade, 14 October 1875.

[106] DVGN 570/2/44, Letter Skene Webster & Peacock to Macleod, 26 July 1876; DVGN 570/2/43, Letter Loch to Macleod, 30 July 1876.

as a pertinent, with the second plea being that the member's possession was sufficient to give him title. In both cases it was the Clyde Trustees who wished to pursue the actions and the participation of the Board was, in effect, in name only, being indemnified as to costs by the Clyde Trustees.[107] In both cases the Inner House of the Court of Session decided that the Association's member was entitled to the foreshore on the basis of proof of possession and did not decide the first plea in law, although the words of Lord Lee, the Lord Ordinary in the Outer House of the Buchanan case, breathed some life into the Association's principal contention.[108] The Blantyre case was appealed by the Clyde Trustees to the House of Lords but without the unfortunate consequences that had troubled the Law Officers in the Agnew case; the House of Lords reached the same conclusions as the Inner House in the Court of Session but did not form an opinion on the principal contention.[109]

In some kind of final acceptance of the position, Donald Beith wrote at the conclusion of the Buchanan case:

> The [case has] today been decided by the First Division of the Court of Session adversely to the Crown thus settling in all time to come I suppose that where a landed proprietor can establish that he has possessed the foreshore by such acts of possession as were found sufficient in the well-known case of Sir Andrew Agnew the Crown has no right to the foreshore.[110]

But surprisingly the dispute lingered on. In a number of cases after 1882, proprietors' titles and a memorandum of facts were submitted by the Association's lawyers to the Board and the Board admitted the claims without litigation or, as in the case of Duncan Darroch of Gourock in 1892, a summons was issued which was not defended by the Crown and a decree in absence was given in November 1892 surprisingly in the same terms as that given in the Argyll case: that the foreshore was found to be the property of Darroch as 'part and pertinent of his lands and estate subject to Her Majesty's right as trustee for public uses'.[111]

[107] NRS, CR11/264, Letters Lowray to Beith, 25 July 1876, 12 November 1878; Letter Beith to Howard, 22 July 1876; CR11/288, Letter Beith to Lowray, 4 February 1882.

[108] See Buchanan and Geils v. Lord Advocate (1882) 9 R 1218, Lord Lee at pp. 1221–2.

[109] Lord Advocate v. Lord Blantyre (1879) 6 R (HL) 72. Lord Mure in the Inner House of the Court of Session said (at p. 79) as an *obiter dictum*: 'Agnew proceeds upon a sound view of the law applicable to that important question' and he approved of Lord Benholme's opinion on the point.

[110] NRS, CR11/288, Letter Beith to A. B. Loch, 20 July 1882.

[111] NRS, AF67/179, The Association Memorandum; Darroch v. Lord Advocate

It is, however, the Agnew case that has been taken as establishing what is now accepted as the modern law,[112] although we might just note that as late as 1899 the ghost of the Association's principal contention and the underlying uncertainty over the law was still apparent with the words of Lord Watson who said, echoing the words of Lord Lee in the Buchanan case:

> the foreshores of a barony . . . according to an opinion expressed by many eminent Scottish Judges, are carried by the mere grant of a barony, without their being expressly mentioned. That doctrine has not been expressly affirmed by a judgement of the Court; but the contrary has never been expressly decided, although, in the majority of cases, an opposite doctrine appears to have been followed.[113]

The Association remained in existence after these cases ended to help proprietors in disputes with the Crown over foreshore questions, and generally to protect proprietors' interests in the foreshore. As we see in Chapter 7, it was to have a prominent role in defeating a legislative proposal in 1891 to give crofters and the public rights to seaware over the foreshore, and it was finally wound up in 1952 having been moribund for a considerable number of years.

## CONCLUSIONS

When discussions opened in 1867 between the Association and the Board to find a way forward in the foreshore dispute, the Association was, in a sense, pushing at an open door because the Board would have been anxious to reach a settlement with the Scottish proprietors so that it could introduce an amendment to the Crown Lands Act 1866 as discussed in Chapter 3. But it was a door that, in the end, the Board felt constrained from letting the proprietors through. Farrer's desire for a compromise was dashed, however, by the fact that the Law Officers in

(1892), DVGN 569/4, Closed Record (including Summons, Condescendence and Answers, Pleas in Law, Interlocutors and Decree in Absence), 1892; NRS, CS46/1892/10/73, Decree of Declarator.

112 Reid, *Law of Property in Scotland*, para. 314; Robbie, *Private Water Rights*, para. 3.39; Lord Advocate v. Blantyre (1879) 6 R (HL) 72 at pp. 79, 83; Luss Estates Co. v. B. P. Oil Grangemouth Ltd 1982 SLT 97 at p. 99.

113 Lord Advocate v. Wemyss (1899) 2 F (HL) 1 at p. 9; but see contra Lord Maxwell in the Luss Estates case at p. 99. Lord Hunter in Mather v. Alexander (1926) SC 139 explained Lord Watson's 'opposite doctrine' as being the doctrine that 'is fully expounded in the leading case on this branch of the law – Agnew v. Lord Advocate'.

1868 said that the Crown had both a right of property in the foreshore and an interest held as trustee on behalf of the public. Farrer seemed to want to reach a legislative compromise with the proprietors but the law was against him; he could not give away the property of the Crown. Nor was he helped by the fact that the Association was not prepared to give him the time he needed to persuade the Treasury of the sense of a compromise. He did not relish the prospect of more litigation but, on the other hand, he considered the Board had a duty to protect the interests of the Crown in the foreshore that the Law Officers said existed. He seems truly to have found himself between the devil and the deep blue sea. When Loch proposed to the Duke of Richmond that the decision in the Agnew case should be regarded as definitive by the Board, we may suppose that, if the duke passed this information on to him, Farrer would have breathed a sigh of relief because he might have hoped that the long-running dispute was reaching closure. And with the advice of the Law Officers that the Board could properly abandon the appeal in the Agnew case, Farrer may well have considered that the Board could, finally, draw a line under the issue of the Scottish foreshore and the private proprietors. He would, however, have been wrong; the dispute continued to be litigated into the 1880s.

The Association's proposals in 1867 for legislation were not accepted but the pressure the Association exerted through its legal actions that culminated with the Agnew decision produced for the proprietors a satisfactory result. While the Inner House in the Agnew case had not accepted the proprietors' main argument, the decision left no room to doubt the importance of possession, and the partial victory of the Crown in getting the main argument of the proprietors defeated would be seen to be a barren one. Partial victory it may have been but, in reality, the Crown had lost a battle. The Crown had not yet, however, lost the war and the continuing efforts of the Crown in attempting to protect its property right in the foreshore are the subject of Chapter 6.

# 6

# 'What remains in the Crown cannot be of great extent'

## INTRODUCTION

THE BATTLE THE CROWN lost with the Agnew decision had shown that possession of the foreshore was a crucial element in the establishment of title. It could be used either to provide evidence that explained a grant of land as including the foreshore, or to establish ownership of the foreshore by prescriptive possession. And, in both cases, the collection of seaware from the foreshore could provide the necessary possession. Donald Beith, the Solicitor in Scotland to the Board of Trade, had given a stark warning after the Agnew case that 'If the possession in Sir Andrew Agnew's case was sufficient in law to establish a right to the foreshore I think that every proprietor in the Island will be able to establish an equal right to the foreshores where his estate abuts on the sea.'[1]

This chapter is principally concerned with the Crown's attempts during the first forty-seven years or so of the twentieth century to prevent the loss of the battle the Crown had experienced with the decision in the Agnew case turning into the loss of the war, by proposing changes to the law relating to the significance of the collection of seaware as a means of proving possession, and to the period required to establish prescriptive possession, but it also touches on recommendations for changes in the law relating to the management of, and public rights over, the foreshore.

## THE ROYAL COMMISSION ON COAST EROSION

The appointment of the Royal Commission in July 1906 to inquire into and report on questions affecting coast erosion, the reclamation of tidal lands and afforestation included as one of its terms of reference 'whether any alteration of the law is desirable as regards the management and

[1] NRS, CR 11/263, Letter Beith to Howard, 10 February 1876.

control of the foreshore', and the Royal Commission heard evidence on the way in which title to the foreshore was acquired by subjects against the Crown.[2] The evidence of the Solicitor to the Board, R. Ellis Cunliffe, the Hon. T. W. H. Pelham, an assistant secretary at the Board, and C. E. Howlett, one of the principal clerks to the Office of Woods, was extremely detailed and explained the issues that concerned the Crown in this area; and Cunliffe prepared an extensive 'Statement as to the Law relating to the Foreshore in Scotland' in conjunction with the Edinburgh solicitors Davidson & Syme and he submitted this as part of his evidence.[3] So far as the issues of adverse claims to the foreshore were concerned, Pelham described the problem to the Royal Commission in the following terms:

> we are constantly finding that the owner of the adjoining property lays claim to the ownership of the foreshore; we find, for instance, that he has been warning people off, he has been exercising powers of ownership; in these cases we tell him that prima facie the foreshore belongs to the Crown and is under the management of the Board of Trade.[4]

The evidence given by Cunliffe as to the problems in Scotland caused by twenty years being the prescriptive period was forthright. He was asked whether he could suggest any alterations to Scottish law that he would like to see effected. Cunliffe said that

> the Scotch proprietor of land adjoining the foreshore seems to get a title to the foreshore a good deal easier than he does in England, and that the limitation of the years which he can prescribe, and so obtain possession, is very short, in my opinion.[5]

As compared with the sixty-year *Nullum Tempus* Act[6] period in England, Cunliffe said that the twenty-year period in Scotland (reduced, in 1874,

[2] PP, 1907, XXXIV, Royal Commission, vol. 1 (part 1), Cd 3683, p. iv. The issues as to the law regarding management and control were an adjunct to the environmental factors that mainly concerned the Royal Commission.

[3] For Scotland, see PP, 1907, XXXIV, Royal Commission, vol. 1 (part 2), Cd 3684, Qs 1–531, 1670–80; PP, 1911, XIV, Royal Commission, vol. 3 (part 2), Cd 5709, Qs 24263–427, 27898–974, Appendix XL (which includes Cunliffe's statement as to the law in Scotland) and Appendix LV (Cunliffe's general comparison of the law of England and Wales, Ireland and Scotland relating to the foreshore). The relevant recommendations of the Royal Commission are contained in PP, 1911, XIV, Royal Commission, vol. 3 (part 1), Cd 5708, pp. 115–17.

[4] PP, 1907, XXXIV, Royal Commission, vol. 1 (part 2), Cd 3684, Q 37.

[5] PP, 1911, XIV, Royal Commission, vol. 3 (part 2), Cd 5709, Q 24302.

[6] 9 George 2 c 16.

from forty years) caused the Crown serious concern in relation to the foreshore.[7] 'It is obvious', he said, that 'it has operated in enabling private owners to claim successfully against the Crown in Scotland. This is one of the points to which I hope your attention may be directed.'[8] Indeed, he wondered (expressing his views here as a private suggestion) whether a right to the foreshore should be capable of being prescribed for as against the Crown at all:

> There has been no attempt, as it were, to say that subject matter of this character is so important that prescription would not run, but it does seem rather outrageous, to my mind, that an individual can prescribe in this way today against the Crown and the public with nothing to stop him.[9]

In the event his suggested amendment of the law given in his official capacity was phrased in more diplomatic terms and was not limited to Scotland. Nor, however, was it limited, in terms, simply to an extension of the prescriptive period: 'It is for serious consideration whether some greater restrictions should not be put upon the power of a subject to acquire foreshore against the Crown by adverse user.'[10]

The recommendations of the Royal Commission were published on 1 June 1911, and the Royal Commission said that they only concerned 'such alterations in the law as seem to us to be absolutely necessary in the interests of the public'. So far as the acquisition of title to the foreshore in Scotland by subjects against the Crown was concerned, the Royal Commission recommended that the twenty-year prescriptive period in Scotland should be extended to sixty years. 'As the law at present stands', the Royal Commission said, 'it seems to us to be difficult for a public body having control of the foreshores adequately to safeguard the proprietary interests of the Crown in the foreshore of Scotland.'[11] There was, however, no mention made of the way in which collection of seaware had fortified claims to title to the foreshore by possession or, indeed, of how, if at all, such collection could or should

[7] For the effect of the Conveyancing (Scotland) Act 1874, see Buchanan and Geils v. Lord Advocate (1882) 9 R 1218; TNA:PRO, MT 10/634, Opinion of the Law Officers, 1 February 1894.

[8] PP, 1911, XIV, Royal Commission, vol. 3 (part 2), Cd 5709, Qs 24302, 24310.

[9] PP, 1911, XIV, Royal Commission, vol. 3 (part 2), Cd 5709, Q 24309 and see Qs 24302–11 for the entirety of Cunliffe's oral evidence on the prescriptive period.

[10] PP, 1911, XIV, Royal Commission, vol. 3 (part 2), Cd 5709, Appendix LV, p. 253.

[11] PP, 1911, XIV, Royal Commission, vol. 3 (part 1), Cd 5708, para. 128, pp. 115–16.

be relied upon in making such claims. As we shall see in the following sections of this chapter, the recommendation as to the extension of the prescriptive period was to be the subject of considerable discussion within the Board of Trade, the Scottish Office and the BoAS, and this discussion went further than the recommendation of the Royal Commission, and extended to a consideration of the significance of the collection of seaware.

As to changes which the Royal Commission believed were necessary in the law relating to the regulation and management of the foreshore in the public interest, it will be recalled from Chapter 3 that parts of the foreshore had been excluded from the transfer provisions in the Crown Lands Act 1866; the Royal Commission thought that the split of the management of the foreshore between the Office of Woods and the Board was 'unscientific, unnecessary, and a source of inconvenience to the public, particularly in view of the fact that the two Departments pursue different policies in their dealings with the foreshore'. The Royal Commission noted that the policy of the Board was to administer the foreshore in the public interest and not with the object of realising a revenue from it, while the policy of the Office of Woods was to be bound by the Crown Lands Acts which prevented them from parting with any property for less than full value.[12] The Royal Commission did not question how it was that the two bodies were able to pursue policies so different on the basis of statutory powers that were identical, but as a memorandum written in 1958 was to say, although this did 'at first sight seem strange', the reason was that 'in practice the differences were differences of emphasis rather than of principle'.[13] The Royal Commission recommended that the administration and control should be unified within the Board in the public interest 'and that for this purpose a transfer of such foreshore as remains under the control of the Commissioners of Woods and Forests should be made to the Board of Trade'.[14] The Royal Commission made no recommendation as to the statutory powers of sale and lease in the Crown Lands Act 1866 that were, as we saw in Chapter 3, thought to be defective; indeed, given that Farrer had been advised in 1866 that the only course open to the Board to relieve itself of the difficulties imposed by the 1866 Act in

[12] PP, 1911, XIV, Royal Commission, vol. 3 (part 1), Cd 5708, paras 23, 24.

[13] TNA:PRO, BT 243/95, Foreshore and Seabed; Memorandum by the Crown Estate Commissioners, 15 May 1958, p. 7; see further in Chapter 9.

[14] PP, 1911, XIV, Royal Commission, vol. 3 (part 1), Cd 5708, paras 130–3; see the evidence given by Pelham and Howlett in PP, 1907, XXXIV, Royal Commission, vol. 1 (part 2), Cd 3684, Qs 1–531.

the administration of the foreshore would be to obtain an amendment of the Act,[15] this subject did not assume the degree of importance we might have expected in evidence given before the Royal Commission, the strongest of the comments being from Howlett from the Office of Woods. Howlett was asked if he thought that the amendments made in the House of Lords to the 1866 Crown Lands Bill that we discussed in Chapter 3 had restricted the Board's powers, and he replied: 'the powers given to [the Board] by the Bill as passed were much more restricted, I imagine, than they would have been had the Bill passed in its original form'.[16] Farrer's hope that a liberal construction of the Crown Lands Acts might allow the Board to pursue its public interest policy appeared to be working.

The Royal Commission also considered the public rights over the foreshore and concluded after reviewing the evidence given by Cunliffe as to the law in Scotland in the extensive statement he had submitted that, apart from public rights of navigation and fishing, further rights 'such as those of bathing, riding, diving, collecting seaweed etc.'[17] were difficult to define and suggested that

> the Board of Trade should be empowered by Order after a local enquiry, at which all persons affected should have the opportunity of being heard, to lay down these rights and their extent in localities where it is shown that it is advisable in the public interest that they should be exercisable, with the right to put limitations and conditions on the use of such rights if necessary.[18]

The Royal Commission also recommended that there should be a clear right of passage along the foreshore.[19]

A provision to put into effect the recommendation to unify management of the foreshore in the Board of Trade was to be included in the Coast Protection Bill of 1929, discussed below, and although there had been no recommendation on the defective statutory powers of sale and lease in the 1866 Act, a provision to rectify the defects was nonetheless to be included in the Coast Protection Bill of 1929.[20] The Royal Commission recommendation on public rights was not to be acted on.[21]

[15] Farrer Memorandum, p. 16.

[16] The evidence of Pelham, Howlett and Cunliffe is in PP, 1907, XXXIV, Royal Commission, vol. 1 (part 2), Cd 3684, Qs 7–18, 146, 157–61, 278–311, 477–81, 488–9, 532–5, 547, 1560–7.

[17] PP, 1911, XIV, Royal Commission, vol. 3 (part 1), Cd 5708, p. 117.

[18] PP, 1911, XIV, Royal Commission, vol. 3 (part 1), Cd 5708, p. 117.

[19] PP, 1911, XIV, Royal Commission, vol. 3 (part 1), Cd 5708, p. 116.

[20] Clause 2 of the 1929 Bill; PP, 1929/30, Bills and Acts, Coast Protection, Bill Number 18; see further in Chapter 9.

[21] The subject was, as we shall see in Chapter 9, considered by the SLC in 2003.

## THE DRAFT COAST PROTECTION BILL 1914–15

Following the Royal Commission's final report, consideration was given by the Board to drafting a Bill to deal with the recommendations and, in particular, the recommendation as to the extension of the prescriptive period. A memorandum circulated within the Board assumed that a Bill would include the recommended extension of the prescriptive period and concentrated, instead, on the advice that had been given to Crown departments in 1864 as to the ownership of seaweed, and questioned whether, in the light of this, an extension of the prescriptive period would be sufficient. The memorandum said:

> In connection with this recommendation [on the prescriptive period], which will presumably be embodied in the draft Coast Erosion Bill, it is necessary to consider the somewhat peculiar question of seaweed rights in Scotland. We have always held that the seaweed grown or cast upon the foreshores of England and Ireland is (in general) the property of the Crown, as being part and parcel of the foreshore itself, but the Crown does not similarly claim the seaweed upon the shore in Scotland; the seaweed there being held to be the property of the adjacent landowner whether such landowner has a title to the foreshore or not. This view was also held by the Woods prior to the transfer in 1866, and is expressly laid down in an interesting statement with regard to seaweed generally.[22]

The result of this official view about seaweed had been that the removal of seaweed from the Scottish foreshore had not, for a considerable time, been reported to the Crown authorities and in many cases landowners had been able to fortify their claims to the foreshore by proof of removal of seaweed in addition to other acts of possession by them.[23]

[22] TNA:PRO, MT 10/197, Memorandum – Royal Commission on Coast Erosion, Seaweed rights in Scotland, 23 January 1914 [hereafter Seaweed Rights Memorandum]; the 'interesting statement' is a memorandum by Horace Watson, the Solicitor in England to the Office of Woods, dated 7 April 1864, a copy of which was attached to the Seaweed Rights Memorandum; see Ferguson, *Law of Water*, pp. 52–3 and Rankine, *Ownership of Lands* (4th edn), pp. 257–61, 272–4 as to contemporary textbook views of the law concerning rights to seaware; the modern textbook view can be seen in Reid, *Law of Property in Scotland*, paras 318, 491, 524–6. There are further discussions of rights to seaware in Chapters 7, 8 and 9.

[23] For an acknowledgement that the removal of seaware from the foreshore had been carried on for years with the tacit consent of the Crown, see PD, Fifth Series, vol. 181, House of Commons, cols 1099–100 (10 March 1925).

This, coupled with the fact that they only had to show such possession for twenty years, had put the *ex adverso* landowner in a strong position as against the Crown. The Seaweed Rights Memorandum is important because it contains the first official suggestion that the collection of seaware should not assist a claim to a title by possession; it shows that the Board had been aware of the implications of the advice as to the law in Scotland on the ownership of seaweed:

> the position with regard to seaweed in Scotland meant that the adjacent owner by first claiming the seaweed could then claim the foreshore on which it grows and Mr Hardinge . . . pointed out that if this were possible it would be difficult to uphold the title of the Crown to foreshore anywhere in Scotland.[24]

The Seaweed Rights Memorandum said that a recommendation had been made that the Crown should, wherever possible, grant permission for the removal of seaweed in Scotland on payment of a small sum by way of acknowledging the Crown's rights. This suggestion was not taken up and, indeed, as late as 1908 it seemed that the Crown was still not taking the point seriously because the Board, the Seaweed Rights Memorandum said, had told the Customs Department that the Crown was not concerned with the cutting of growing seaware in Scotland and suggested that a footnote to this effect should be appended to their instructions to local officers.[25] In these circumstances the writer of the Seaweed Rights Memorandum questioned whether the Royal Commission's recommendation to extend the prescriptive period

> is in itself sufficient to safeguard the Crown's title in Scotland in so far as it may be ousted by adverse claims built up by the taking of seaweed, to which we have no power to object. It would appear that the recommendations if given effect to in an Act would at best only lengthen the period necessary for the building up of a claim.
>
> It is therefore also for consideration whether some provision should not be included in the proposed Bill to the effect that the letting, selling or taking of seaweed from the foreshores of Scotland shall not in itself be deemed an act of possession supporting a claim to foreshore.[26]

There was, it seems, already a suggestion that such a provision should be included in relation to Ireland and it was thought that Scotland's need

24 TNA:PRO, MT 10/197, Seaweed Rights Memorandum, p. 3.
25 TNA:PRO, MT 10/197, Seaweed Rights Memorandum, p. 3.
26 TNA:PRO, MT 10/197, Seaweed Rights Memorandum, p. 4.

in this respect was greater than that of Ireland. An internal Board note commented on the Seaweed Rights Memorandum:

> This memo. puts the position of the Crown as regards seaweed in Scotland very clearly. It is plain that a mere extension of the prescriptive period will not help us, since, as the law stands at present, we cd. not at any time during the extended period, prevent an adjacent owner taking, selling (or authorising others to take) seaweed and thus building up a title to the foreshore.[27]

Cunliffe was asked for his opinion as to whether

> the taking of seaweed in Scotland as an element in the building up of a title to foreshore against the Crown is of sufficient importance to warrant the inclusion of a clause in the Coast Protection Bill dealing specifically with the point.[28]

Cunliffe was, at the time, in the throes of the claim by the Duke of Argyll to the foreshore of the island of Tiree that is discussed in Chapter 8 and so he would have been very aware of the significance in that case of the collection of seaweed, and, as we have seen, he had given evidence to the Royal Commission that serious consideration should be given to introducing greater restrictions on the powers of the subject to acquire foreshore against the Crown by adverse use. It is no surprise, therefore, that he supported the clause. It was agreed between the under secretary for Scotland and the Board in June 1914 that, given these issues involved questions of law, they should be considered by the Law Officers and they were instructed, together with James Pitman, at the end of 1914.[29] As we shall see in Chapter 8, the Law Officers had advised in May 1914 on the Tiree claim; they would, therefore, have had all the relevant issues, including, in particular, the importance of the collection of seaware, very much in the forefront of their minds. Indeed, it was because of this that the Lord Advocate expressly asked for Pitman also to be instructed as junior counsel as he had, as we shall see in Chapter 8, been advising the Board on the Tiree claim since April 1910.[30] The Law Officers were specifically reminded of the Tiree claim in the instructions and of

[27] TNA:PRO, MT 10/197, Minute, 27 January 1914.

[28] TNA:PRO, MT 10/197, Minute, 6 April 1914.

[29] NRS, AF 43/60, Letter Craig to Assistant Secretary Board of Trade, 8 October 1914. The Law Officers at the time were Robert Munro as the Lord Advocate and T. B. Morison as the Solicitor General. James Campbell Pitman (1864–1941) was appointed Sheriff of Caithness, Orkney and Zetland on 4 February 1920 and a Lord Ordinary on 3 January 1929.

[30] NRS, AF 43/60, Letter Craig to Assistant Secretary Board of Trade, 8 October 1914.

the fact that the Lord Advocate had at the time attached considerable importance to the views of Lord Watson as to the value of taking loose or drift seaware as an act of ownership.[31] The instructions referred to the proposals to extend the prescriptive period to sixty years and the detailed drafting which was necessary for such a clause to be effective. The instructions also drew attention to the previous advice referred to in the Seaweed Rights Memorandum that had been given to the Crown on the position in Scotland as to the ownership of seaweed:

> It has been the custom of the Board of Trade and Office of Woods to regard seaware as belonging to the proprietor of the adjoining lands in Scotland whether he owned the foreshore or not. It is submitted that the more correct view would have been to regard the seaweed as belonging to the owner of the foreshore, whether the Crown or a subject, and the removal of it as an act of possession of the foreshore just as in the same way as the removal of any other foreshore material was regarded. The removal of seaware from the shores in Scotland was in this way for a considerable time not reported to the authorities, and in many cases landowners were able to fortify their claims to foreshore by proof of removal of seaweed in addition to other acts of possession by them.[32]

The instructions posed the question whether a clause – the seaware clause – should be inserted in the draft Bill to provide that the letting, selling or taking of seaweed from the foreshore in Scotland should not, of itself, in a question with the Crown be deemed an act of possession supporting a claim to foreshore and should not be held, in a question with the Crown, to add to the possession which any claimant of foreshore may have had.

The Law Officers and Pitman gave their opinion in May 1915. They had no doubts that an extension of the prescriptive period was a perfectly legitimate course of action to take and recommended wording for the draft clause to extend the prescriptive period from twenty to sixty years in the following form:

> Notwithstanding the provisions of the Act of the Parliament of Scotland 1617 cap.12 anent prescription of heritable rights and of Section 34 of the Conveyancing (Scotland) Act 1874, the period of prescriptive possession necessary to constitute, establish or validate any right or title to any foreshore in Scotland or any interest therein shall be 60 years and subject to this alteration

[31] Young v. North British Railway Company (1887) 14 R (HL) 53 at p. 55.

[32] NRS, AF 43/60, Case for the Board of Trade with regard to Proposed Amendments of the Law relating to Coast Protection for Opinion of Counsel, and Opinion, 25 May 1915 [hereafter 1915 Instructions and Opinion], p. 7.

> in the said period the law regulating such prescriptive possession shall remain as at the passing of this Act.[33]

They also gave their opinion that the correct interpretation of the law as to the ownership of seaware was that the Crown's *prima facie* title to foreshore in Scotland included drift and growing seaware on the foreshore. But on the question whether the seaware clause should be included, they were, given their involvement in the Tiree case, strangely reticent: 'We regard this as a question of policy rather than one of law; and, that being so, we do not feel justified in expressing an opinion regarding it.'[34]

There was one other issue on which the Law Officers and Pitman were asked for their opinion. It concerned the effect which section 12 of the Crofters Holdings (Scotland) Act 1886 might have on the Crown's *prima facie* title to the foreshore. They were asked whether a clause should be inserted in the Bill to amend section 12 to safeguard the Crown's title to foreshore in Scotland. The background to this section of the 1886 Act is discussed in Chapter 7 but it suffices to say here that it made provision for the Crofters Commission to draw up a scheme regulating the use of seaweed by crofters on the same estate for the reasonable purpose of their holdings. The Board was concerned to be sure that where such schemes were drawn up and, in fixing rents for the croft holding, a sum was included for the facility of getting seaweed, that fact should not be evidence as against the Crown of any title to the foreshore. The Law Officers and Pitman agreed that there should be included in the Bill a provision that

> No transaction or proceedings which have taken place or shall hereafter take place under section 12 of the Crofters Act 1886, shall be evidence as against the Crown of any right or title in the Landlord or tenant or smallholder, to any foreshore in Scotland or to any interest therein.[35]

The opinion of the Law Officers and Pitman, and the instructions, were sent by the Board to the Scottish Office in August 1915 and the accompanying letter made it clear that despite the fact that the Law Officers and Pitman had 'refrained from expressing any Opinion' on the seaware clause, the Board considered it desirable, subject to any observations which the secretary for Scotland might wish to make, that there should be included in the Bill a clause to provide that 'the letting, selling or taking of seaweed from the foreshore in Scotland shall not, of

[33] NRS, AF 43/60, 1915 Instructions and Opinion, pp. 11–12.
[34] NRS, AF 43/60, 1915 Instructions and Opinion, pp. 11–12.
[35] NRS, AF 43/60, 1915 Instructions and Opinion, pp. 8–12.

itself, be deemed an act of possession supporting a claim to foreshore as against the Crown'.[36] The Scottish Office wondered whether legislation was needed. It was accepted that 'Probably adjacent landowners would protest against what they would consider as filching away their rights', but that the economic significance should not be underestimated: 'with the possible revival of the kelp industry the right to seaweed is of importance. Perhaps we should have the observations of the [BoAS] on the question.'[37] But before the BoAS was consulted, the Scottish Office took the advice of P. F. Wood, the counsel who advised the secretary of state for Scotland on the drafting of Scottish Bills. He noted the apparent inconsistency inherent in the suggestion that the Crown's *prima facie* right to seaware should be recognised by statute:

> the whole question of seaware rights is complicated both in law and practice. I think it would be well to have the observations of the [BoAS].
>
> The suggestion to insert a declaratory clause enacting the [Law Officers'] opinion . . . that the Crown's title to foreshore includes drift and seaware seems to need careful consideration. It is precisely the strong presumption in favour of that view which founds the landowner's claim to foreshore whence he has taken or sold ware for the prescriptive period: 'seaware pertains to the owner of the shore: A took the seaware: the Crown did not prevent him, or exact a price: ergo the shore is A's and not the Crown!'
>
> No doubt it would be possible – if apparently inconsistent – to insert <u>both</u> a clause declaring that all ware etc. on Crown foreshore is the Crown's, and also . . . a clause providing that the taking of such ware shall not support a claim to the foreshore as against the Crown: the latter would suffice by itself if the opinion of [the Law Officers] is well founded: the former by itself would be dangerous.
>
> It is obvious that the Prescription proposal as well as that about seaware, would be highly controversial.[38]

On the prescription clause, Wood suggested, 'with diffidence' given that the Law Officers had settled the wording, that the clause should make it clear it was only to apply to questions with the Crown, as the Royal

[36] NRS, AF 43/60, Letter Roper to Under Secretary for Scotland, 26 August 1915.

[37] NRS, AF 43/60, Copy minutes from S. O. File No. 20569.8, 1 September 1915, initialled G. W. M. The Scott Committee had pointed out in 1914 the possibility of an increased demand for iodine from seaweed and that, given favourable circumstances, the kelp industry was capable of 'very great expansion'; PP, 1914, XXXII, Report to the Board of Agriculture for Scotland on Home Industries in the Highlands and Islands, Cd 7564, p. 120.

[38] NRS, AF 43/60, Copy minute from S. O. File No. 20569.8 addressed to Mr Lamb the Assistant Under Secretary, 17 September 1915, initialled by P. F. Wood (emphasis in original).

Commission had recommended. He also suggested an amendment to make it clear that the clause had retrospective effect, although he agreed that this 'might be difficult to justify on the merits'.[39] The views of the Scottish Office and the counsel to the secretary of state were not, however, at this time communicated to the Board and, in the event, the BoAS had no amendments to suggest.[40] The exigencies of the War caused discussions on the draft Bill to be dropped.

## THE DRAFT COAST PROTECTION BILL 1923–9

Discussions on the Bill were revived during 1923 and the Scottish Office turned, again, to consider the issues that had been raised by the Law Officers, Pitman and the Board in 1915. As to the extension of the prescriptive period, the Scottish Office now saw no reason, as a matter of policy, why the department should not agree with the proposal; the Royal Commission had, after all, recommended it. As to detail on the proposal, the Scottish Office limited itself to two questions: first, should the extension apply only to cases against the Crown, the answer to which was 'yes'; and second, should it be prospective or retrospective, the answer to which was that it should be prospective, notwithstanding Wood's suggestion in 1915. As to the proposed seaware clause, we saw that in 1915 the Scottish Office took the view that such a clause would be controversial (as indeed they had also thought about the extension of the prescriptive period clause), but had reached no conclusions on it. The internal minutes on the question in 1923 are, frankly, confusing, but they suggest that there may have been a difference of opinion within the department. One minute recommends that the Board should be told that the Scottish Office agreed to the inclusion of such a seaware clause.[41] Another minute states, with the unhelpful use of a double negative, that 'the Secretary for Scotland does not think the clause . . . re seaware need not be included'. However, the remainder of the minute suggests that the author of the minute does, in fact, believe that such a clause should *not* be included.[42] In the event, the Scottish Office came off the fence over the seaware clause and replied formally in January 1924 to the Board's letter of August 1915:

[39] NRS, AF 43/60, Copy minute from S. O. File No. 20569.8 addressed to Mr Lamb the Assistant Under Secretary, 17 September 1915, initialled by P. F. Wood.

[40] NRS, AF 43/60, Note HMC, 2 February 1916.

[41] NRS, AF 43/60, Secretary for Scotland No. 20569/9. Coast Protection. Coast Protection Bill, minute, 15 December 1923, initialled G. W. M.

[42] NRS, AF 43/60, Minute, 15 December 1923, initialled T. F. M.

> As regards the Board's letter . . . of the 26th August 1915 . . . the Secretary for Scotland has no objection to offer to the insertion of a clause providing that the letting, selling or taking of seaweed from the foreshore in Scotland shall not, of itself, be deemed an act of possession supporting a claim to foreshore as against the Crown.[43]

Hugh Pattison Macmillan was now the Lord Advocate[44] and John Charles Fenton the Solicitor General,[45] and so the Board submitted the questions of extending the prescriptive period and including the seaware clause to the new Law Officers for a fresh opinion. They considered that the questions raised were largely matters of policy (as Munro, Morison and Pitman had themselves considered in relation to the seaware clause) but said that as their views had been invited, they would give their view on the issue. Their view was that it was undesirable to introduce a new and longer prescriptive period for the acquisition of rights in the foreshore, particularly as the tendency of modern legislation was all in favour of shortening the prescriptive period regarding heritable rights. Furthermore, so far as the combined effect of an extension of the prescriptive period and the seaware clause were concerned:

> if it were enacted, as proposed, that the taking of seaware should not in law be evidence of possession, the effect of this coupled with the extension of the prescriptive period would be to render it practically impossible to acquire a right to foreshore by prescription. If this is the real object of the proposed legislation it would be preferable to enact directly that a subject should no longer be entitled to prescribe a title to foreshore against the Crown.[46]

On the proposed seaware clause, the Law Officers were no less emphatic in their views:

> It is well-established law in Scotland that the gathering of seaware from the foreshore is good evidence of possession for the purpose of prescribing a title to the foreshore. Indeed as seaware may fairly be called the harvest of the foreshore the taking of it is commonly the most distinctive act of beneficial use to which the foreshore can be put. We do not think it is advisable to alter the law in this respect.[47]

[43] NRS, AF 43/60, Letter Scottish Office to Board of Trade, 1 January 1924.

[44] And a Lord of Appeal in Ordinary in 1930.

[45] And Sheriff of Fife in 1925.

[46] NRS, AD 54/53, Coast Protection Bill – Case for the Board of Trade for opinion of Crown Counsel – Opinion, 4 November 1924.

[47] NRS, AD 54/53, Coast Protection Bill – Case for the Board of Trade for opinion of Crown Counsel – Opinion, 4 November 1924.

The Law Officers did, however, agree with their predecessors about the need for the clause dealing with section 12 of the 1886 Act. They also added as a general remark that

> in our view the main object of the proposed Bill could be attained and the public interest sufficiently safeguarded by empowering the Department with the duty of coast protection to intervene when necessary to prevent erosion and to prohibit operations upon the foreshore which are prejudicial to the community.[48]

The lack of special or summary powers for enforcing public rights was an issue which had troubled Farrer when he wrote his Memorandum.[49]

One might have expected that, in the face of the unequivocal view expressed by the Law Officers, the Board would draw back from their proposals. However, given that the Royal Commission had recommended an extension of the prescriptive period, the views of the Law Officers on this point were noted but not accepted; the prescription clause was included but with a sub-clause the effect of which was that where the necessary degree of possession could be proved to have been had for a period of not less than twenty years before the commencement of the Act, the sixty-year extension did not apply. The seaware clause was more controversial, but it was still included in the new draft Bill. The clause provided that

> From and after the passing of this Act, the letting, selling or taking of drift seaweed as distinct from growing seaweed from the foreshore in Scotland, whether such has been done before or after the passing of this Act, shall not be deemed an act of possession supporting a claim to the foreshore as against the Crown.[50]

There is little doubt that the legal department within the Board and its external lawyers, Davidson & Syme, were very keen to see the seaware clause becoming law. They had been frequently thwarted in their efforts successfully to challenge claims to the foreshore by *ex adverso* landowners by evidence of possession through the collection of seaweed (as the Tiree case discussed in Chapter 8 shows) and keenly anticipated the benefits which would flow from such a clause, particularly as the clause was drafted with retrospective effect. In a letter of advice in 1925

48 NRS, AD 54/53, Coast Protection Bill – Case for the Board of Trade for opinion of Crown Counsel – Opinion, 4 November 1924.

49 Farrer Memorandum, p. 3.

50 The draft Bill is to be found at NRS, AF 43/60, Draft Coast Protection Bill, 24 December 1925.

concerning an adverse claim to the foreshore at Sandsend Bay in Reay, Caithness, Davidson & Syme highlighted the advantage: 'The taking of seaweed is also relied upon and if the clause as to the removal of seaware is passed as drafted . . . these acts of ownership might be discounted as this clause is made retrospective.'[51] There was another important change to the clause included in the 1925 draft of the Bill compared with what had been under discussion earlier: the clause did not apply to growing seaware as the draft of the Bill discussed in 1915 had provided.

It was not, however, until 1929 that a Bill was finally presented to Parliament. In answer to a parliamentary question on 16 July 1929, William Graham, the President of the Board in Ramsay Macdonald's Labour government (which had been formed in June 1929), replied that the government intended to introduce a Coast Protection Bill before the summer recess to give effect to the recommendations of the Royal Commission, and the Bill was presented on 25 July 1929. The clause in the Bill which dealt with the extension of the prescriptive period (clause 11) and the seaware clause (clause 12(3)) were, in all material respects, the same as the clauses in the 1925 draft of the Bill except that the seaware clause was not limited to Scotland. A provision (clause 1) was also included to take account of the recommendation of the Royal Commission that the management of the foreshore should be unified in the Board; and the Bill included a provision (clause 2) which remedied, with retrospective effect, the defective powers of management in the Crown Lands Act 1866 by giving the Board the power to sell, lease and grant licences of the foreshore on such terms and conditions and in such manner as the Board might think fit.[52] There was no provision dealing with the recommendations of the Royal Commission concerning public rights over the foreshore. The first business after the summer recess on 29 October would be the Bill's second reading.[53]

As to the views of private proprietors, the Bill was considered shortly after the second reading in October 1929 in a lengthy memorandum drawn up by the Scottish Land and Property Federation (SLPF), an organisation of proprietors that had originally been set up for the purpose of preventing the passing of the Small Landholders (Scotland)

[51] NRS, CR 11/249, Letter Davidson & Syme to Board of Trade, 28 October 1925.

[52] PP, 1929/30, I, Bills and Acts, Coast Protection, Bill Number 19; TNA:PRO, CRES 36/60. Minute Sheet. E.859/26 – Coast Protection Bill, minute, 23 June 1926.

[53] See PD, Fifth Series, vol. 230, House of Commons, col. 210 (16 July 1929).

Act 1911,[54] and by other representatives of private proprietors. The SLPF's views on the prescription and seaware clauses were unremarkable. As to the prescription clause, they simply questioned whether the proposed alteration to the law should be 'objected to by the owners of seaboard estates', without offering a view, and as to the seaware clause noted, without further comment, the fact that the clause was 'apparently to protect the Crown against [the] use of seaweed being set up as evidence of a right of private ownership in the foreshore'.[55] George Fraser, the factor to Lord Macdonald, was a little more specific in his comments. He saw no objections to the prescription clause given the limitations contained in the sub-clause. He did, however, object to the seaware clause, in particular to the fact that it had retrospective effect:

> This . . . in my view is much too wide and should be restricted to the period after the Act. A large quantity of sea-weed taken in the West Highlands is drift weed and in the past the taking of it has been one of the Acts of Possession tending to set up a prescriptive title to the foreshore by possession.[56]

In observations on Fraser's comments, May, May & Deacon, the London solicitors to the Land Agents' Society, noted simply that the prescription clause 'purports to carry into effect the recommendations of the Royal Commission' and as to the seaware clause, merely restated what the clause actually said without commenting one way or the other as to its acceptability.[57]

## THE DEBATE ON THE SECOND READING OF THE COAST PROTECTION BILL 1929

The long summer recess gave ample time for detailed consideration of the Bill. The bulk of the Bill dealt with the coast erosion concerns that had been discussed by the Royal Commission and it was clear that the whole Bill would be subject to criticism,[58] but we look now at the extent to which the prescription clause and the seaware clause were considered in Parliament.[59] Given that this was a sensitive, indeed controversial,

[54] Cameron, *Land for the People?*, pp. 161–2.

[55] NRS, GD 325/1/170, Memorandum, Coast Protection Bill [n.d.].

[56] NRS, GD 325/1/170, Notes on the Coast Protection Bill, Geo. M. Fraser, 6 November 1929.

[57] NRS, GD 325/1/170, Observations on Mr Fraser's Notes, 12 November 1929.

[58] See, for example, *The Times*, 16 August 1929.

[59] The debate is covered in PD, Fifth Series, vol. 231, House of Commons, cols 29–127 (29 October 1929).

area it is perhaps surprising that Graham, when he spoke to move the Bill for its second reading, did not mention, in his outline of the provisions of the Bill, the clauses dealing with these issues. Sir Philip Cunliffe-Lister,[60] Graham's predecessor as President of the Board, drew attention to this:

> There are one or two other clauses which call for comment. Clauses 11 and 12, upon which the Right Hon. gentleman was silent, and which, I frankly admit, I do not altogether understand, seem to take away something from the inhabitants of Scotland and Northern Ireland – some rights which they had.[61]

Graham apologised for not dealing with these clauses but said that they did not take away any public rights. 'On the contrary', he said, 'they both protected public rights'.[62] Cunliffe-Lister retorted that he had not been referring to public rights but to 'private rights of crofters in Scotland and occupiers in Northern Ireland'.[63] In making this comment, Cunliffe-Lister had, on the face of it, entirely missed the main mischief that clauses 11 and 12 were really aimed at, which was to protect the Crown against the claims, not of crofters but of *ex adverso* estate owners, to acquire the foreshore by proving possession; in this context, the crofters and the inhabitants of Northern Ireland were a sideshow.[64] But this comment by Cunliffe-Lister is even more strange when we consider that the clauses he said he did not understand had, in all material respects, been the same as the clauses in the draft 1925 Bill which his department had produced while he was President of the Board, as to which, Graham, when he introduced the Bill, had said:

> Since [the publication in 1911 of the Royal Commission's final report], on one or two occasions draft legislation has been prepared, and during the previous year my predecessor in office at the Board of Trade indicated that a Bill, substantially on the lines of the Bill which I am now recommending to the

[60] Cunliffe-Lister (previously known as Philip Lloyd-Greame until 1924) had been the President of the Board from October 1922 to January 1924 and from November 1924 to June 1929 in the Conservative governments of Bonar Law and Baldwin, and from August to November 1931 in Ramsay Macdonald's National government.

[61] PD, Fifth Series, vol. 231, House of Commons, col. 45 (29 October 1929); see also *The Scotsman*'s report of this debate, 30 October 1929.

[62] PD, Fifth Series, vol. 231, House of Commons, col. 45 (29 October 1929).

[63] PD, Fifth Series, vol. 231, House of Commons, col. 45 (29 October 1929).

[64] *The Times* had similarly missed the mischief aimed at by the clauses in its report of 16 August 1929.

House, would be one of the early legislative efforts of the late Government if it were returned to office.[65]

There is no satisfactory explanation why Cunliffe-Lister should have said he did not understand clauses 11 and 12 that he must surely be taken to have known about from his time in office. But if this was odd, so was Graham's response to Cunliffe-Lister. He explained that clauses 11 and 12 'turn really on the point of the establishment of prescriptive rights against the Crown in regard to foreshore'. He said that all clause 11 did was 'to bring the practice in Scotland into line with the 60-year prescriptive period in England'. Clause 12, he said, did not interfere in any way with the provisions of section 12 of the 1886 Act but 'merely ensures that it will not enable [the collection of seaweed by crofters] necessary to the crofters for the cultivation of the soil, to build up a claim to the foreshore against the Crown'.[66] This, of course, was absolutely correct, but only so far as it went. What Graham failed to explain and, indeed, was never explained in the debate, was that there was a third sub-clause in clause 12, the seaware clause; that this was the crucial element in the protection the Crown was seeking in extending the prescriptive period; that the effect of the seaware clause was to diminish the ability of *ex adverso* owners to claim a title to the foreshore as against the Crown by proving possession through the collection of seaware; and that, on any view, this was an interference with private rights. Cunliffe-Lister ended his contribution to the debate by saying that he was satisfied that 'if all these clauses do is to bring the Scottish pilferers into line with the more law-abiding subjects of the Crown; he would not challenge them'.[67] But, of course, this was definitely not what the clauses were aimed at, as Cunliffe-Lister must surely have known.

The parliamentary secretary to the Board, W. R. Smith, was no more forthcoming on the point and, indeed, further confused the issue because he wrongly described section 12 of the 1886 Act as giving substantive rights to crofters, saying that 'when the crofters were given the right to take seaweed from the foreshore it was surely never intended that the exercise of that right should give them a prescriptive right to the ownership of the foreshore from which they gathered the material'. But of course section 12 of the 1886 Act had not given any such substantive rights to the crofters. And Smith failed to mention the more far-reaching seaware clause.[68]

[65] PD, Fifth Series, vol. 231, House of Commons, col. 429 (29 October 1929).
[66] PD, Fifth Series, vol. 231, House of Commons, cols 45–6 (29 October 1929).
[67] PD, Fifth Series, vol. 231, House of Commons, col. 46 (29 October 1929).
[68] PD, Fifth Series, vol. 231, House of Commons, cols 89, 90 (29 October 1929).

But right at the end of the debate, Graham came perilously close to giving the game away when, in response to a complaint from Archibald Skelton about the extension of the twenty-year prescriptive period, he said: 'All that we are now considering is the claim to the foreshore as against the Crown for a trifling act which no one can justify.'[69] The trifling act that he was, of course, referring to, was the letting, selling or taking of drift seaweed. Given the history of the Scottish kelp industry over the centuries, this could hardly be described as a 'trifling act'; certainly the Law Officers had not regarded it as such and nor had Lord Watson in the Young and North British Railway case. Other speakers also drew attention to what they saw as the iniquities of the extension of the prescriptive period and, interestingly, they objected to such an extension on largely the same grounds as the Law Officers had in their 1924 opinion. Skelton said that 'the method of dealing with well-established principles of Scottish land legislation in a statute such as this is a most improper way of proceeding'. He concluded 'that the Scottish Office cannot have been consulted about this, and that the Law Officers of the Crown can hardly have been consulted'.[70] No reply came on behalf of the Board that both the Scottish Office and the Law Officers had indeed been consulted and that one set of Law Officers had declined to express an opinion on the seaware clause save to say that it was a matter of policy, and the other set of Law Officers had said that both the proposed extension of the prescriptive period and the seaware clause were undesirable; and that the advice of the Scottish Office was that the proposals would be highly controversial. Skelton urged Graham to reconsider the provisions and said that in future 'even a Labour Government should not alter the law of Scotland in such a ludicrous and illogical manner'.[71] All in all the second reading of the Bill proved a less than enlightening experience for those who wanted to understand these important provisions of the Bill.

In the event, however, the Bill did not proceed any further than the second reading. When he had introduced the Bill, Graham had said that it 'was hardly controversial in character'.[72] It had, in fact, proved anything but uncontroversial and as there was considerable dissatisfaction with most of the Bill, it was dropped. Explaining this, the prime minister

[69] PD, Fifth Series, vol. 231, House of Commons, col. 113 (29 October 1929). Skelton was the Conservative Member of Parliament for Perth, who had been an advocate at the Scottish bar from 1906.

[70] PD, Fifth Series, vol. 231, House of Commons, cols 113–14 (29 October 1929).

[71] PD, Fifth Series, vol. 231, House of Commons, col. 36 (29 October 1929).

[72] PD, Fifth Series, vol. 231, House of Commons, col. 114 (29 October 1929).

said that the government 'informed the House when the Bill was introduced that if it was to go through, it had to be treated practically as a non-contentious Bill. This has not happened.'[73] Further questions and answers during 1930 and at the beginning of 1931 confirmed that the position had not changed. Progress could not be made in the absence of agreement between the interests concerned.

## THE CROWN REVIVES AND THEN ABANDONS ITS PROPOSAL TO EXTEND THE PRESCRIPTIVE PERIOD

After the Second World War, the government turned its attention, again, to consider the extension of the prescriptive period, and also the outstanding question of the unification of the management of the foreshore that is discussed in Chapter 9. In a memorandum for the Official Committee on the Machinery of Government on the subject of Crown Foreshore and Coast Erosion, it was said that 'It is estimated that during the period 1866 to 1937, 2,300 miles of foreshore in Scotland out of a total of 5,250 were successfully claimed by private owners'. The memorandum suggested that the Royal Commission proposal to extend the prescriptive period for Scotland to sixty years should be given effect to, or even that the right to establish claims against the Crown by the exercise of acts of possession over any period should be abolished. It was recognised, however, that the proposal to abolish the right to establish claims by prescription 'might meet with considerable opposition'.[74] The discussion on the matter took place in the context of a claim being made to the foreshore of the island of Islay and minutes reveal a reluctance to concede the claim: 'The alienation of the foreshore from the Crown to private ownership is, to my mind, closely akin to the enclosure of the Commons in the past. I cannot believe that it will be tolerated after the War.'[75] It was decided that the whole

[73] PD, Fifth Series, vol. 234, House of Commons, cols 841–2 (28 January 1930). It 'was not proceeded with', the Board later noted, 'in view of the great opposition which it encountered'; TNA:PRO, T 163/120/4, Note by Board of Trade. Coast Protection Bill, 14 November 1938; see also NRS, AF 43/61, Coast Erosion: Coast Protection Bill 1929–1939.

[74] TNA:PRO, MT 45/117, Ministry of War Transport – Memorandum for the Official Committee on the Machinery of Government; TNA:PRO, BT 297/943, Minute extracted from PT/H.94/45, 7 March 1945, initialled A. C. The figure of a total of 5,250 miles of Scottish foreshore should be taken to refer just to the foreshore in the Highlands and Western Isles.

[75] TNA:PRO, BT 297/943, Minute, 21 March 1945, initialled P. J. N. B.

issue should be considered in a paper produced for the Lord President's Committee. Aubrey Clark, an assistant secretary at the Ministry of War Transport, prepared a draft memorandum for the Committee that said that foreshore belonging to the Crown, which might be regarded as a national asset, ought not to be subject to loss by prescription. As to the extension of the prescriptive period to sixty years, the draft memorandum said that, even if this change had been made as the Royal Commission had recommended, it would be unlikely that it would have done more than slow down the process of loss of foreshore and so the draft memorandum suggested the more radical move that first, the acquisition of title to the foreshore by prescription should not be possible at all after the passing of the relevant legislation and that, second, after say five years from the passing of the legislation no title to foreshore previously acquired by prescription should be admissible unless it had previously been expressly admitted on behalf of the Crown or established in legal proceedings. These were extremely far-reaching proposals and reflected the earlier minutes exchanged on the subject and the previous memorandum submitted to the Official Committee on the Machinery of Government.

However, an exchange of minutes between Sir Gilmour Jenkins, deputy director-general at the Ministry of War Transport,[76] and Aubrey Clark about the draft memorandum suggests that, in reality, the appetite for extending the prescriptive period was waning and that Clark's heart was not really in the matter. Clark said to Jenkins that he had endeavoured in his draft to make out the best case he could for legislation. But he said that the person who had helped him in its preparation had personally doubted whether there was really a sufficient case for such dramatic change and there were, in Aubrey Clark's mind, certain fundamental weaknesses in the suggestion, in particular that the foreshore should be selected for protection from amongst other Crown lands. Clark confessed that he had no appetite for proceeding with such a proposal in isolation, and that it should form part of general legislation relating either to Crown and public lands, or to coast erosion and foreshore. In any event, he advocated that action should be postponed until a decision was taken on the proposals that were then being discussed for departmental responsibility for the foreshore to be transferred; Jenkins

[76] Jenkins became permanent secretary at the Ministry of Transport in 1947; G. Wardale, 'Jenkins, Sir (Thomas) Gilmour (1894–1981)', in *Oxford Dictionary of National Biography*, Oxford University Press, available at <http://www.oxforddnb.com/view/article/66858> (last accessed 25 October 2017).

agreed and decided that further consideration of the issue should be decided by the department that became responsible.[77] As we shall see in Chapter 9, the Commissioners of Crown Lands took responsibility for the foreshore on an agency basis in April 1947[78] and they consulted T. Menzies McNeil, the Solicitor in Scotland to the Commissioners, on the issue. After analysing the background to the proposal and, in particular, the history of the ownership of the foreshore and the prescriptive period in Scotland, McNeil concluded that

> it is difficult to find any conclusive argument in favour of an extension now to 60 years ... Any attempt to extend the period to 60 years in Scotland would, in our opinion, raise very substantial and powerful opposition ... [to extend the period would be] inappropriate and uncalled for ... the Commission would not be well advised to press for the extension of the prescriptive period to 60 years.[79]

This advice, of course, was consistent with the advice from the Law Officers given in 1924. The Commissioners of Crown Lands decided not to press for the extension:

> In view of the Scottish Solicitor's opinion the question of the extension of the prescriptive period in Scotland should be shelved indefinitely. It should be borne in mind, however, in case an opportunity occurs at some time in the future to introduce it into legislation affecting land in Scotland generally.[80]

A Coast Protection Act was eventually passed in 1949 and under section 37 of the Act the management of the foreshore was, as we shall see in Chapter 9, formally transferred to the Commissioners of Crown Lands. But, while Clark's draft memorandum had suggested considering the proposals in the context of future legislation relating to coast erosion and the foreshore and the Commissioners of Crown Lands had not ruled out a reconsideration of the issue if a suitable legislative opportunity presented itself, there was no mention in the Act of the extension of the prescriptive period or of the seaware clause.

[77] TNA:PRO, BT 297/943, Minutes, 14 May 1945, 23 January 1946. Clark's draft memorandum is attached to these minutes.

[78] PD, Fifth Series, vol. 436, House of Commons Written Answers, col. 150 (25 April 1947). The Commissioners of Crown Lands were the successors to the Commissioners for Woods and Forests; see Chapter 9.

[79] NRS, CR 11/1553, Letter McNeil to Office of Commissioners of Crown Lands, 13 September 1947.

[80] NRS, CR 11/1553, Minute, 15 October 1947.

## CONCLUSIONS

We have seen how concerns over the ramifications of the Agnew case and the extent to which the Scottish foreshore had fallen into private ownership had led, at the beginning of the twentieth century, to proposals to change the law, and we might conclude that the battle the Crown had lost with the decision in the Agnew case in 1873 had, in effect, turned into the loss of the war with the final rejection of the proposals to legislate to extend the prescriptive period and to deny title to Scotland's foreshore being obtained by possession through the letting, selling or taking of seaweed. By 1947 the Crown appears to have accepted that there was little point in trying to lock the stable door, perhaps accepting the words of the Scottish jurist John Rankine that 'similar titles and similar possession [as in the Agnew case] could be produced for almost every yard of foreshore in Scotland',[81] and of the Solicitor to the Commissioners of Crown Lands that

> Most of the foreshores of Scotland have been included in express grants by the Crown or in claims by adjoining proprietors admitted by the Crown. Consequently it would seem that what remains in the Crown cannot be of great extent.[82]

The horse had well and truly bolted.

[81] Rankine, *Ownership of Lands* (4th edn), p. 276.

[82] NRS, CR 11/1553, Letter McNeil to Commissioners of Crown Lands, 13 September 1947, p. 4.

# 7

# 'The proposals amount to the most bare-faced confiscation'

## INTRODUCTION

As previous chapters have shown, the collection of seaware from the foreshore was a critical element in the battle over the ownership of the foreshore. The early litigation about the foreshore from the end of the seventeenth century through the eighteenth century had, indeed, mostly been about disputes over the right to collect seaware from the shores, and in the nineteenth century the collection of seaware was probably the most important element in proving the possession that determined ownership in the absence of a grant in the cases that finally determined the question of ownership of the foreshore. As we noted in Chapter 1 and as we see in Chapter 8 in the case study of the island of Tiree, the use by crofters and cottars of the foreshore and their collection of seaware from it played an important role in the battle over the ownership of the foreshore. Running alongside the importance of the collection of seaware for the determination of ownership of the foreshore is the question of what rights, if any, crofters and cottars had to collect seaware from the foreshore. We saw in Chapter 1 how crofters believed they had a customary right to seaware and we examine in this chapter the Napier Commission recommendations as to seaware and the debate in the House of Commons that gave rise to provisions being included in the Crofters Holdings (Scotland) Act 1886 that regulated the collection of seaweed by crofters for the use of their crofts. We also look at proposals in 1891 for legislation that would have given crofters (and others) substantive rights to seaware, and at the position taken by the Association of Seaboard Proprietors of Scotland over this proposed legislation. There is a further discussion in Chapter 9 of crofters' rights to seaware in the context of the review of the law of the foreshore by the Scottish Law Commission in 2003.

## SEAWARE, THE FORESHORE AND THE CROFTERS HOLDINGS (SCOTLAND) ACT 1886

In its report on the conditions of crofters and cottars in the Highlands and islands, the Napier Commission had recommended that

> the township should possess the right, in case of necessity, of cutting and gathering sea-ware without payment on the shores of lands belonging to the proprietor and occupied by him or his tenant adjacent to the township, or conveniently situated, for use of the township, full provision having first been made for the service of the lands on which the privilege is exercised. In the case of existing leases this privilege should not be enforced, but all future leases should be contracted subject to such a claim on the part of the townships.[1]

This recommendation gave limited recognition to the communal and customary rights to, and division of, seaware that, as we saw in Chapter 1, had existed in Gaelic Scotland up to the beginning of the eighteenth century and had continued in the minds of the crofters late into the nineteenth century. It was, however, a recommendation in special circumstances and did not acknowledge that the communal arrangements had amounted to a right as such; and while the Napier Commission had noted the 'impression indigenous to the country' that the crofters had 'inherited an inalienable title to security of tenure in their possessions', the Commission had said this had never been legally recognised and that the proprietors had long repudiated it by their actions.[2] And indeed no provision dealing with the recommendation had been included in the Bill.[3] Proposals to include a provision relating to seaware were, however, debated in committee in April 1886. Leonard Lyell, the Member of Parliament for Orkney and Shetland, proposed the inclusion of a clause giving to crofters the right, where the croft was contiguous to the foreshore, to cut and to gather seaware for the use of the croft. Sir Herbert Maxwell, the Member of Parliament for Wigton, wondered if any provision was required because he understood that under 'the law of Scotland, there is no property at all in seaweed'. At this, the Lord Advocate, J. B. Balfour, said:

> I think the Committee ought to be made aware of the exact manner in which the law stands. According to the law of Scotland, where a landlord has an

[1] Napier Report XXXII, p. 23.

[2] Napier Report XXXII, p. 8.

[3] PP, 1886, Bills and Acts, Bill to amend Law relating to Tenure of Land by Crofters, Bill Number 118.

> express grant of sea ware, or, without such an express grant, has exercised an exclusive enjoyment of it for 40 years, the property in it is his.[4]

Otherwise it would belong to the Crown. The Lord Advocate suggested that there might be a distinction, however, as between drift seaware and growing seaware. He believed it was necessary to include a provision 'to meet the case of the landlord who now possesses the absolute right in the sea ware' because 'the use of sea ware, in many places, is absolutely essential to the cultivation of the croft'.[5] We might, therefore, have expected that the Lord Advocate would approve of the inclusion of a substantive right to seaware, but he preferred the suggestion of Dr R. Macdonald, the Member of Parliament for Ross-shire,[6] which would give to the Land Commission the ability to draw up a scheme for regulating the use by crofters of seaware and that charges for this use should be included in the croft rent.[7] While Macdonald's suggestion was limited in scope, it nonetheless gave rise to a number of Members of Parliament voicing their concerns on behalf of the proprietors of Highland estates as to the potential damage it would do to the economic interests of these proprietors in the foreshore. John Ramsay, the Member of Parliament for Falkirk, was concerned that such a clause would deprive proprietors 'of that which, in many instances, brings him a considerable revenue' and he wanted to know 'if the Committee are to understand that the Government are contemplating the desirability of taking from the landlords this source of revenue and giving it to those who never enjoyed any right of ownership?'[8] Lyell's original proposal would not have allowed crofters to cut or gather seaware for the purposes of kelp manufacture, the right that he proposed being limited to the use of seaware for the croft, but alarm bells were ringing that the proprietors could be threatened by the proposal. Other members drew attention to the value of seaware for the purposes of kelp and were concerned that proprietors may have a valuable asset taken away from them. The Lord Advocate suggested that, to meet this concern, there should be a provision to make it clear that the Land Commission scheme should permit crofters to take seaware only to the extent that

[4] PD, Third Series, vol. 304, House of Commons, col. 927 (6 April 1886). The Lord Advocate, J. B. Balfour, was later Lord President from 1899 to 1905.

[5] PD, Third Series, vol. 304, House of Commons, col. 927 (6 April 1886).

[6] Lyell himself had, in fact, been happy not to press for his own wording but to accept Macdonald's amendment.

[7] PD, Third Series, vol. 304, House of Commons, cols 926–8 (6 April 1886).

[8] PD, Third Series, vol. 304, House of Commons, col. 928 (6 April 1886).

was reasonable under the circumstances, and he further suggested that the scheme should relate only to crofters whose crofts were contiguous to the foreshore. At this proposal, Hansard noted cries of 'No', and the Lord Advocate, in response, said: 'I think that we ought not to give rights which do not at present exist to persons whose holdings are at a considerable distance from the seashore.'[9] The Lord Advocate advised further limitations on the provision so that only crofters on the same estate should be allowed to be party to the scheme. But even this did not go far enough for the members who were concerned that proprietors might suffer in the context of the kelp industry. Ramsay said that, without expressly providing that the scheme should be limited to the gathering of seaware for the purpose of manuring the croft, the crofters would be able to use the seaware for the manufacture of kelp, particularly if, as he said, kelp again became a valuable commodity. The Lord Advocate did not believe such a restriction was necessary because, he said, 'Surely there can be no idea that the crofters will set up any large business for the manufacture of kelp.'[10] In the event however, in the face of the pressure from Members of Parliament on behalf of the proprietors, a specific provision was included to restrict the use by crofters of seaweed gathered under the Land Commission scheme to the reasonable purpose of their croft; in other words for agriculture and not for kelp manufacture. The section finally included in the 1886 Act provided:

> It shall be competent for the Crofters Commission to draw up a scheme regulating the use by crofters on the same estate of seaweed for the reasonable purposes of their holdings . . . and to include the charge for all these in the fixed rent.[11]

It is important to understand that this provision in the 1886 Act did not give to crofters a substantive right to gather seaware. There was acceptance that

> A crofter could acquire rights to gather seaweed from his landlord only by way of a grant under his lease, and that such a right could not be acquired through prescription or any other method in the absence of such a grant.[12]

It was recognised by the Court of Session in 1896 that crofters may have such a right as a pertinent of their crofts if they could show they had

[9] PD, Third Series, vol. 304, House of Commons, col. 933 (6 April 1886).

[10] PD, Third Series, vol. 304, House of Commons, cols 938, 940 (6 April 1886).

[11] Crofters Holdings (Scotland) Act 1886, section 12. The Land Commission spoken of in the Bill was named the Crofters Commission in the Act.

[12] SLC Discussion Paper, para. 6.6.

collected seaware over a long period.[13] The substantive rights of crofters in relation to seaware after the 1886 Act was passed were, therefore, no greater than they had been before the Act was passed other than, to the extent they could show a pertinent right to seaweed, that right became part of the security of tenure of the croft under the 1886 Act, and the Act did provide an administrative power for ensuring seaware was properly shared out amongst a township's crofters.[14] In respect of the foreshore itself, the 1886 Act excluded any possibility that the foreshore could be part of the croft by defining a holding as consisting of arable and pasture land; there is also some doubt that the foreshore can be part of the common grazings.[15]

## THE SEA WARE (CROFTING COUNTIES, SCOTLAND) BILL

The passing of the 1886 Crofters Act did not bring tranquillity to the Highlands and islands but rather a series of encounters between the crofting community, proprietors and the forces of law and order, which have been characterised as more bitter and more violent than those that had given rise to the appointment of the Napier Commission.[16] And in South Uist and Barra there was marked crofter and cottar agitation, unrest and public disturbances.[17] It was this general state

[13] Macdonald v. Macdougall (1896) 23 R 941; Sir C. Agnew, *Crofting Law* (Edinburgh, 2000), pp. 11–13; see also Mackinnon v. Macdonald (1905) 7 F 589, a dispute as between crofters over entitlements to collect seaware in which Lord Kyllachy questioned whether the pertinental privileges of collecting seaware were of the nature of legal rights or were rather privileges held at the landlord's pleasure and subject to estate regulations; and the early case of Campbell v. Campbell (1795) Mor. 9646 where the question was whether an entitlement to take and burn seaweed was implied in a lease. The right of crofters to take seaweed for agricultural purposes was considered in John MacInnes v. Hamilton & Kinntail Estates Ltd and Alginate Industries Ltd (1959) SLCR App 79 and (1960) SLCR App 79, and the Scottish Land Court Report as to Proceedings, 1959, Cmnd 1038 at pp. 19–20, and 1960, Cmnd 1382 at p. 20; the Land Court held that the pertinental right to have seaweed for manurial purposes of the crofts was not an exclusive right to the whole seaweed of the areas but was a right only to take what the crofters required for their crofts and was a right which had to be exercised *civiliter*, i.e. 'in a reasonable fashion'.

[14] A power that could not be used to alter or restrict any rights there may be; Agnew, *Crofting Law*, pp. 42, 151.

[15] Agnew, *Crofting Law*, p. 8, but cf. SLC Discussion Paper, para. 6.2 that suggests that it is possible for the foreshore to be included in the croft; the basis for this is not explained.

[16] Hunter, *Making of the Crofting Community*, p. 164.

[17] See, for example, NRS, HH 1/713, Report of Skene Edwards & Bilton to the Marquis of Lothian, 4 February 1888.

of affairs, and specifically a claim made in 1890 by the South Uist crofters that Lady Gordon Cathcart had no legal right to the drift seaware cast up on the shores of the island, that was the genesis of the Sea Ware Bill.[18] The crofters had been dissatisfied with the price the estate had paid for the kelp the crofters manufactured from the drift seaware and asked Charles Fraser Mackintosh, the Member of Parliament for Inverness-shire, to find out whether they were bound by contract to sell the kelp they manufactured to the estate. Fraser Mackintosh asked the Lord Advocate in a parliamentary question in March 1890:

> whether he is aware that the crofters on the South Uist estates are by their contracts compelled to sell all their kelp to the proprietrix . . . and whether such contract is by the Law of Scotland obligatory on the people; and, if so, whether he will introduce a measure providing absolute freedom of sale of the products of sea and land?[19]

The Lord Advocate responded that he was informed no such contract did exist.[20] It is interesting to note that, in answering this question, the Lord Advocate relied heavily, if not exclusively, on a report by Skene Edwards & Garson. We last came across the firm in Chapter 5 under its then name of Skene & Peacock and then as Skene Webster & Peacock,[21] as the law agents for the Association of Seaboard Proprietors of Scotland. In this chapter we will find the firm acting as the law agents for Lady Gordon Cathcart and, still, the Association. During the period 1860–91 the firm had been developing its reputation and contacts with the proprietors of large estates in the Highlands and islands and, through this work, with government departments, including, of course, the Lord Advocate.[22] The Lord Advocate's Crown Agent had written to the firm on 12 March with the text of Fraser Mackintosh's questions and 'requested [the firm] to furnish [him] with such informa-

[18] Lady Gordon Cathcart, the owner of South Uist, was the widow of Lt. Col. John Gordon of Cluny; on the death of her husband she had married Sir Reginald Cathcart and took the name Lady Gordon Cathcart; Mackenzie, *History of the Outer Hebrides*, p. 496.

[19] PD, Third Series, vol. 342, House of Commons, col. 988 (17 March 1890).

[20] The Lord Advocate was J. P. B. Robertson, later Lord President in 1891 and a Lord of Appeal in Ordinary in 1899.

[21] And between 1878 and 1890 as Skene Edwards & Bilton.

[22] See Cameron, *Land for the People?*, pp. 44, 92, 149–52, 171, 185 for references to the firm acting for Lady Cathcart and other proprietors on estate and crofting matters, and relationships with the BoAS and Scottish Office.

tion as will enable the Lord Advocate to answer the question'.[23] The Lord Advocate's answer given in the House of Commons on 17 March 1890 was modelled almost exactly on the lines of Skene Edwards & Garson's response, although, interestingly, while the Lord Advocate's answer stated categorically that no such contract existed as had been alleged, Skene Edwards & Garson's letter had not, in terms, denied the existence of such a contract.[24]

Acting on the Lord Advocate's response, the crofters attempted to sell their kelp on the open market but the estate intervened to stop them by serving an action of suspension and interdict on seventeen of the crofters, prohibiting them from removing or disposing of the drift seaware, and the estate also refused to purchase the kelp which they had manufactured.[25] At an open-air public meeting at Daliburgh near Lochboisdale on 16 June 1890, some 500 crofters gathered to discuss the estate moves against them. Fraser Mackintosh chaired the meeting that passed resolutions condemning Lady Gordon Cathcart for insisting that all the kelp the crofters manufactured should be sold through the estate, for indicting the crofters and for refusing to have any further dealings with the crofters on the issue. The meeting also passed a resolution calling for Parliament to be petitioned:

> That this meeting in view of the conduct of the proprietrix of South Uist and officials on her estate of South Uist and Barra is making exactions for the use of the foreshores which hinder the development of the country and stifle important industries, is of opinion that the only practical remedy is the declaration by the legislature of an inalienable public right to the foreshores of the realm for all purposes connected with the prosecution and development of fishings and the collection and utilising of seaware and tangle, as there is now for the purposes of navigation, and that a petition be presented from this meeting to both Houses of Parliament praying for an amendment of the law to this effect.[26]

23 NRS, AF 67/179, Letter Skene, Edwards and Garson to Jamieson, 12 March 1890.

24 NRS, AF 67/179, Letter Skene Edwards & Garson to Jamieson, 12 March 1890.

25 *Scottish Highlander*, 19 June 1890, pp. 2, 4, 6; A. Goodrich-Freer, *Outer Isles* (London, 1902), pp. 164–5. The objectivity of the *Scottish Highlander* edited by Alexander Mackenzie, which was to play a prominent role in reporting the events described in this chapter, might be questioned: it has been described as 'more of a mouthpiece of the [Highland Land Law Reform Association] than a newspaper of record'; Cameron, *Land for the People?*, p. 49. On Alexander Mackenzie, see B. Thomas, '"The Clach": Alexander Mackenzie and the land question in the late-nineteenth century Highlands and islands', *Northern Scotland*, 8 (2017), pp. 68–86.

26 *Scottish Highlander*, 19 June 1890, p. 2.

The mention in the crofters' resolution of the public right to use the foreshore for fishing shows that the concerns over the estate actions were not just about kelp manufacture, but also involved the Barra fishermen. As we see in Chapter 9, fishing was one of the public rights over the foreshore that was firmly acknowledged as existing in the law, and the common law public right was supplemented by statute, notably by the White Herring Fisheries Act 1771 which provided that

> all and every person or persons engaged in [the British white herring fisheries] . . . shall have and exercise the free use of all . . . shores and forelands in Great Britain . . . below the highest water mark, and for the space of one hundred yards on any waste or uncultivated land beyond such mark, within the land, for landing their nets, casks, and other materials . . . and for erecting tents, huts, and stages, and for the landing, pickling, curing, and reloading their fish, and in drying their nets, without paying any foreland or other dues, or any other sum or sums of money, or other consideration whatsoever.[27]

It also provided that any persons obstructing the exercise of these rights would be subject to a penalty of £100.[28] John Seymour Keay, the Member of Parliament for Elginshire, had asked the Lord Advocate in March 1890 whether the 1771 Act was still in force and whether the Lord Advocate was aware that fees were being 'exacted by the landlords on the East and West Coasts of Scotland, and in the islands?' The Lord Advocate had replied that the relevant sections of the Act were still in force and said that if Keay could give specific instances of the alleged charges being made, he would investigate them.[29] Keay wrote to the Lord Advocate telling him that the fishermen of Barra had erected fish-curing buildings on the foreshores, and that the estate was, under the direction of Lady Gordon Cathcart, now claiming rent for these buildings, and asked the Lord Advocate for his views on this issue. In May 1890 he asked the Lord Advocate in Parliament whether he had reached any conclusions on his letter. The Lord Advocate responded that while he had just received information about the cases referred to by Keay, he had not yet had time to consider them.[30] After due consideration, the conclusion of Keay's correspondence with the Lord Advocate was that the Lord Advocate confirmed that 'the 1771 Act was passed to encourage fishermen by providing means whereby they might utilise what was

[27] 11 George 3 c 31, section 11.
[28] 11 George 3 c 31, section 11; Ferguson, *Law of Water*, pp. 551–2.
[29] PD, Third Series, vol. 342, House of Commons, cols 118–19 (6 March 1890).
[30] PD, Third Series, vol. 344, House of Commons, cols 948–9 (15 May 1890).

otherwise useless ground for drying their nets, and upon which they might erect temporary structures for the purpose of fish curing' but that he declined to bring proceedings saying that it was for the aggrieved persons to do so.[31]

Fraser Mackintosh returned to his own attack on Lady Gordon Cathcart in the House of Commons in July 1890. In a question to the Lord Advocate, he summarised the events that had given rise to the 16 June open air meeting, in particular the fact that 'the crofters have been in use to gather for sale the perishable commodity of sea ware called tangles, not only on the shores of their own lands, but also on those of the large farmers without let or hindrance' and that the crofters had 'demanded legislative redress'. He asked the Lord Advocate 'whether he will take steps to legislate for the relief of the people primarily interested, and against the closing of a valuable chemical trade?'[32] The Lord Advocate did not respond to this himself but through one of the Lords of the Treasury, Sir Herbert Maxwell, who gave Fraser Mackintosh little ground for comfort. He told him that

> I am informed that it is not the fact that the crofters have been in use to gather tangle on the shores of South Uist; nor is it the fact that they have sold the tangles to the proprietor. The industry which is comparatively of modern growth, has always been conducted by the proprietor of the foreshore on the island, who pays to those crofters employed to gather the tangles the whole proceeds under deduction of expense of supervision and incidental outgoings, and these crofters are under no obligation to work if they are dissatisfied with the remuneration the proprietor is able to give them . . . My information being that no valuable chemical trade has been closed, and that no change has taken place in the manner of conducting this industry, I am unable to discover any legitimate grievance which calls for remedy by legislation.[33]

Fraser Mackintosh tried again in February 1891 but the Lord Advocate told him that he had no information of exceptional poverty and distress, that the interdicts as to the gathering and sale of seaware for kelp had not had the disastrous consequences Fraser Mackintosh alleged they

[31] Letter Mure to Keay, 27 May 1890, reproduced in *Scottish Highlander*, 3 July 1890, p. 2.

[32] PD, Third Series, vol. 342, House of Commons, col. 329 (21 July 1890); *Scottish Highlander*, 24 July 1890, p. 6.

[33] PD, Third Series, vol. 344, House of Commons, cols 329–30 (21 July 1890); see also *The Scotsman*, 22 July 1890; NRS, AF 67/411, The Uist Report, p. *c*; *Scottish Highlander*, 24 July 1890, p. 6; DVGN 570/8/2, Letter Skene Edwards & Garson to Macleod, 25 April 1891 discussed below.

had, and he repeated that he could find no legitimate grievance calling for remedy by legislation.[34] In the absence of any legislative proposals from government, Fraser Mackintosh prepared his own Bill and on 10 April 1891 the Sea Ware (Crofting Counties, Scotland) Bill was presented to Parliament and had its first reading. It was explicitly modelled on, and referred to, the White Herring Fisheries Act 1771. The preamble to the Bill explained the Bill's purpose:

> Whereas in certain parts of Scotland known as its crofting counties, exceptional legislation has recently been found necessary, in order to alleviate the impoverished condition of many of the people; and whereas permanent and remunerative employment at their doors can be had by utilizing sea ware, at present, and to the value of many thousands per annum, unproductive and allowed to decay, and it is therefore necessary to make certain provisions for encouraging the industry of gathering and manufacturing sea ware.[35]

The *Scottish Highlander* was, as might have been expected, characteristically clear in its view of the effect this Bill would have:

> If the Bill becomes law, as we have every reason to believe it may, Lady Cathcart and her advisers will have no small cause to rue their recent conduct towards the industrious crofters of South Uist and Barra . . . The circumstances should also prove a salutary lesson to other northern proprietors . . . Their grasping instincts in connection with the foreshores and the appropriation of the salmon and trout in our seas and rivers, and all the birds fit for food in the heavens above, will, unless they hold their hand, very soon bring about a revolution and set all the fish in the sea and the fowls of the air, as well as tangles and seaware, free for the use of the people.[36]

The Members of Parliament shown as being supporters of the Bill were Joseph Chamberlain; Dr Charles Cameron, the Member of Parliament for Glasgow College and a supporter of land law reform; Colonel John Malcolm of Poltalloch, the Member of Parliament for Argyllshire and a member of the committee of the Association of Seaboard Proprietors of Scotland; Dr Roderick Macdonald, the Member of Parliament for Ross and Cromarty; and James Caldwell, the Member of Parliament for Glasgow St Rollox.

The 1891 Bill gave to the public, and not just to crofters, the substantive right to collect seaware and, more importantly, the right to do so

[34] PD, Third Series, vol. 350, House of Commons, cols 1346–7 (23 February 1891).

[35] PP, 1890–1, Bills and Acts, Sea-Ware Bill, Bill Number 274.

[36] *Scottish Highlander*, 16 April 1891, p. 4; 23 April 1891, p. 5.

not just for agricultural purposes, but also for kelp manufacture.[37] The Bill extended the rights that fishermen had to use the foreshore and land above the high water mark without payment or obstruction, to crofters and the public generally to collect, dry and manufacture seaware on the foreshore. The Bill provided, in clause 2, that the 'right to gather, manufacture, use, and dispose of all sea ware of every description, whether drift or fixed, on the sea coasts of the crofting counties of Scotland . . . is and shall be, open and free to the public' and, rather confusingly, provided in clauses 3–6 that people who wanted to manufacture seaware should obtain a licence from the clerk of the relevant county on payment of a fee of one shilling; gave to all licence holders access to the foreshores and to a distance of 100 yards above the high water mark, for the purposes of the Bill in the same way, and to the same extent, as was provided in the 1771 Act; and required county councils to produce such bye-laws as may be required 'for the nurture of fixed ware, for the preservation of amenity, and the maintenance of good neighbourhood and order'. Any person interfering with a licence holder in the exercise of his rights was to be liable to a fine of £5 for each offence.[38]

We saw in Chapter 5 that the Association of Seaboard Proprietors of Scotland had remained in existence to help proprietors in disputes with the Crown over foreshore questions and generally to protect proprietors' interests in and to the foreshore notwithstanding that, with the decision in the Agnew case, the principal purpose of the Association had been achieved; indeed, it was only in 1952 that the Association was finally wound up, as we note in the final section of this chapter. The Association reacted swiftly to the threat that the 1891 Bill posed to the economic interest of proprietors in the foreshore. The secretary, Norman Macleod of Macleod, now retired from the civil service and living in Paris, wrote in April 1891 to the Secretary for Scotland, the Marquis of Lothian, to draw his attention to the Bill. Macleod told Lothian that if the kelp industry was ever to be revived, the manufacture of kelp would, as in the past, be reserved to the estate proprietors and 'there is no apparent reason for transferring this property that would not equally apply to the grass of the adjoining estate'. Macleod also told Lothian that the Bill's proposals for county councils to regulate access to the foreshore were ill conceived. In a barbed reference to the effects

[37] As we see in Chapter 9, the right to collect seaware from the foreshore was not one of the common law public rights over the foreshore.

[38] PP, 1890–1, Bills and Acts, Sea-Ware Bill, Bill Number 274. The Bill gave, in clause 4, an incorrect citation to the 1771 Act.

of the 1886 Crofters Act and the creation of the Crofters Commission, Macleod told Lothian that 'The experience of the last year or two shows that good neighbourhood and order are not promoted by depriving the proprietor of all power, and transferring it to distant authorities.'[39] Macleod also wrote to the Dukes of Argyll and Richmond and to the Lord Advocate, and to Skene Edwards & Garson asking for the firm's advice on the Bill.

Skene Edwards & Garson – who were also the law agents to Lady Gordon Cathcart and, therefore, had a particular interest in the Bill from her standpoint, not to mention the other estate proprietors for whom they acted – responded at length on 21 April and gave their first thoughts on the Bill: 'After the money that has been spent and the trouble that has been taken by yourself and other seaboard proprietors in vindicating a right to the foreshores it is certainly disappointing to find the question again raised by the Bill.' The firm took exception to the preamble to the Bill, believing it to be a 'complete misstatement of the case'. They were concerned that the right of county councils to make bye-laws would give them 'the right to cultivate seaware on the foreshores of any estate in the crofting counties'.[40] Overall, Skene Edwards & Garson considered that

> the proposals contained in the Bill amount to the most bare-faced confiscation. We agree with you that the Foreshore Association should use all of its influence to prevent such a measure from becoming law, and we are pleased to observe that you have already written to the Dukes of Argyll and Richmond, Lord Lothian and the Lord Advocate. We have received a letter from the Lord Advocate in which he mentions having heard from you and asks us to put before him any facts which we think he ought to be informed of.[41]

Skene Edwards & Garson told Macleod that they were surprised that Chamberlain, Caldwell and, in particular, Colonel Malcolm of Poltalloch who had been a member of the committee of the Association, were named as supporters of the Bill and said: 'we feel confident that Colonel Malcolm has allowed his name to be put on the back of the Bill under some misapprehension as to its contents'.[42] As to immediate action, Skene Edwards & Garson told Macleod that they had already contacted Martin & Leslie who were specialist parliamentary agents and who had recommended:

[39] NRS, GD 40/16/51, Letter Macleod to Lothian, 15 April 1891.
[40] DVGN 570/8/1, Letter Skene Edwards & Garson to Macleod, 21 April 1891.
[41] DVGN 570/8/1, Letter Skene Edwards & Garson to Macleod, 21 April 1891.
[42] DVGN 570/8/1, Letter Skene Edwards & Garson to Macleod, 21 April 1891.

> that notice of opposition on the second reading should be at once given. It will also be necessary that a statement should be prepared for the Government showing cause why the Bill should not be allowed to pass, and we think the statement should be printed and circulated among those Members of Parliament who are likely to vote against the Bill. We shall at once put in hand the preparation of the necessary statement which we shall submit to you.[43]

Edwards and Garson then commenced a considerable programme of work over the next sixty days to ensure that the Bill did not receive a second reading.[44] On 24 April 1891 Edwards had a meeting with one of the Orkney seaboard proprietors and explained to him the effect the Bill would have on seaboard proprietors in that county.[45] He then had a meeting in London on 25 April with Martin & Leslie, to discuss with them the necessary parliamentary steps to oppose the Bill. On the same day, Edwards met with Colonel Malcolm of Poltalloch who told him that he had not been aware of the provisions of the Bill when he permitted his name to be printed as a supporter and he told Edwards that he had given notice of a motion to oppose the second reading of the Bill. Edwards concluded the day in London by making arrangements to inform Members of Parliament generally of the provisions of the Bill and to secure their votes against the Bill on a second reading. On 30 April 1891 Edwards met with Sir John Orde, the proprietor of North Uist and a member of the Association, and explained the provisions of the Bill to him and the steps that were being taken to oppose it. Orde would, of course, have had a particular interest in the Bill given his ownership of North Uist and the fact that he had let the North Uist foreshores for the purposes of kelp manufacture to the British Seaweed Company. Garson travelled to London and, on 11 May 1891, spent

43 DVGN 570/8/1, Letter Skene Edwards & Garson to Macleod, 21 April 1891.

44 The following detail of Edwards' and Garson's programme of work is derived from the business account of Skene Edwards & Garson for 1891 sent to the Association of Seaboard Proprietors of Scotland, at DVGN 544/3–12.

45 In fact, the Orkney proprietors were well aware of the issues that the Bill presented and one of the proprietors, Andrew Gold of Kirkwall, had already written to the Earl of Zetland on the subject. Gold suggested to Zetland that whereas the other Highland proprietors may not have cause for complaint over the Bill, the Orkney proprietors should have particular protection. The Earl of Zetland wrote to the Secretary for Scotland: 'May I ask you to cast your eye over the enclosed [Bill] which seems a serious matter and a very unfair proposal as far as the Orkney proprietors are concerned. Would it be possible to get Orkney excluded from the Bill?'; NRS, GD 40/16/51, Letter Gold to Zetland, 22 April 1891; Letter Zetland to Lothian, 27 April 1891.

the day at Dover House with members of the Scottish Office, including the Lord Advocate, discussing the Bill and the contents of the draft memorandum on the Bill that his firm was to submit, on behalf of the Association, to government. An exchange of notes between the assistant under secretary for Scotland, William Dunbar, and the Lord Advocate's legal secretary, William Mure, suggest that in his discussions on the Bill at Dover House, Garson may have been pushing at an open door; in his response to Fraser Mackintosh's question in February 1891, the Lord Advocate had made it clear that he saw no need for legislation, and his legal secretary Mure wrote in a note to Dunbar that he presumed that the Bill 'will not be allowed to pass'. Dunbar's response, in red ink, was unequivocal: 'This Bill cannot be accepted.'[46] The draft memorandum was finalised on 20 May and was printed. On 25 May Skene Edwards & Garson wrote to the Lord Advocate and a number of proprietors, including Colonel Malcolm of Poltalloch, sending them a copy of the memorandum, and a copy was also sent to the Scottish Office. Edwards undertook to travel again to London to influence Members of Parliament to vote against the Bill on a second reading. At the same time as providing a memorandum on behalf of the Association, Garson was also engaged in drafting a memorandum on the Bill on behalf of Lady Gordon Cathcart, dealing with the specific South Uist and Barra aspects.

The memorandum written by Skene Edwards & Garson on behalf of the Association made two principle points. The first was that the Bill's proposals amounted to an unjust expropriation of, and interference with, private property without compensation. So far as the foreshore was concerned, the memorandum stated that under the auspices of the Association, a number of cases had been tried in the Court of Session and the House of Lords 'which have had the effect of setting the Law of Scotland as regards Foreshore rights on a clear footing' and 'the result of the action of the Foreshore Association has been to establish the seaboard proprietors' right of property in the foreshore of their estates, subject always to certain recognised and definite public uses, such as navigation and the like'.[47] The memorandum also said that 'in all cases

[46] NRS, AF 67/179, Exchange of minutes, 24 April 1891.

[47] NRS, AF 67/179, Memorandum for the Foreshore Association of Seaboard Proprietors in Scotland with reference to the 'Seaware (Crofting Counties, Scotland) Bill 1891', May 1891 [hereafter Association Memorandum], p. 2. The leading cases cited which the Association had brought were the Maclean of Ardgour, Agnew, Blantyre (although as we noted in Chapter 5, the Association had, in fact, declined to take up Blantyre's case) and Buchanan cases discussed in Chapters 2 and 5. As

seaware has been recognized to be the property of the landowner' and that this had 'long been clearly settled in the law of Scotland'.[48] The memorandum then stated that the manufacture of kelp had, in the past, been an important industry in Scotland and that the

> manufacture was invariably in the hands of the proprietors ... [and] ... This was a recognised element in the value of estates, and many transactions, both of purchase and loan, have taken place on the faith of the proprietors' right to the kelp.[49]

If the kelp industry was ever to become valuable again, the proposal in the Bill that the public should have free access to the seaware

> without compensating proprietors or tenants ... [was] ... a proposal altogether without precedent, which, if passed, would operate most unfairly and injuriously against proprietors and tenants. The proposal is not justified by the facts, and is without warrant either in justice or expediency.[50]

The proposals in the Bill, the memorandum said, would not be limited to an interference with the rights of property to the foreshores but to 'a zone of land extending inland 100 yards from high water mark'. The value of grazing land adjacent to the foreshore would be seriously affected and 'the stock would be continually disturbed, and the pretence of collecting ware could always be used by unauthorised persons of all kinds to justify their presence on land where they have no right to be'.[51] The extension to 100 yards inland was the result of the Bill applying the 1771 Act to the right to collect seaware, and was a point that had been made to Lady Matheson, the proprietor of the island of Lewis. In a letter that was also seen by the Scottish Office, Lady Matheson was told:

far as the foreshore of South Uist was concerned, Lady Cathcart had established in 1879 to the satisfaction of the Board that the foreshore was owned by her, a fact which was noted in the memorandum on the Bill drafted on her behalf by Skene Edwards & Garson.

[48] The Association Memorandum cited as authority for this Paterson v. Marquis of Ailsa (1846) 8 D 752 and Pirie v. Rose (1884) 11 R 490, a case that was also cited in an opinion of the Lord Advocate (J. B. Balfour) in 1895 where he said: 'It has been decided that a proprietor whose lands are *de facto* bounded by the sea even although he may have no express grant of the foreshore is entitled to prevent persons from taking seaware from the foreshore unless those persons can show that they have acquired a right to take the seaware by grant or by prescription referable to some title to land'; NRS, AF 67/179, Association Memorandum.

[49] NRS, AF 67/179, Association Memorandum, p. 2.

[50] NRS, AF 67/179, Association Memorandum, p. 3.

[51] NRS, AF 67/179, Association Memorandum, p. 3.

> if this old Act is to be made applicable to the crofters, and the taking of seaware, it will greatly injure your shootings and Deer Forests. The crofters will squat along the shores of Park, Athline, Morsgail and other places, under the pretence of collecting and manufacturing seaware but really and truly for poaching and annoying the Shooting Tenants and disturbing the game.[52]

The second point made by the Association Memorandum arose out of the way in which Fraser Mackintosh had drafted the Bill. While the dispute that had given rise to the Bill concerned the crofters of South Uist, the Bill's proposals were not limited to crofters or cottars, but gave rights to the public at large. This approach left open a door which allowed another attack on the Bill, and one, moreover, which did not depend on arguing the case for the protection of private property or arguing that proprietors were disadvantaged. It allowed the Bill's opponents to argue that, far from benefiting the crofters as, no doubt, was the intention, the Bill would in reality act to their disadvantage. This was a door through which Skene Edwards & Garson were, not surprisingly, happy to go. The Bill, the memorandum stated, would disadvantage the crofters for three reasons. First, the crofters would be deprived of the seaware they needed for manurial purposes. Second, their crofts would suffer through the free access afforded to the public. Third, the crofters would be deprived of the benefit they currently had from being employed in the kelp industry. Worse still, the memorandum argued, if it was a correct principle that the impoverished people of the crofting counties should have the benefit of free access to the foreshore and seaware, then why should this benefit not be extended to the impoverished people of the whole country? And if this were so, the proprietors and tenants of several million acres would suffer serious loss without compensation. The memorandum concluded that 'The Bill is framed in ignorance of the facts, in total disregard of the rights of proprietors and tenants alike, and in violation of all principles, political and economical, applicable to the circumstances.'[53]

Skene Edwards & Garson took exception to the statements already made by Fraser Mackintosh and others, including the *Scottish Highlander*, about the actions of their client Lady Gordon Cathcart and her estate officials in South Uist; statements which the firm believed were grossly untrue. They were also concerned about the implications the Bill would have for her estates in South Uist and Barra, and about

[52] NRS, AF 67/179, Letter Mackay to Matheson, 16 April 1891.
[53] NRS, AF 67/179, Association Memorandum, pp. 3, 4.

the kind of statements Fraser Mackintosh would be likely to make about her estate management in Parliament on the second reading of the Bill. Macleod had sent Skene Edwards & Garson copies of a leading article in the *Scottish Highlander* of 16 April 1891, in which, under the heading 'Estate oppression in South Uist and its lessons', Lady Gordon Cathcart and her estate officials were accused of practically destroying the profitable kelp industry on South Uist. The effect of the interdicts obtained against the crofters had, the *Scottish Highlander* said, been to debar the crofters from utilising the drift seaware as in previous years. But worse was the fact that, the *Scottish Highlander* alleged,

> the estate officials closed all other markets against [the crofters] and at the same time refused to take the manufactured material off their hands, as they were in the habit of doing in the past, with the result that, at the present moment, there are thousands of pounds worth, made ready for the market after great trouble and labour, rotting on the sea shore or at the roadside.[54]

Skene Edwards & Garson took some trouble to put the estate position in a letter to Macleod. They explained that although

> We have so often been made the subject of attack in [the *Scottish Highlander*] that we no longer take any notice of what they write, the more especially as we believe nobody reads the paper . . . we have considered it due to Lady Cathcart as well as to you to give this explanation although you very generously state that you do not believe a word of the statements made against Lady Cathcart's administration.[55]

The account given by Skene Edwards & Garson to Macleod was rather different from that given by Fraser Mackintosh and the *Scottish Highlander*. Far from destroying the kelp industry in South Uist, the firm said, Lady Gordon Cathcart had in fact rescued it, and the people of South Uist had benefited because she had allowed to the people engaged in the industry all the proceeds of sale less a small deduction for expenses. The proceeds of the sale of kelp were paid by the estate through the estate factor who deducted the croft rent and paid the balance to the crofters. While this may well have been sound economics on the part of the estate, and there are arguments that it was to the benefit of the crofters because it prevented them falling too far behind in the payment of rent, it is an interesting example of the controls exerted by the estate over the lives of the crofters and it was a practice that was not appreciated by the crofters. However, it was the view of

[54] *Scottish Highlander*, 16 April 1891, p. 4.

[55] DVGN 570/8/2, Letter Skene Edwards & Garson to Macleod, 25 April 1891.

Skene Edwards & Garson that the problems in South Uist had arisen, not out of general discontent on the part of the crofters, but as a result of 'Several local agitators . . . who have been trying to induce the people to pay no rent.'[56] These agitators, they said,

> were very much outraged at the idea that the proceeds of the kelp passed through the Factor's hands and a few years ago a cottar who is a leading agitator among them informed the people that he would undertake the manufacture of kelp and the gathering of tangles on his own account. We understand he informed the people that Mr Fraser Mackintosh and other politicians were to back him . . . A number of the people acted on his advice and exercised all the rights proposed by Mr Fraser Mackintosh's Bill to be conferred on the public.[57]

Skene Edwards & Garson explained that the crofters had gone onto the foreshore of one of the farms, miles from their own township, and cut trenches in the machair and brought their horses and dogs among the farmer's stock. The damage to the machair was something that the estate had found particularly reprehensible given the importance of the machair to South Uist. In the circumstances, the firm's letter said, 'it became imperatively necessary for the protection of the estate that Lady Cathcart should take proceedings' and so the interdicts were brought in the Court of Session.[58] The estate succeeded in the interdicts and Skene Edwards & Garson went on to explain why the estate had found it necessary to prevent the crofters from marketing the kelp. The estate could not be seen to have been defeated by the crofters, and the whole issue on behalf of the crofters was politically driven:

> Lady Cathcart waived her claim against the crofters for expenses and they asked that they should be allowed to remove the tangles they had illegally gathered and placed on the farms. It was however thought that if they were allowed to carry away the tangles and dispose of them this would be represented by the agitators, and would be believed by the people, to be the practical defeat of the proprietor on an important question and Lady Cathcart therefore decided that the people should not be allowed to remove the tangles. Mr Fraser Mackintosh and others thereupon got up an outcry that thousands of pounds worth of tangles were left rotting on the ground. The writer visited the ground about the time of the proceedings and instead of there being thousands of pounds worth there certainly was not more than £50 worth of tangles . . . So far as Lady Cathcart's estates were concerned

[56] DVGN 570/8/2, Letter Skene Edwards & Garson to Macleod, 25 April 1891.
[57] DVGN 570/8/2, Letter Skene Edwards & Garson to Macleod, 25 April 1891.
[58] DVGN 570/8/2, Letter Skene Edwards & Garson to Macleod, 25 April 1891.

> this whole business is entirely political. The people are treated with the greatest liberality and if agitators would only leave them alone matters would soon be tranquil in the Islands.[59]

In addition to the letter to Macleod, which was written so that he should not be misled by what Fraser Mackintosh had said or might in the future say, Skene Edwards & Garson also strove to ensure that the Scottish Office and the Lord Advocate should be under no misapprehension as to the effects the Bill would have for Lady Gordon Cathcart's estates in South Uist and Barra, and to ensure that the Scottish Office and the Lord Advocate were clear that the facts given by the firm to enable the Lord Advocate to reply to Fraser Mackintosh's parliamentary questions remained as they were when the replies had been given. The memorandum that the firm drafted on behalf of Lady Gordon Cathcart was, accordingly, directed at these issues, and copies were sent to the Lord Advocate and the Scottish Office.[60] As to the effects the Bill would have in South Uist and Barra, the memorandum pursued the line that one of the principal effects of the Bill would be that the crofters would suffer. The memorandum made it clear that Lady Gordon Cathcart accepted that the crofters had a pertinent right to seaweed for the purposes of manure and that the fair rents for their crofts had been fixed on the assumption that the crofters had this right. To give 'to the public without compensation the right to all the seaware on the crofts might be materially to affect holdings for which fair rents have been fixed under the [1886] Act'.[61] Furthermore, if the public had free access to the foreshores of South Uist and Barra, a large acreage of machair and adjoining pasture would be damaged: 'On a modest computation . . . the effect of the Bill would be to throw open to the public some 30,000 acres of ground without any compensation to either proprietors or tenants.' Finally, if the kelp industry was to be revived, 'it would be altogether unjust and unworkable to deprive the proprietors and the crofters, who have shared the benefit of the manufacture in the past, of the prospects of its continuance in the future'.[62] As to the comments made by Fraser Mackintosh over the administration of the estates of South Uist and Barra, the Estate Memorandum reprinted all of Fraser Mackintosh's

[59] DVGN 570/8/2, Letter Skene Edwards & Garson to Macleod, 25 April 1891.

[60] NRS, AF 67/179, Skene Edwards and Garson to Under Secretary for Scotland, 27 May 1891.

[61] NRS, AF 67/179, Memorandum for Lady Cathcart with reference to the 'Seaware (Crofting Counties, Scotland) Bill 1891' [hereafter Estate Memorandum], p. 4.

[62] NRS, AF 67/179, Estate Memorandum, p. 5.

parliamentary questions and the answers given by the Lord Advocate and stated that 'the facts remain as they were when the replies above quoted were given and nothing has taken place in South Uist to justify the statement in the preamble of Mr Fraser Mackintosh's Bill'.[63] The Estate Memorandum reminded the Lord Advocate that in 1879 'the Board of Trade [had] abandoned the claim put forward on behalf of the Crown to the ownership of the [South Uist] foreshores'[64] and that 'the foreshores admittedly belong to Lady Cathcart'.[65]

Following the lodging of the two memoranda, there then followed an intensive period during which Edwards was engaged on behalf of the Association for five consecutive days: two of which were taken up in travel and the other three with meetings and discussions in London. On 26 May Edwards had a meeting with William Mure, when he delivered further copies of the Association Memorandum, and later in the day he had a meeting with the Lord Advocate at his house, when it was arranged between the two men that the Conservative whips would be asked to ensure that a sufficient number of members should be present in the House of Commons when the Bill came up for its second reading, which had been put down for the next day, to ensure that it was rejected. It was, in fact, hoped that the Bill would not come up for its second reading because a motion for the adjournment of the House was to be proposed and, if passed, the Bill would not be heard. However, as a further precaution, Edwards and the Lord Advocate agreed that if the motion for the adjournment failed, the Solicitor General should be telegraphed to come to London to make a statement in the House against the Bill. On the next day, 27 May, Edwards met with William Dunbar at the Scottish Office and agreed to send to the Secretary for Scotland, Lord Lothian, a further copy of the Association Memorandum. In the afternoon Edwards attended the House of Commons, but the motion for the adjournment had been passed the previous day and the Bill did not come up for its second reading. On 28 May Edwards had a further meeting with Malcolm of Poltalloch and agreed with him that Malcolm should speak to Mr Chamberlain, one of the named supporters of the Bill, and explain to him the serious objections to the Bill. Edwards also had a meeting with Lord Lorne at Kensington Palace explaining to him the Association's objections to the Bill, and arranged that papers should be submitted to the Duke of Argyll and that the duke's support and

63 NRS, AF 67/179, Estate Memorandum, p. 3.

64 NRS, AF 67/179, Estate Memorandum, p. 3.

65 NRS, CR 11/380, Memorial and Opinion of the Law Officers, 1879, p. 14.

influence should be sought in opposing the Bill. At the beginning of June, Skene Edwards & Garson wrote to Duncan Darroch of Gourock, Mr Bankes of Letterewe and Lady Matheson of Lewis explaining the position which had been reached on the Bill and the steps taken to oppose it, and on 8 June 1891 they wrote to the Duke of Argyll in similar terms. The Bill was now expected to come up for its second reading on 24 June, but in the face of the considerable opposition that had been mounted against it, it was, in fact, withdrawn.[66]

Fraser Mackintosh made one further attempt to have his Sea Ware Bill adopted. The Bill was presented and read for the first time on 11 March 1892.[67] Skene Edwards & Garson wrote to the Secretary for Scotland sending further copies of their 1891 memoranda and expressed the hope 'that the Government will oppose the second reading of the present Bill'.[68] Macleod also wrote to William Dunbar at the Scottish Office asking him to get in touch with Skene Edwards & Garson for any information he might need and to 'tell the Lord Advocate that it is important the Bill should be opposed'.[69]

The Bill was withdrawn shortly after these letters were sent and nothing further was heard of it until 1919 when the issue of crofters' rights to seaware in South Uist was raised again with complaints being made by the crofters about the monopoly which they said the estate had over the kelp industry in the island. The BoAS had, before these complaints were made, been considering proposals to stimulate the production of kelp and the revival of the kelp industry on the north and west coasts of Scotland in the context of alginates and the fertiliser business.[70] The BoAS had also been considering the terms on which crofters were involved in the kelp industry. The ownership of the kelp shores played a significant part in the extent to which the BoAS felt able to intervene in any revival of the industry or the terms on which crofters participated in the industry. At a mass meeting of the South Uist kelp

66 PD, Third Series, vol. 354, House of Commons, col. 1363 (24 June 1891).

67 See PP, 1892, Bills and Acts, Sea-ware Bill, Bill Number 217. This time the Bill was not supported by either Chamberlain or Colonel Malcolm of Poltalloch; PD, Fourth Series, vol. 2, House of Commons, col. 727 (11 March 1892).

68 NRS, AF 67/179, Letter Skene Edwards & Garson to Lothian, 24 March 1892.

69 NRS, AF 67/179, Letter Macleod to Dunbar, 25 March 1892.

70 The Scott Committee had, as we noted in Chapter 6, pointed out in 1914 the possibilities for expansion of the kelp industry for the production of iodine. The optimism for revival has not been borne out; see G. Kenicer, S. Bridgewater and W. Milliken, 'The ebb and flow of Scottish seaweed use', *Botanical Journal of Scotland*, 52:2 (2000), pp. 119–48.

workers held in December 1919, a number of resolutions were passed, echoing the complaints made in 1890. The resolutions protested against the monopoly of the kelp industry held by the estate, asked for arrangements to be made so that the crofters could participate in the industry outside estate control, and asked for the kelp shores to be declared free, or if this was not possible, asked that a fair rent should be fixed for the use of the shores for gathering seaware and making kelp. A memorial was also drawn up which explained, in some detail, the problems that the crofters were labouring with in prosecuting the kelp industry under estate control, and asked for the reintroduction of the 1891 Bill; and a letter was written to the BoAS sending the resolutions and the memorial.[71] The BoAS felt constrained from taking any action on behalf of the kelp workers noting, in a minute to the Scottish Office, that

> in view of what appears to be an undoubted right of property in kelp vested in the proprietrix, the Board are not in a position to force any improvement in the conditions of employment of kelp workers in South Uist as far as that depends on arrangements between the workers and the Estate.[72]

The kelp workers were told that the BoAS could not intervene in the dispute.[73]

There was another attempt made in 1935 by the crofters to ask the Crown to intervene in South Uist and help them; in particular they asked the Board of Trade how the crofters could claim the foreshore. The letter expressed the crofters' concern over what they saw as the odd state of the law regarding ownership:

> It is a very funny position here; I can go down to the Shores and Rocks and pick up limpets and whelks, but I am not allowed to break the Tangles without the permission of the Estate Factor . . . we think the Board of Trade should have a say in this Industry, because the Tangles grow miles out at Sea, when they are ripe, they break off the rocks, and come to the surface of the ocean where they are as we might term them, floating wreckage until they are washed ashore, when the Estate claim them . . . So, Dear Sir, please let us have all particulars relating to the above including what steps if any, for us to claim the Rights of the Shore.[74]

[71] NRS, AF 43/73, Resolutions 22 December 1919; Memorial to BoAS and letter Doherty to BoAS, 27 December 1919.

[72] NRS, AF 43/73, Secretary for Scotland No. 5077/36 Minute 24, April 1920, John M. Ramsay.

[73] NRS, AF 43/73, Letter Scottish Office to Doherty, 7 June 1920.

[74] NRS, AF 43/74, Letter Maclellan-Boyle to Board of Trade, 1 February 1935.

The Board asked the Scottish Office for its comments and the Scottish Office responded that because Lady Gordon Cathcart owned the foreshore, 'the Secretary of State appears unable to intervene'.[75] The Board responded to the crofters:

> I am directed to state that the Board of Trade, on behalf of the Crown, do not contest the claim of Lady Gordon Cathcart or of her successors in title, to the ownership of the foreshore below high water mark of ordinary spring tides of the Island of South Uist and of the adjacent islands. The Board are, therefore, unable to intervene in any question of the disposal of the seaweed, or products therefrom, which are found on the shores of the Island of South Uist.[76]

The unhappiness over estate control of the kelp industry in the Uists and the royalties levied on behalf of the estate on the gathering of seaware by crofters from the island's foreshores did not die out in the 1930s. More recently, in 1998, there were protests over royalties being levied by the North Uist estate on kelp harvested by crofters from the estate foreshores that was then sold to an alginate company; and correspondence in the *West Highland Free Press* made it clear that the concerns expressed in and since the 1890s had not disappeared.[77]

## THE ASSOCIATION IS FINALLY WOUND UP

As the Association had, as it modestly put it in the Association Memorandum on the Sea Ware Bill, 'established the seaboard proprietors' right of property in the foreshores of their estates', and had seen off the challenge of Fraser Mackintosh's Sea Ware Bill, its raison d'être had all but gone. It was not, however, until August 1938 that steps were taken to wind it up when a petition was presented by its bankers Coutts & Co.[78] The petition, drafted by Skene Edwards & Garson, said

[75] NRS, AF 43/74, Note 'TDF', 27 February 1935.

[76] NRS, AF 43/74, Letter Wright to Maclellan-Boyle, 16 February 1935; for the ownership of the foreshore in South Uist, see NRS, CR 11/380, Memorial and Opinion of the Law Officers, 1879, p. 14.

[77] 'Anger over "greedy" estates seaweed royalty demands', *West Highland Free Press*, 7 April 1998; *West Highland Free Press*, 24 April, 1 May, 8 May, 15 May 1998; see also *The Scotsman*, 30 April 1998; SLC Discussion Paper, para. 6.17; SLC Report on Law of the Foreshore and Sea Bed, March 2003, No. 190 [hereafter SLC Report], para. 4.7, p. 27. This is discussed in Chapter 9.

[78] The following information is taken from the documents at NRS, CS 46/1952/628, William McKay Campbell, Judicial Factor of the Foreshore Association of Scotland: Discharge, 1952 and NRS, GD 325/1/394, Foreshore Association of Scotland: Correspondence and opinion of counsel, 1938.

that in 1911 the committee of the Association had comprised the Dukes of Sutherland and Richmond and Colonel Malcolm of Poltalloch but that since then all the members had died, no new members had been appointed and all the original subscribers were dead, and

> For a considerable number of years the Association has not been asked for assistance and as most of the questions between the Crown and seaboard proprietors regarding foreshores have been settled or allowed to remain in abeyance, it appears that in the meantime all events the object for which the Association was formed have ceased to exist. In these circumstances it has been decided to apply to the Court for the appointment of a Judicial Factor on the said fund in order that he may be able to make up a title thereto and take such steps as he may be advised to take for the proper winding-up of the Association and distributing the fund amongst those who may be found entitled thereto.

John Macdougall Scott was appointed the Judicial Factor of the fund that amounted to £1,100 in Consols, £700 in Funding Loan and cash. Scott sought special powers to distribute the fund due to the 'hopeless task of finding the heirs of the original subscribers to the fund'. Scott was advised that in these circumstances he should obtain a power from the court to hand over the fund to the Scottish Land and Property Federation as it appeared 'to be the natural successor of the Foreshore Association', being 'the only organisation in Scotland representing owners of land' and 'many of the subscribers to the Federation [were] descendants of the landlords who were the original subscribers to the Foreshore Association'. However, the representative of the Crown as *ultimus haeres* objected to this suggestion in language that provides an interesting post hoc opinion on the motivations of the Association. He said:

> It is denied that the Federation is the natural successor of the Association . . . In particular it is denied that the Association was a charitable association or one designed to promote the interests of the public or of any section thereof. On the contrary it is believed and averred that the interests of the Association are adverse to those of the public in respect that it was formed in order to oppose the Crown in litigation in which the Crown was acting on behalf of the public . . . The objects of the Federation [being] the promotion of the interests in land of persons dwelling on the land and engaged in agriculture thereon and relief from imperial and local taxation affecting the land [are entirely distinct from those of the Association which] relate entirely to the foreshore which is incapable of habitation or agriculture and is not subject to taxation.

It was decided that the Association was moribund and that its funds had become *bona vacantia* and fell to the Crown as *ultimus haeres*. On 20 April 1951 the Court ordered the fund to be handed over to the Lord Advocate as representing the Crown as *ultimus haeres*, and finally, on 14 May 1952 the balance of the fund was paid by the Judicial Factor to the Crown, the Judicial Factor was discharged and the Association wound up.

## CONCLUSIONS

The Crofters Holdings (Scotland) Act 1886 gave no substantive rights to the crofters over seaware and so did not settle the concerns crofters had over the access to the foreshore or their use of the seaware growing or cast on the foreshore, and there is still unrest as to the ability of proprietors to charge royalties for seaware collected by crofters and sold to commercial users of kelp. As we see in Chapter 9, the SLC considered crofters' rights to seaware in the context of its 2003 review of the law of the foreshore, and while it noted the concerns of the crofters in North Uist mentioned above, the SLC declined to recommend that the law should give crofters the right to collect seaware for commercial exploitation. If Charles Fraser Mackintosh's Sea Ware Bill had become law, these concerns and unrest might have been settled, although drafted in the way it was to give rights to the public rather than a more measured proposal to give crofters and cottars specific rights to seaware for kelp while reserving the traditional manurial rights, the Bill would not have wholly settled these concerns. However, in the face of determined opposition from the Association and, in particular, Skene Edwards & Garson, and a government that had a veneration for private property, whose traditional constituency was the proprietors and that was disposed to pursue policies that reflected the demands of proprietors,[79] the 1891 Bill failed.

There is a delicious irony in the fact that demise of the Association led to the Crown, the long-time adversary of the Association, being paid the funds of the Association when it was finally wound up.

[79] Cameron, *Land for the People?*, pp. 81, 76.

# 8

# 'The Argyll influence in Tiree is paramount'

## INTRODUCTION

THIS ACCOUNT OF THE dispute between the Crown and the 9th Duke of Argyll over the island of Tiree foreshore contributes to the story told by this book for a number of reasons.

First, the nature of the Tiree foreshore meant that the arguments over ownership were decided, almost wholly, as a result of the degree of possession of the foreshore which could be proved through the gathering of seaware for manure and, especially, for the kelp industry. The kelp industry in Tiree was of considerable importance in the social and economic history of the island and the creation of the crofting community on the island. It is thought that the kelp industry began in Tiree in 1746, although the first specific reference is not made until 1778; but by the end of the century and beyond to 1812 the island was producing kelp in such quantities that it exceeded the whole agricultural rental of the island. In the years 1800–8 the amount of kelp being produced in the island was some 200 tons per annum. Relative to its population, Tiree people were producing as much kelp as those of the island of Lewis, and the dukes of Argyll were among the five leading kelp proprietors in the Highlands and islands. Tiree could truly be called a 'kelp isle'.[1] Lord Moncrieff in the Agnew case had, as we have seen, referred to the practically universal possession of the foreshore by *ex adverso* proprietors for the purposes of the kelp industry and, as we discussed in Chapter

[1] Duke of Argyll, *Crofts and Farms in the Hebrides* (Edinburgh, 1883), pp. 11, 46; PP, 1902, LXXXIII, Report by the Crofters Commission on the Social Condition of the People of Lewis in 1901, p. lxxxii; Gray, *Highland Economy*, pp. 127, 129; J. Macdonald, *General View of the Agriculture of the Hebrides or Western Isles of Scotland* (Edinburgh, 1811), p. 78; J. R. Coull, 'The island of Tiree', *Scottish Geographical Magazine*, 78:1 (1962), pp. 17–32; Goodrich-Freer, *Outer Isles*, pp. 25–40.

1, the extensive use of the foreshore by the adjacent landowners during the boom years of the kelp industry had played a significant part in the growth by the early years of the nineteenth century of the assumption that the foreshore was owned by the adjacent proprietor as a pertinent of their lands. The Tiree case study is a fine example of the significance of the kelp industry in the story of Scotland's foreshore.

Second, Tiree had experienced some of the more serious incidents in the disturbances in the Highlands and islands during the Crofters' War of the 1880s, and disturbances were still taking place at the time of the dispute. The underlying sensitivities between crofters and landowners and, specifically the relationship between the duke and the crofters and cottars, were to be important issues which exercised the minds of the Board of Trade and its lawyers during the dispute.

The third reason relates to the identity of the lawyers on the Crown's side of the dispute. The Solicitor to the Board at the time, R. Ellis Cunliffe,[2] had been heavily engaged since 1906 in preparing for, and giving evidence to, the Royal Commission on Coast Erosion which was discussed in Chapter 6, and he had produced with, as he put it, 'the great assistance' of the Edinburgh firm of solicitors, Davidson & Syme who had acted for the Board for many years, a detailed 'Statement on the Law relating to the Foreshore in Scotland' for the Royal Commission.[3] He was, therefore, fully aware during the dispute of the relevant law and, indeed, its finer points, as, of course, were Davidson & Syme, the solicitors used by the Board during the dispute. And James Pitman, the Crown Counsel used by the Board during the dispute, was no stranger to the issues. He had given a number of opinions to the Board on foreshore disputes both on his own and together with the Law Officers; and, as we saw in Chapter 6, the Lord Advocate specifically requested him to advise with the Law Officers on the seaware and prescription clauses in the proposed Coast Protection Bill, because of his experience with the Tiree case. This chapter provides a detailed, indeed a blow-by-blow, account of how the Crown's representatives went about considering a foreshore claim in the aftermath of the Agnew case.

[2] Cunliffe was knighted in 1910.

[3] PP, 1911, XIV, Royal Commission, vol. 3 (part 2), Cd 5709, Appendix XL. Davidson & Syme merged with Dundas & Wilson in 1972 and the merged firm practised as Dundas & Wilson until it combined with CMS in 2014.

## THE ORIGINS OF THE DISPUTE

In November 1881 Lindsay Howe & Co.,[4] the Edinburgh solicitors to the 8th Duke of Argyll, wrote to the harbour department of the Board saying that the duke was minded to construct a pier at Gott Bay on Tiree. The letter made two points. First, there could be no question but that the construction of the pier was for the public good; the island had a large export trade of agricultural produce, of fish and of kelp and the lack of a suitable harbour was damaging to this trade. Second, the duke was the sole proprietor of Tiree including, and the letter was specific on this, the foreshore. The Board's consent, on behalf of the Admiralty, to the construction of the pier was requested.[5] We should remember that this letter was written only thirteen years after the Crown's somewhat bruising experience with the duke over the ownership of the Scottish foreshores described in Chapter 4. It is therefore no surprise that the Board regarded this, on the face of it, innocent letter as raising a number of delicate questions, the most important being that of foreshore rights:

> The Duke of Argyll has always been one of the prominent and, when out of office, the most assertive of the members of the Scotch Foreshore Association. It is therefore, in my humble opinion a matter for consideration whether either of the delicate questions raised by Messrs. Lindsay Howe's [letter] . . . (1) foreshore rights . . . should be raised, at all events until we have the plans of the work before us . . . I should be inclined to think that the Duke will fight – and we know how harmful the costs of these cases which are invariably pushed to the House of Lords are qua mere ownership of the foreshore – if the Crown raises [this] point.[6]

The Board's response was to play for time before having to confront this delicate matter, and to ask for plans of the pier.[7] The duke's solicitors sent the plans but also explained that they were not yet settled because the engineers wanted to observe the winter storms to see what modifications might be required. This was helpful to the Board; the letter from the duke's solicitors gave 'an excellent, nay, almost a cogent reason for postponing the matter', and the Board replied that when the details were

[4] Lindsay Howe & Co. is still in practice under the name Lindsays.

[5] TNA:PRO, MT 10/1813, Letter Lindsay Howe to the Board of Trade, 7 November 1881.

[6] TNA:PRO, MT 10/1813, Minute of Harbour Department, 8 November 1881.

[7] TNA:PRO, MT 10/1813, Letter Board of Trade to Lindsay Howe, 10 November 1881.

settled they would be prepared favourably to consider the proposal. No mention of the ownership of the foreshore was made.[8]

Nothing further was heard of the proposal until Lindsay Howe asked, in October 1887, for copies of the correspondence that had passed in 1881, because the proposal was being revived. The Board was still sensitive to the duke's claims as to ownership of the Tiree foreshore; in an internal minute concerning proposals to lay submarine cables between the islands of Coll and Tiree, there were two notes that acknowledged that the duke claimed the Tiree foreshore.[9]

## THE QUESTION OF OWNERSHIP OF THE FORESHORE IS RAISED

It was not until 1909 that firm proposals to build the pier at Gott Bay were, at last, received by the Board. The engineer to the Gott Bay pier trustees, G. W. Brenan, wrote to the Board about plans for the pier and said that because the foreshore was owned by the duke, the Pier Trustees would not need to trouble the Crown for the title to the foreshore but would obtain it from the duke. The Board sought Cunliffe's advice about the duke's alleged ownership of the foreshore.[10] Cunliffe took note of the reference to the kelp industry in Lindsay Howe's letter of November 1881 and advised that, given what Lord Benholme had said in the Agnew case about the cutting of seaware for kelp being one of the most decisive symptoms of property,[11] he was afraid that, assuming the kelp had been obtained and worked under licence or permission from the duke, the duke may have a strong title on possession alone, especially if the industry had been carried on continuously from 1881. He noted that the Board had not asserted the Crown's title in 1881 when the pier was first mooted, and this, he felt, might be held against the Crown now. But he accepted that the Crown had never admitted the duke's title and so he suggested that Brenan should be told that, unless evidence could be produced that

[8] TNA:PRO, MT 10/1491, Letter Lindsay Howe to Board of Trade, 23 November 1881; Minute, 24 November 1881; Letter Board of Trade to Lindsay Howe, 23 November 1881.

[9] TNA:PRO, MT 10/500, Minutes, 12 March 1888.

[10] TNA:PRO, MT 10/1813, Letter Brenan to Board of Trade, 28 May 1909.

[11] Lord Benholme, speaking of the nature of possession required to establish a title, had said: 'possession for a series of years . . . of the right of cutting from the rocks sea-ware for the purpose of manufacturing kelp is one of the most decisive symptoms of property that can well be imagined in the shape of possession . . . The enjoyment of mere waif and stray cast upon the shore is very different, and much less important'; Agnew v. Lord Advocate (1873) 11 M 309 at p. 331.

the Crown's title had been displaced, the pier trustees would be required to obtain the necessary title from the Crown.[12] Cunliffe asked to see all the old 1881 papers and proposed to pass the matter to Davidson & Syme. In July Lindsay Howe wrote to the Board making it clear that, in their view, the duke owned the Tiree foreshore. They said that the duke and his tenants had exercised all the rights of ownership of the foreshore such as the removing of stones and sand, and seaware for the manufacture of kelp. The Board made no substantive response to this letter and in September Lindsay Howe asked for a firm response, stating that their letter had provided sufficient evidence to support the duke's claim. The Board simply replied that the matter was 'of a somewhat complicated nature and involves considerable research'.[13]

By the end of October 1909 nothing further had been heard from the Board and the duke's solicitors were concerned that no progress was being made. The pier trustees were anxious for a start to be made on the pier. Lindsay Howe did not believe that considerable research was required and drew the Board's attention to the fact that

> the Duke of Argyll has repeatedly vindicated his right [to the foreshore] in the Courts here by interdict against third parties taking seaware, that at one time the kelp industry gave employment to many in Tiree, and that it was carried on under Leases granted by His Grace's ancestors, that in 1818 the then Duke of Argyll was one of the parties to a Memorial about the Salt Tax presented to the Lords of the Treasury on behalf of the Proprietors of Kelp Shores in Argyll and other Counties, including the Western isles, and that we have papers here giving accounts of the kelp sales so far back as the first years of the last century.[14]

The duke's solicitors said that the duke's title to the foreshore was so obvious that further debate and delay was unnecessary. It is clear from the outset that the gathering of seaware and the kelp industry on the island were to be the cornerstone of the duke's argument that he had title to the foreshore.

Cunliffe instructed Davidson & Syme in October to consider the duke's claim and told them that he considered it to be a strong one.[15]

[12] TNA:PRO, MT 10/1813, Memorandum, 11 June 1909.

[13] TNA:PRO, MT 10/1813, Letters Lindsay Howe to Board of Trade, 12 July, 23 September 1909; Letter Board of Trade to Lindsay Howe, 1 October 1909.

[14] TNA:PRO, MT 10/1813, Letter Lindsay Howe to Board of Trade, 2 October 1909. For the 1818 Memorial, see MacAskill, 'Highland kelp proprietors', p. 61.

[15] TNA:PRO, MT 10/1813, Letter Cunliffe to Davidson & Syme, 14 October 1909.

Davidson & Syme requested information from Lindsay Howe and in response they were sent, as evidence of the duke's title, an instrument of sasine dated 13 May 1848 and copies of correspondence dated June 1811 which showed that the duke had sold 'the whole of the Tiry Kelp 1811' to a firm in Newcastle. They were also sent a copy of an interdict obtained in 1889 by the 8th Duke of Argyll prohibiting two crofters from gathering seaware, whether drift or growing, from the shores of Tiree opposite one of his farms.[16] It is worth considering this interdict in a little more detail because actions taken by *ex adverso* landowners to protect what they saw as their rights are important considerations in the view taken over the degree of possession of the foreshore had by proprietors. In the condescendence to the interdict, the then duke said that he and his predecessors had since time immemorial given the tenants of the farm at Hough the right to take seaware from the shores *ex adverso* the lands of the farm, for the use of the farm. They had also let seaware not required for farm use to the tenant of the farm, and sometimes to other parties, for the purpose of making kelp. The condescendence also said that the crofters occupying the adjacent townships had been allowed to obtain seaware from the shore but only if they agreed, in return, as consideration to provide labour and services to the tenants. While these agreements may, from time to time, have been varied, the crofters had never, the condescendence said, been allowed to take seaware from the shores except under such agreements and subject to providing the said consideration. The 8th duke had not been a party to these agreements but he had not objected to them. For two or three years before the interdict was sought, the two crofters, Donald Brown and Malcolm Campbell, had, apparently, asserted a right to take the seaware without any need to seek permission or pay any consideration. The 8th duke and the farm tenants had complained and in March 1889 the duke's chamberlain had sent to the crofters what was, in effect, a letter before action: if the crofters persisted in taking the seaware in such a fashion, legal proceedings would be taken against them. They were, however, offered the olive branch that if they confirmed their willingness to 'conform to such reasonable conditions as His Grace may deem necessary in the interests of the farm of Hough, he will consider favourably any application by you for a renewal of the privilege of taking seaware for your croft'. The crofters evidently were not prepared to agree to this rather uncertain offer and perhaps considered that the

16 TNA:PRO, MT 10/1813, Correspondence regarding Tiry Kelp, 6 June, 8 June, 10 June 1811.

taking of seaware for their crofts was not a privilege but their right. They continued, therefore, taking the seaware, proceedings were issued and on 17 October 1889, the Lord Ordinary gave the interdict asked for by the duke.[17]

Lindsay Howe believed that this evidence should satisfy the Board and that the Board would have no further objections to work on the pier starting, saying:

> proprietary rights exercised by the Duke and his ancestors in the foreshore of Tiree are so well recognised in the District that very little enquiry on the part of the Board of Trade there would have satisfied them on the point. We think, however, that the documents sent you will be sufficient for your purpose.[18]

Davidson & Syme were not, however, satisfied and asked for evidence of specific examples. Lindsay Howe believed this was unnecessary. They said that the exercise of *any* proprietary rights was sufficient without the need for cumulative proof, but they undertook to seek further evidence from the duke's chamberlain in Tiree. In their advice to Cunliffe, Davidson & Syme made vaguely encouraging sounds and said that as no boundaries were stated in the instrument of sasine, the question was one of possession of the foreshore. The evidence of possession which Lindsay Howe had supplied had all related to the taking of seaware for kelp or manure and that, 'as none of the decided cases have gone so far as to hold that that alone is sufficient', they had asked the duke's solicitors for evidence of possession through the taking of sand, gravel and other materials from the foreshore.[19] Cunliffe, however, continued to believe that the duke's claim to the foreshore was a strong one but that, until the further information requested from the duke's solicitors had been produced, he could not say whether or not the Board should contest the duke's claim.[20]

Lindsay Howe's response to the request for further information was sent to Davidson & Syme on 7 December 1909. As to evidence of possession through taking sand and gravel, the duke's solicitors said that, as yet, they could not produce any documentary evidence of payment

[17] TNA:PRO, MT 10/1813, Copy Note of Suspension and Interdict, 17 October 1889. The views of crofters on their rights to take seaware are discussed in Chapters 1 and 7.

[18] TNA:PRO, MT 10/1813, Letter Lindsay Howe to Davidson & Syme, 18 October 1909.

[19] TNA:PRO, MT 10/1813, Letter Davidson & Syme to Cunliffe, 8 November 1909.

[20] TNA:PRO, MT 10/1813, Memorandum, 11 November 1909.

having been made for taking stones, sand or gravel from the foreshore or for any regulations made by the duke in relation thereto. They did, however, refer to the fact that the 8th duke had given to the Tiree School Board consent to take stones from one part of the island's foreshore when the school at Balemartin was being built. They pointed out that in Tiree, stone, sand and gravel could easily be obtained from places other than the foreshore so there would have been no need for any regulation as to taking these materials. They reiterated, however, their position that the exercise by the duke and his ancestors of proprietary rights in kelp and seaware was sufficient, and that those rights had formerly been of a very valuable nature, quoting the remarks of Lord Gillies in Macalister v. Campbell as to the significance of the great value of sea-wreck.[21] Davidson & Syme were not impressed with this:

> The only clear cut acts of possession on the part of the Duke, which his Agents have produced evidence of, are . . . his dealings with kelp and seaware. Although such dealings are no doubt very important we know of no decided cases in which these alone have been held sufficient to confirm the frontage proprietor's rights, and we therefore suggest that before the Duke's right is admitted an Opinion of Counsel should be obtained.[22]

Cunliffe wanted precise information as to any acts of ownership of the foreshore by the Crown, such as conveyances, leases or acknowledgements, before deciding whether to take counsel's advice. He also asked, in an internal memorandum to the harbour department, for the 'official papers in which I refer to the Scotch decisions set out in my evidence'.[23] The Office of Woods was now informed of the claim by the duke and was asked for any dealings that the department may have had with the foreshore at Tiree or any mines or minerals under the foreshore.[24] The response of Charles Howlett on behalf of Sir Stafford Howard at the Office of Woods was that the department had no documentary or other information apart from the copy of a Crown charter granted to a former Duke of Argyll dated 23 February 1774. Sir Stafford confirmed that the charter did not grant or refer to the foreshore but he offered

21 TNA:PRO, MT 10/1813, Letter Lindsay Howe to Davidson & Syme, 7 December 1909; Macalister v. Campbell (1837) 15 S 490 at p. 493.

22 TNA:PRO, MT 10/1813, Letter Davidson & Syme to Cunliffe, 14 December 1909.

23 TNA:PRO, MT 10/1813, Memorandum, 17 December 1909. A reference to the Statement prepared by Cunliffe and Davidson & Syme for the Royal Commission on Coast Erosion, referred to in Chapter 6.

24 NRS, CR 11/152, Letter Board of Trade to Office of Woods etc., 4 January 1910. The Office of Woods had retained, since 1866, responsibility for minerals.

the observation that it appeared to be a barony title and thus one which would allow the doctrine of prescriptive possession to apply.[25]

## THE OPINION OF THE LAW OFFICERS AND CROWN COUNSEL IS TAKEN

In April 1910 Cunliffe decided that James Pitman should be asked for his opinion on the duke's claim. It appears that Cunliffe still considered the claim of the duke to be a strong one and that, furthermore, the evidence of contrary possession by the Crown was very slight. The question, he believed, turned almost entirely on possession of a particular nature – the taking of seaweed for the manufacture of kelp.[26] The case for the opinion of counsel prepared by Davidson & Syme contained, amongst other documents, the bound volume of the 1774 charter showing the title of the duke to be a barony title and that it was *habile* thus enabling a right to the foreshore to be acquired by prescriptive possession, and referred to the duke's evidence of possession as relating solely to the taking of seaware and manufacturing kelp.[27] Pitman's opinion was clear and, on the face of it, unequivocal:

> The extent of possession required to establish a right to the foreshore must depend on the circumstances of each case, the nature of the foreshore, and uses to which it could be put. In the case of an island such as Tiree the regular leasing of the right to take seaware for kelp and for the use on the farms and the protection of the right by interdict is very strong evidence of the assertion of a right of property and is in my opinion sufficient to fortify the title even where unsupported by other evidence. There are other indications in this case of the exercise of proprietary rights on the part of the Duke and no indication of counter-possession. I therefore think that the Duke's claim is well founded.[28]

We might have expected that this would have been the end of the matter; Pitman's advice confirmed Cunliffe's own view and had rejected Davidson & Syme's point about possession through kelp alone not being suffi-

[25] NRS, CR 11/152 and TNA:PRO, MT 10/1813, Letter Office of Woods etc. to Board of Trade, 2 February 1910.

[26] TNA:PRO, MT 10/1813, Letter Cunliffe to Davidson & Syme, 11 April 1910.

[27] TNA:PRO, MT 10/1813, Case for the Board of Trade for the Opinion of Counsel. The fact that the case to Pitman enclosed the bound volume of, and made specific mention of, the 1774 charter is significant given that in 1914, as we shall see, the Solicitor General was to say that when the action was raised none of the material documents, in particular proof of a barony title, had been seen by counsel.

[28] TNA:PRO, MT 10/1813, Opinion of James Pitman, 28 May 1910.

cient. And, importantly, he found no evidence of counter-possession. But Cunliffe decided that, before Pitman's opinion was acted on, the duke's claim should be submitted to the Law Officers for their view.[29] In his letter asking Davidson & Syme to prepare a case for the opinion of the Law Officers, Cunliffe suggested that, in view of the fact that Pitman's opinion was adverse to the Crown, the instructions should 'set forth more specifically the decisions which are in the Crown's favour' and he mentioned Lord Benholme's words in the Agnew case, saying that 'the taking of seaweed was just one of the decisive symptoms of property' and that there were other decisive symptoms of property in the case. Cunliffe accepted that there was no indication of counter-possession of the foreshore, but he took issue with Pitman's opinion that there were other indications of the exercise of proprietary rights besides the taking of seaware for kelp. He also referred to a 1904 case in which the Lord Justice-Clerk had said that he was 'not prepared to say that the possession of a small portion of the foreshore would necessarily establish a prescriptive right to the whole' and he wanted the Law Officers to consider whether possession of a limited part of the foreshore of the island was sufficient to give the duke title to the whole of Tiree's foreshore; this was, he felt, an open question.[30] The case put before the Law Officers asked them:

1. Is the possession by the cutting and gathering of seaware and manufacturing of kelp, without other possession except as before stated, sufficient to give the Duke of Argyll right to the foreshore?
2. If such possession were confined only to part of the foreshore of the Island, would that be sufficient to prescribe a right to the whole?
3. Are Counsel of the opinion that the Duke of Argyll has now right to the whole foreshores of the Island?[31]

[29] TNA:PRO, MT 10/1813, Memorandum, 1 June 1910. The Law Officers at the time were Alexander Ure, the Lord Advocate and Lord President from 1913, and William Hunter, the Solicitor General and a Lord Ordinary from 6 December 1911.

[30] Aitken's Trustees v. The Caledonian Railway and the Lord Advocate (1904) 6 F 465 at p. 468; but Cunliffe omitted to quote the immediately following sentence that said: 'I am equally not prepared to hold that partial possession, where that is all that is possible, may not entitle the proprietor of the lands to prescribe a right to the foreshore.' Davidson & Syme and Pitman had been the Lord Advocate's agents and counsel in the case; TNA:PRO, MT 10/1813, Letter Cunliffe to Davidson & Syme, 15 June 1910 (emphasis in original).

[31] TNA:PRO, MT 10/1813, Island of Tiree. Claim by the Duke of Argyll. Queries. The case to the Law Officers enclosed all the relevant details of the 1774 charter. This is significant given that in 1914, as we shall see, the Solicitor General was to say that when the action was raised counsel had seen none of the material documents, in particular proof of a barony title.

The Law Officers replied:

1. In our opinion the gathering of seaware and manufacturing of kelp is sufficient of itself to give a title to foreshore if that is the only use to which the foreshore can naturally be put and there is no counter-possession. Before giving a definite answer to the question put to us we desiderate further information on these points from an independent source.

2/3. In certain circumstances possession of part of the foreshore may, in our view, be sufficient to prescribe a right to the whole foreshore belonging to one proprietor. In the case before us further information on the points referred to in answer 1 is necessary to enable us to answer these questions.[32]

In an internal memorandum to the harbour department, Cunliffe concluded that these views of the Law Officers were not as decided as those of Pitman's original opinion.[33]

Cunliffe put proceedings in motion to collect the further information the Law Officers had asked for. He suggested to Davidson & Syme that, before instructing a local agent on the island, a review of local histories, works on geology and the *Ordnance Gazetteer of Scotland* might produce the necessary information on the history of the kelp industry in Tiree and the formation of the foreshore.[34] Davidson & Syme responded in October 1910. Information and a description of Tiree which they had gathered from the *Ordnance Gazetteer of Scotland* and books by A. Goodrich-Freer and Erskine Beveridge[35] suggested to them that Tiree was an island where the proprietor who possessed the whole of the island on one title (as the Duke of Argyll did) and possessing the foreshore of parts of it, would prescribe rights to the whole of the island foreshore, and that the fact that the foreshores were flat and sandy and not precipitous might explain why there had been no other acts of possession shown by the duke. There was clear evidence that there had been a flourishing kelp industry on the island for many years. Finally, their reading of the books also suggested that the inhabitants used the foreshores as roads.[36] On the face of it, then, this was not

[32] TNA:PRO, MT 10/1813, Island of Tiree. Claim by Duke of Argyll. Replies, 6 July 1910. Pitman also signed the opinion.

[33] TNA:PRO, MT 10/1813, Memorandum, 11 July 1910.

[34] TNA:PRO, MT 10/1813, Letter Cunliffe to Davidson & Syme, 8 August 1910.

[35] F. H. Groome (ed.), *Ordnance Gazetteer of Scotland: A Survey of Scottish Topography* (London, 1893–5); Goodrich-Freer, *Outer Isles*; E. Beveridge, *Coll and Tiree: Their Prehistoric Forts and Ecclesiastical Antiquities* (Edinburgh, 1903).

[36] TNA:PRO, MT 10/1813, Letter Davidson & Syme to Cunliffe, 11 October 1910 and enclosures. As to the use of the foreshore as roads: the inhabitants will

information that was helpful to the Crown's position, apart, perhaps, from the use of the foreshore as roads by the inhabitants. And, indeed, it was this last point that appealed to Cunliffe. He considered that, having regard to the

> habitual user of the foreshores around the Island by the inhabitants for roads and the possible user of the foreshores for other purposes than the taking of seaware which has not been exercised by the proprietor I think that [the question: was possession of the foreshore by gathering seaware sufficient?] must be answered in the negative, subject to anything that local enquiries may bring out.[37]

While it is true that the use of the foreshore as roads was, of course, a use which meant that gathering of seaware for the manufacture of kelp was not the *only* use to which the foreshore could be put, it is difficult to understand Cunliffe's optimism as to the other possible use of the foreshore as there was nothing in Davidson & Syme's letter or the enclosures which gave any suggestion that there was any. But Cunliffe clearly thought that the foreshore might also be used for the removal of sand, shingle and stones, that the duke had not produced any evidence that he or his tenants had done this, and that it might be possible to show that the local inhabitants had used the foreshore for these purposes, without the consent of, or payment to, the duke. This would provide evidence not just of other uses, but also, crucially, of counter-possession.[38] He would, no doubt, have had in mind Lindsay Howe's letter of 7 December 1909 in which the duke's solicitors had said that, because stone, sand and gravel could easily be obtained in Tiree without the trouble of going to the foreshore, the duke had not found it necessary to make regulations as to the use of the foreshore for this purpose. Was there, Cunliffe may have thought, a suggestion that the inhabitants did, indeed, make use of the foreshore for this purpose without any consent or regulation by the duke? Cunliffe did not, at this stage, raise the possibility that the inhabitants may also have been taking seaware from the foreshore for their crofts without the consent of, or payment to, the duke or his farm tenants. But, as we shall see, the further

'tell you that they have "the best of good roads which is mended twice a day", which means that, no one being in a hurry in Tyree, it is usual to go from point to point along the seashore'; p. 10 of the enclosures.

[37] TNA:PRO, MT 10/1813, Copy letter Cunliffe to Davidson & Syme, 28 November 1910.

[38] TNA:PRO, MT10/1813, Copy letter Cunliffe to Davidson & Syme, 28 November 1910.

enquiries made by the Board's agent in Tiree suggested that this might be so and, also, the evidence given to the Napier Commission carried the suggestion that this did occur, albeit that the bulk of the evidence suggested that it was of limited significance.

Steps were, accordingly, taken in December 1910 to instruct Mr D. M. Mackinnon, a solicitor in Oban, to deal with the requests for further information made by the Law Officers. Lindsay Howe were informed of this development and they told Davidson & Syme that they noted the action now being taken and could not object to the Board making the enquiries.[39]

## MACKINNON'S REPORT

Mackinnon produced his report on 29 December 1910. It contained much interesting material and made a number of important observations, and was clearly influential in a more favourable view of the Crown's case being reached. We now look at it in some detail.[40]

Mackinnon began by stating that the community of the island of Tiree at the date of the last census numbered some 2,195 people and that the community was comprised of three classes: the farmer who paid a yearly rent of over £30 (and so was outside the provisions of the crofting legislation); the crofter who had a tenancy which was within the provisions of the crofting legislation; and the cottar or squatter who occupied a dwelling house on the common grazings but without any title or tenancy and so rent and tax free. Mackinnon reported that the bulk of the population was comprised of the crofters and cottars, that the crofters earned their living principally by working their crofts and also, to some extent, by gathering seaware for kelp, and that the cottars earned their living by gathering seaware for kelp and also through fishing, while in the summer many of them earned their living as seafarers. He said that there were four uses to which the foreshores of the island were put. The first was the gathering of seaware, the second the removal of stone and gravel, the third was the erection of piers and other structures, and the fourth was the passage of vehicle and foot traffic. Mackinnon reported in detail on each of these uses.

[39] TNA:PRO, MT 10/1813, Copy Letter Lindsay Howe to Davidson & Syme, 12 December 1910. The firm of D M Mackinnon is still in practice in Oban.

[40] TNA:PRO, MT 10/1813, Report of Inquiry made by D. M. Mackinnon, solicitor, Oban, regarding use of the foreshore of the Island of Tiree, 29 December 1910 [hereafter Mackinnon's Report].

## *The collection of seaware*

Mackinnon confirmed that the collection of seaware was, indeed, the principal use to which the foreshore was capable of being put. The seaware collected was won by gathering, not by cutting, and this process had been carried on over practically the whole of the foreshore of the island for over a century, with the exception, somewhat ironically, of the foreshore at Gott Bay from which none, or very little, seaware was ever collected. The report also drew Cunliffe’s attention to the evidence taken by the Napier Commission that, it said, contained frequent mentions of the use of the foreshore for the collection of seaware.[41] The recipients of Mackinnon’s Report would have noted from their reading of the evidence given to the Napier Commission when it visited Tiree on 7 August 1883 that, out of fourteen crofters and cottars who had given evidence to the Napier Commission, only four of them did not mention the collection of seaware, whether for manure or kelp. Donald McDougall, a fifty-two-year-old crofter from Balephuil, said that their forefathers had possessed a shore from which they had taken seaweed to manure their ground but that this had been taken away when their common pasture had been taken from them because ‘the shore belongs to the piece of land’ which they had been deprived of.[42] McDougall went on to say that, although they no longer possessed the shore, they continued to obtain seaware from it without any impediment through the goodwill of the tenant of the land. Asked if they made any payment for the seaware, McDougall replied that ‘we do not, because it belongs to ourselves, if we get it out’.[43] The Board’s lawyers may have regarded the fact that crofters at Balephuil collected seaware without payment as significant. But none of the other nine crofters and cottars who answered questions about seaware were able to say that they made free use of seaware, something about which they strenuously objected. Donald McDonald, a crofter, and Hector McDonald, a cottar, both from Balemartin and both aged thirty-eight, explained that they had to pay the factor for seaweed to manure their ground in the form of three or four days’ work at harvest time and three other days in winter time. They had petitioned the Duke of Argyll on this grievance, saying that they should not have to pay for the seaware, but had been

[41] Mackinnon’s Report referred to the evidence contained in the Napier Report XXXV.

[42] Napier Report XXXV, Q 33430.

[43] Napier Report XXXV, Qs 33433–7.

refused.[44] Asked whether they thought that, upon a great estate such as Tiree, it was proper that they should pay for seaware, particularly given that they said they could not work their crofts without it, they answered that as all they collected was the drift ware from the beach they did not believe that any value should be exacted for it. Donald Campbell, a thirty-six-year-old crofter, and Donald MacLean, a sixty-five-year-old cottar, from Kilmolang, told the Napier Commission that they also had to pay for the seaware they used as manure, either in money or by providing twenty cart-loads of seaware to the farmer from whose shore they collected the ware.[45] As to the estate regulations concerning the collection of seaware, Hugh MacDiarmid, the sub-factor, explained that the rules which the Balemartin crofter had been speaking of were already in place when he took over his farm; he did not make any new rules and when he was asked if the crofters or cottars ever complained about, or objected to, these regulations he replied in a somewhat enigmatic manner that 'we talked about it'. Asked whether it would be possible to make arrangements for a limited part of the shore to be set aside for the crofters to take the seaware they needed for their crofts while the rest could go to his farm, he replied that that 'would be a very difficult arrangement to make, because the seaware all comes in a sort of common, and it would be difficult to arrange to give them a share of it – in fact, almost impossible'.[46]

So far as kelp manufacture was concerned, it appeared from evidence given to the Napier Commission that the British Seaweed Company rented shores from the Duke of Argyll and had the right to purchase, at a price fixed by the company, all the kelp manufactured on the island either directly by the company or indirectly by the crofters and cottars.[47] James Sleven, the resident manager of the company, was asked about the employees of the company and, from the answers he gave, it was clear that the crofters and cottars who collected the seaware and sold it to the company were effectively free agents; they were emphatically not employed by the company.[48] When asked about the seaware collected, Sleven confirmed that it was all drift seaware cast up by the sea; none of it was cut.[49] We will see that these points were considered to be of particular significance to the Crown's case against the duke.

[44] Napier Report XXXV, Qs 33607–25.

[45] Napier Report XXXV, Q 34143.

[46] Napier Report XXXV, Qs 33938–54.

[47] Napier Report XXXV, Qs 33535, 33536, 34181, 34252, 34295.

[48] Napier Report XXXV, Qs 34313, 34316.

[49] Napier Report XXXV, Qs 34344, 34345. This is interesting because it appears that at the end of the eighteenth century the manufacture of kelp in Tiree was almost

Reference was made at the Napier Commission to regulations made by the duke or his agents for the collection of seaware, and Mackinnon reported that, in some cases, the farmers had included in their leases provisions giving them a right to collect the seaware for their farms and that in those cases where no such express right was included the farmers exercised, *de facto*, such a right. So far as the crofters were concerned, Mackinnon reported that they exercised a like right to collect seaware from the foreshore *ex adverso* of their croft holdings where, by custom or express arrangement, part of the foreshore had been assigned to them for this purpose. The cottars gathered seaware from the foreshore *ex adverso* of the croft holdings where their houses were built but subject to the understanding that the crofters' requirements should first be satisfied. The crofters would require virtually all of the seaware until the month of May but the cottars were permitted to make kelp from the part of the seaware known as tangle, which was of no value for manurial purposes. Mackinnon reported that it was the practice of the crofters and cottars in certain of the townships to make arrangements for the foreshores to be partitioned between them and for shores to be allocated by lot. He also said that it appeared that the duke regarded the right of farmers and crofters to take seaware to be a pertinent of the farm tenancy or of the croft.[50] Mackinnon said that there was no information available to him as to whether the right exercised by the crofters and cottars flowed from an express grant by the duke. Indeed, it appeared that a number of the crofters and cottars who were interviewed by Mackinnon, some while actually gathering the seaware, had:

> strongly resented the suggestion that [they were collecting the seaware] at the Duke's will, and on being asked to whom the foreshore belonged replied 'the Crown'. Further that so long as they did not trespass over the lands not in their own occupation in order to do so, the Duke had no right to interfere with them.[51]

Mackinnon went on to say that there did not appear to exist any regulations laid down by the Argyll estate authorities generally regarding

wholly from cut, not cast, ware: 'The quantity and quality of [cast ware] being altogether precarious and uncertain, and it being made mostly by cottars & idle people in the country during harvest season'; see Cregeen, *Argyll Estate Instructions*, p. 21.

50 There had, as we saw in Chapter 7, been judicial authority since 1896 for the proposition that a pertinent of a croft could include a right to collect seaware for fertiliser; Macdonald v. Macdougall (1896) 23 R 941; see Agnew, *Crofting Law*, pp. 11–13.

51 TNA:PRO, MT 10/1813, Mackinnon's Report, pp. 4–5.

the gathering of seaware. Mackinnon's view was that the estate only intervened in seaware-gathering disputes where the dispute was, in reality, one over access to land and he regarded the example of the 1889 interdict produced by Lindsay Howe as being designed, not so much to prevent the taking of seaware, as to regulate and control the passage of the crofters whose holdings were not *ex adverso* the relevant foreshore.

Mackinnon's Report on the use of the seaware for kelp was interesting. He referred to the fact that for many years the British Seaweed Company had manufactured kelp on Tiree. He had not ascertained the number of years but we know that the company had started operations in 1863[52] and so at the time of the dispute had been manufacturing kelp on the island, and lately on the mainland, for some forty years. We also know that the duke and his predecessors had been manufacturing kelp on the island since, at least, 1778[53] but that the kelp trade had entirely ceased and failed long before 1846. There was, therefore, no doubt that the kelp trade had been a fundamental and defining influence on the social and economic status of the island of Tiree and its people for a considerable number of years. But the key question was whether the manner in which this trade had been carried on in the last forty years or so gave the 9th Duke of Argyll the possession of the foreshores that he needed to prescribe a title to them. Mackinnon was not so sure on this and he questioned, crucially, whether the collection of the seaware for kelp was, in fact, under the duke's authority. He examined in some detail the methods adopted by Stanford's company in obtaining and paying for the seaware used in the manufacture of the kelp. The seaweed was, he said, collected by crofters and cottars and piled up above the foreshore from where it was taken to the factory by the company's employees. The crofters and the cottars were paid by the company on an individual basis. They were, he said,

> not employees of the Company in the ordinary sense, not being under obligation to work unless they chose. They were truly sellers of seaweed etc to the Company. This situation might raise the question as to whether during the subsistence of this arrangement, the Crofters and Cottars in their operations collected the seaweed etc in virtue of the Company's rights derived from the

[52] Argyll, *Crofts and Farms*, p. 45; E. C. C. Stanford and W. M. Wood, 'On the economic applications of seaweed', *Journal of the Society of Arts*, 32:1646 (1884), p. 723.

[53] And indeed Lindsay Howe in one of their earliest letters in the dispute had established the key role of Tiree and the duke in the kelp-making industry since the early years of the nineteenth century.

> Duke, or at their own hand . . . Consideration of the whole circumstances disclosed by the investigation made, points to the possession had by the Duke of the foreshore through others in the matter of gathering seaweed etc not being exclusive and that the use had by others free from regulation by the Duke is not of such a character as to be described as precarious or casual.[54]

The evidence given to the Napier Commission by Sleven as to the employment status of the crofter and cottar gatherers of the seaweed had also been very clear. Mackinnon concluded his report on the use to which the foreshore was put in the context of seaware by saying that

> The reporter feels satisfied from his enquiries and from his knowledge of the conditions obtaining in the Island that His Grace would be slow to challenge at the present time the landless cottars or squatters in the pursuit of their collection of tangle etc. Thus, even although the Duke's contention that the farmers and crofters derived right from him be sound, there would remain the fact that a similar and practically equally extensive use was and is being made of the foreshore by an equally numerous class, namely cottars.[55]

The important message from this was that there was a considerable degree of counter-possession of the foreshore on the part of the cottars. The 8th duke had confirmed that there were a considerable number of cottars on the island and the important role these people had played in the kelp industry. He had spoken of the cottars as the 'detritus' of the old sub-divided crofting population that comprised 'the remains of the old kelp-burning or kelp-gathering population' on the island.[56] As we shall see, this 'detritus' would have a defining role in the way the case was decided.

## *The removal of stone, sand and gravel*

So far as the removal of stone, sand and gravel was concerned, Mackinnon pointed to instances over the last forty years where stone had been removed with the permission of the duke (the latest being in connection with the Gott Bay pier works themselves) but he also pointed to instances of stone being taken by crofters and cottars for the rebuilding of their houses, without the permission of the duke, or the estate authorities questioning the practice. Over the last twenty years gravel had been taken from the foreshore on behalf of the Argyll

54 TNA:PRO, MT 10/1813, Mackinnon's Report, p. 7.
55 TNA:PRO, MT 10/1813, Mackinnon's Report, p. 7.
56 Argyll, *Crofts and Farms*, pp. 15, 43–4.

County Council roads authority, again without, apparently, the permission of the estate. Crofters and cottars had similarly removed gravel, but to no great extent. None of this showed any significant use by the duke or his tenants that might go towards an argument of possession. Indeed, it was probably arguable, on the basis of this evidence, that such use of the foreshore for these purposes was, if anything, evidence of counter-possession.

### *The erection of piers and other structures and the use of the foreshore as roads*

If we are to take at face value the evidence given by Donald McDonald and Hector McDonald to the Napier Commission, the Argyll estate had never built any piers or harbours on the island. Asked by the Commission whether 'the proprietor expended any money in making a pier or harbour of any description in this island since you can remember?' the crofters replied: 'Not a penny since I can remember.'[57] So far as the position of a harbour is concerned, the 8th duke had accepted the need for one, but given the exposed coasts of the island he was not encouraged to believe that a safe harbour could be constructed at 'any moderate, or indeed almost at any cost'.[58] Although we know, of course, that the duke had been considering, since at least 1881, the construction of the pier at Gott Bay, no progress had been made until the turn of the century and so the McDonalds were not far wrong; there was still no safe harbour on the island.[59] The evidence adduced by Mackinnon as to the existence of piers was, we should not therefore be surprised, hardly conclusive in favour of the duke. There were two small piers at Scarnish used by the ferry, built by the then duke some years before, and there was a pier at Hynish belonging to the Northern Lights Commissioners in connection with the Skerryvore Lighthouse[60] but Mackinnon was unable to say whether or not the duke's permission for this pier had been obtained. There were remains of piers (at four other points) whose condition was beyond use and, in any event, there was no information available as to any consent sought for their construction. As to other structures, the only instance that Mackinnon's Report referred to was an assertion contained in a postscript to Lindsay Howe's letter of 20

[57] Napier Report XXXV, Q 33680.
[58] Argyll, *Crofts and Farms*, p. 44.
[59] See Goodrich-Freer, *Outer Isles*, pp. 2, 4, 19.
[60] B. Bathurst, *The Lighthouse Stevensons* (London, 1999), p. 160.

October 1909 that the duke had exercised his proprietary rights by granting permission in 1904 for a sewage pipe to be laid across the foreshore.[61] However, according to Mackinnon, no such permission had ever been requested. Indeed, he went further and, by reference to the feu charter which was granted by the estate in connection with the building site concerned, he drew attention to the fact that not only did the feu charter not contain any grant of a right to lay the pipe across the foreshore, but the wording of one of the clauses inserted on behalf of the duke's estate indicated, he said, that there was doubt in the minds of the duke's agents as to whether their client had, indeed, any right to give permission for such a structure on the foreshore. Mackinnon confirmed that the sandy beaches at four locations on the island were, to all intents and purposes, part of the island's road system.

Cunliffe received Mackinnon's Report on 30 December 1910. He had a number of questions on it and he wrote to Davidson & Syme requesting that Mackinnon should be asked to give his comments on these questions. Cunliffe's letter makes it clear that he was interested in pursuing the distinction, of which he said he was previously unaware, between the gathering of drift seaware as against cut seaware in the context of the quality of possession, and he was encouraged by Sleven's evidence to the Napier Commission that all the kelp was made from drift, not cut, seaware. Cunliffe apparently thought that, having regard to the remarks of Lord Benholme in the Agnew case as to the importance of the right of cutting seaware from the rocks, as opposed to the collection of drift seaware, it might well be possible to argue that in this case the gathering of drift seaware, which comprised the bulk (if not the whole) of the collection should not be regarded as such an important incident of possession. From originally taking the view that Lord Benholme's words might prove fatal to the Crown's case, Cunliffe now seemed to believe – because Mackinnon's evidence pointed to the importance of drift, rather than cut, seaware – that they might prove helpful. He wanted, however, to be sure that this had still been the case in the period since the 1880s.[62] Mackinnon confirmed that it was indeed

[61] TNA:PRO, MT 10/1813, Letter Lindsay Howe to Davidson & Syme, 20 October 1909.

[62] TNA:PRO, MT 10/1813, Letter Cunliffe to Davidson & Syme, 6 January 1911. It is significant, in view of what a new set of Law Officers would say in 1914 as we see below, that Cunliffe referred only to what Lord Benholme had said in the Agnew case and not to what Lord Watson had said in Young v. North British Railway Company (1887) 14 R (HL) 53 at p. 55: 'with regard to the relative importance of taking loose ware and the cutting of growing tangle as acts evidencing property

the case that all the types of seaweed collected were drift seaweed. He had referred, in his report, to seaware and tangle. Tangle grew below the low water mark and was a deep sea tangle called *Herminaria digitata*. The other seaweeds collected were knobbed wrack and bladder wrack. In their collection, however, cutting was never resorted to and the most suitable time for collection was after strong weather. He confirmed that this had been the case since 1883.[63]

But perhaps the most significant question Cunliffe put to Mackinnon was the following: 'Does it seem likely that cottars would be willing to furnish statements in the event of the Law Officers advising the Crown to contest the Duke's claim?'[64] It was, of course, one thing for Mackinnon's Report to have produced evidence favourable to the Crown's case, but quite another if there was no reasonable prospect of the Crown being able to present this evidence to the court. Mackinnon's answer was carefully phrased. He acknowledged that the question was, as he put it, 'not unattended with difficulty'.[65] He had, indeed, found numerous cottars and crofters who had resented the suggestion that the duke could control the gathering of seaware, but

> it must be borne in mind that in a case of conflict in Court between the Board of Trade and the Duke, the cottar, dependent as he is for his house on the goodwill of the Duke, might not unnaturally be disinclined to do or say anything tending to bring himself into open opposition with the Duke, and so perhaps imperil his precarious tenure.[66]

But Mackinnon went on to suggest that the duke, even if he was disposed to evict cottars who gave evidence against him, might, in the then current conditions in the Highlands and islands, be slow to act, if in so acting he might create a disturbance; a reference, no doubt, to the legacy left by the Crofters' War of the 1880s and, in particular, to the fact that the disturbances which had taken place after the Napier Commission had reported had, to a large extent, been directly related to the fact that the cottar population had been so badly dealt with; and the

rights, I can only say, in my opinion, it depends not so much upon attachment or non-attachment to the foreshore as upon the beneficial character of the right'.

63 See also Argyll, *Crofts and Farms*, p. 56.

64 TNA:PRO, MT 10/1813, Observations on Mr Mackinnon's Report, 29 December 1910 and Replies, p. 3.

65 TNA:PRO, MT 10/1813, Observations on Mr Mackinnon's Report, 29 December 1910 and Replies, p. 3.

66 TNA:PRO, MT 10/1813, Observations on Mr Mackinnon's Report, 29 December 1910 and Replies, p. 3.

disturbances were still taking place. At the time of the dispute over the Tiree foreshore, there had been over twenty years of continual protest about land rights in the Highlands and islands, with serious disturbances in particular in Tiree itself, and the Board would have been sensitive to the strong feelings of the crofters and the cottars.[67] But Mackinnon also drew attention to the fact that the duke had, some years before, offered to the cottars on the island a feu of each house site, an offer that the cottars had turned down. Mackinnon concluded, on balance and having particular regard to his experience in the island when he visited it, that the cottars would be willing to give evidence.

But Cunliffe was still concerned. We know that he was aware of the fact that the Tiree crofters and cottars had been hesitant about giving evidence to the Napier Commission because of possible repercussions from the then duke and he worried about the implications this might have for the case.[68] Donald McDougall, a crofter from Balephuil who had been elected as the representative of the Tiree crofters and cottars, had asked for an assurance from the duke's factor, Mr MacDiarmid, 'that no-one will suffer prejudice in consequence of what he says here on this occasion'. The factor said he was unable to give such an assurance. He had not been aware that he was to be asked for such an assurance and had no instructions or permission to give one. He did, however, say that no one telling the truth would suffer but when, again, asked to 'give a positive assurance that no prejudice will occur to anyone on account of what is said here today', he replied: 'I am not going to say that.' Lord Napier then went on to tell McDougall that it was not in the power of the Commission to give any such assurance and that the crofters and cottars who gave evidence would have to trust to the goodwill of the duke. This was far from satisfactory. One may imagine that some hurried discussion must have taken place between the duke's factor and advisers present while McDougall was being examined, because

[67] The most serious disturbances that occurred in July 1886 resulted in a force of policemen and marines being sent to the island: 'There is war in Tiree', said *The Times*, 24 July 1886. The disturbances that had taken place during the thirty years after the Napier Commission reported in 1884 carried on until the outbreak of the Second World War. For the disturbances in Tiree during the Crofters' War, see I. M. M. MacPhail, *The Crofters' War* (Stornoway, 1989), pp. 186–92; D. E. Meek, *Tuath Is Tighearna* (Edinburgh, 1995); D. E. Meek, 'The role of song in the Highland land agitation', *Scottish Gaelic Studies*, 16 (1990), pp. 1–53; A. MacArthur, *The Tiree Crofters' Struggle* (Tiree, 1986).

[68] See his note about this contained in the internal memorandum he wrote to the Harbours Department on 21 March 1911, TNA:PRO, MT 10/1813.

MacDiarmid suddenly intervened to say, 'I have had this moment put into my hands a letter from the Duke's Chamberlain.' The letter said that 'the crofters are at liberty to make any statement they have to make without any fear of after consequences'. McDougall then said, rather confusingly, that it was not really the actions of the duke they were concerned about, but rather those of his factors.[69] That the 8th Duke of Argyll was upset by what was said at the Tiree hearing of the Napier Commission is clear from the pamphlet he wrote just under two months later which he addressed to Lord Napier. He wanted, he said, to give some authentic information to the Commission about his estate in Tiree and the Ross of Mull. As to the grievances and complaints that the Commission had heard from the Tiree crofters and cottars, the duke said that they did not, for the most part, reflect the circumstances in Tiree. They were, he said, 'the mere echo of complaints which have been stereotyped elsewhere'.[70] He did not, however, blame the crofters and cottars but, rather, suggested that others were putting the words in their mouths, describing them as simple-minded people who found it hard to resist being influenced by propagandists, of being affected by what he called the 'Phenomena of Suggestion'.[71]

The issue as to whether the crofters and, in particular, the cottars might be expected to give evidence did not, however, go away and it was a matter which continued to trouble the Board.

## THE LAW OFFICERS AND CROWN COUNSEL RECONSIDER THE DUKE'S CLAIM

The Law Officers and James Pitman were asked at the end of February 1911 to reconsider, in the light of Mackinnon's Report, their views as to the strength of the Crown's case against the duke. The instructions that were sent to counsel included a copy of the original instructions in July 1910 together with all the documents that had been sent with the origi-

[69] Napier Report XXXV, Qs 33423–9. When the Commission took evidence the next day at Bunessan, the chamberlain made an opening statement on the part of the duke that all the duke's tenants were 'at perfect liberty to make any statement that they wish without any fear of after consequences'; see Napier Report XXXV, p. 2183. The practice during the hearings of factors withholding assurances that witnesses would not be prejudicially treated for criticising their estates happened elsewhere too, e.g. in Sutherland (the author is grateful to Dr Annie Tindley for this information) and in Skye; Hunter, *Making of the Crofting Community*, p. 144.

[70] Argyll, *Crofts and Farms*, p. 53.

[71] Argyll, *Crofts and Farms*, p. 60.

nal instructions, copies of the relevant passages from the Napier Report, copies of the literature on Tiree that Davidson & Syme had produced and, of course, Mackinnon's Report and his replies to Cunliffe's questions on the report. They drew the attention of counsel, in particular, to the fact that Mackinnon's Report said that the seaware gathered in Tiree was drift, not cut, and directed counsel's attention towards the words of Lord Benholme in the Agnew case which Cunliffe had identified as being of possible significance, suggesting that 'It may perhaps be questioned whether the gathering of drift seaware can be regarded as of the same importance.'[72] The opinion of the Law Officers and James Pitman was given on 15 March 1911. It was short and to the point and contained no explanation or justification, something which, in the light of later circumstances, may be thought to be unfortunate:

> On the information now before us we are of the opinion that the Duke of Argyll has not right to the whole foreshore of the Island of Tiree. We consider that the counter-possession had by the inhabitants, as disclosed in that information, is sufficient to oust the Duke's claim. The appropriate mode by which to vindicate the rights of the Crown, if they are disputed, is by an Action of Declarator at the instance of the Crown directed against the Duke.[73]

## THE ISSUE OF GETTING THE CROFTERS AND COTTARS TO GIVE EVIDENCE IS CONSIDERED FURTHER

The decisive factor for counsel was counter-possession and if the Crown was to prove its case for counter-possession, the evidence of the crofters and, in particular, the cottars would be crucial. Cunliffe's concerns as to the prospects for actually getting the crofters and cottars to give evidence were, therefore, of some significance, and he proposed, before any proceedings were begun, to ask Davidson & Syme for further information on the likelihood of getting this evidence. His internal memorandum with which all the papers were sent to the Board for their consideration

[72] TNA:PRO, MT10/1813 Supplementary Case for the Board of Trade regarding claim by the Duke of Argyll to the foreshores of the Island of Tiree for Opinion of Crown Counsel, February 1911.

[73] TNA:PRO, MT10/1813, Supplementary Case for the Board of Trade regarding claim by the Duke of Argyll to the foreshores of the Island of Tiree for Opinion of Crown Counsel, Opinion, 15 March 1911. It is interesting that, given the importance of drift rather than cut seaware on Tiree, counsel's attention was drawn to Lord Benholme's words in the Agnew case rather than to Lord Watson's in the Young case as referred to above.

highlights his concern, but ended with the hope that things might be different from 1883 when the Tiree crofters and cottars gave evidence to the Napier Commission.[74] Cunliffe was also concerned that the case might be expensive and troublesome, in particular because of, as he put it, the inaccessibility of the island and also because of the difficulty there might be in obtaining satisfactory evidence. He wanted to know from Davidson & Syme how many witnesses the Crown might have to produce. It would also appear that Cunliffe was not particularly anxious to get the case before the court with any speed; he had before him at that time a good many similar cases. He told Davidson & Syme that 'the matter does not press' and that he did not expect to hear from them on the point until after Easter.[75] He would, therefore, have been somewhat surprised to receive a response by return.

There then followed a flurry of letters exchanged between Cunliffe, Davidson & Syme and Mackinnon on the issue of the number of witnesses and how the Crown could be certain that what witnesses said in their statements would be repeated in the case itself. While these might be seen as mere matters of detail of the sort usually discussed between lawyers, there are, underlying them, the more important issues of the relationship between the duke and the Tiree crofters and cottars, and the wider question of the disturbances in the Highlands and islands and the extent to which these might affect the case.

Cunliffe was anxious to get signed statements from the witnesses because he believed that this would give him a greater hold over what they would eventually say in the case. Davidson & Syme explained to him that in Scotland, signed statements were not accepted in evidence, which had to be given in person or failing that because of age or illness, the witness's evidence had to be taken before a commissioner appointed by the court. It was, however, the general practice of Mackinnon to get precognitions signed where he was not 'absolutely certain of witnesses, and the West Highlander, though not untrustworthy, is inclined to be evasive in the witness box'.[76] This would not have come as particularly welcome news to Cunliffe, nor would the fact that Mackinnon returned, again, to the difficulties of even getting statements from the crofters

[74] TNA:PRO, MT 10/1813, Memorandum, 21 March 1911. 'I dare say,' Cunliffe said, 'the conditions have altered since 1883.'

[75] TNA:PRO, MT 10/1813, Memorandum note 27, March 1911; Letter Cunliffe to Davidson & Syme, 4 April 1911.

[76] TNA:PRO, MT 10/1813, Letters Cunliffe, Davidson & Syme and Mackinnon, 5 April, 6 April, 7 April 1911.

and cottars. He explained that when he had visited the island for the purposes of his original report he had not given the people he spoke to any indication of the reasons for his visit or for the questions he was asking. He explained:

> The Argyll influence in Tiree is paramount, and had it been known that any interest was on behalf of a probable challenge of the asserted ducal rights in the foreshore, apprehension as to their future relations with the Estate would have interposed against the frank expression of their views and knowledge as to the use of the foreshore.[77]

He went on to say that the bulk of the evidence would have to come from the cottar class who had no security of tenure for their dwellings, possessing them at the will of the duke, a point he had made in his report, and it was likely that, out of self-interest, their evidence would be flavoured by 'sympathy towards the Duke'. But as against this he said that he believed the underlying potential for disturbances in the island would act as a deterrent against 'any disposition towards reprisals in the form of determination of precarious possessions of parties favouring the view of the Crown to the extent of giving evidence in support of its challenge to the ducal claim'. While the fear that was expressed by the crofters and cottars to the Napier Commission still affected the community, he thought, on balance, that such a fear 'in a question between the Crown and the Duke . . . might be reckoned an inconsiderable factor'.[78] He concluded that it should be practicable to obtain sufficient evidence on behalf of the Crown. However, he suggested a somewhat unusual prelude in an attempt to prepare the ground for an official approach to the crofters and cottars. He believed that if the crofters and cottars were made aware of the background to the case through the publication of correspondence between the Board and the duke's agents in the *Oban Times*, correspondence which, he suggested, should emphasise that the Board was acting in the interests of the public and that the practice of crofters and cottars and other inhabitants on the island would not be interfered with by the Crown, then any latent apprehension should be assuaged and that they would see it as in their interests to support the Crown's claim. Mackinnon also warned Cunliffe that he thought that the Argyll estate had been preparing its position for just such a challenge by the Crown, piling up, as he put it, instances of possession of the foreshore

[77] TNA:PRO, MT 10/1813, Copy letter Mackinnon to Davidson & Syme, 7 April 1911.

[78] TNA:PRO, MT 10/1813, Copy letter Mackinnon to Davidson & Syme, 7 April 1911.

in support of the duke's claim and compiling a 'large body of carefully accumulated evidence in support of his claim'.[79] While Cunliffe was still concerned about the ability of the Crown to obtain a sufficient number of witnesses[80] and, moreover, to be sure that the evidence they eventually gave was strong enough, he was not prepared to adopt the procedures suggested by Mackinnon. He was not, in particular, prepared at this stage to give the suggested assurances to the crofters and cottars. It was, he said, the duty of the Board to administer the foreshore in the interests of the public generally rather than to safeguard the alleged interests of particular persons. Publication of the correspondence in the *Oban Times* would, he thought, be contrary to the Board's ordinary practice. He was, however, prepared to consider that the Board could indicate publicly at the time the action commenced what the Crown's attitude would be as to the public user of the foreshore. And while he was not ready to give the suggested assurances, he did seem to accept that the interest of the public generally in the Tiree foreshore was not great and that the crofters and cottars in Tiree, where the kelp industry still existed, might, perhaps, be entitled to more consideration than those on the mainland.[81]

## THE CROWN DECIDES TO COMMENCE PROCEEDINGS

An internal note was prepared in October 1911 summarising the case and the potential difficulty of obtaining evidence. By this stage, as the note discloses, it is apparent that the permanent officials at the Board were prepared to recommend to the President of the Board that the islanders could be given an assurance that the practice of taking seaweed would not be interfered with in any way. It was considered that there were good grounds for treating the inhabitants, so far as the gathering of seaware was concerned, on the analogy of tenants of estates adjacent to the sea in Ireland.[82] The permanent officials at the Board had taken

[79] TNA:PRO, MT 10/1813, Letter Davidson & Syme to Cunliffe, 22 April 1911.

[80] Mackinnon had recommended that thirty witnesses would need to be cited – double the number cited by the Crown in Young v. North British Railway Company (1887) 14 R (HL) 53; TNA:PRO, MT 10/1813, Letter Mackinnon to Davidson & Syme, 7 April 1911.

[81] TNA:PRO, MT 10/1813, Memorandum, 27 April 1911.

[82] TNA:PRO, MT 10/1813, Claim of the Duke of Argyll to the foreshore of the Island of Tiree H5742/11 27, October 1911, initialled CHG. For the position of Irish tenants and the actions of landlords in connection with the removal of seaweed which is referred to in this note, see PP, 1911, XIV, Royal Commission, vol. 3 (part 2), Cd 5709, Qs 25356–64.

matters as far as they could and now required a political decision. It was decided that the papers should be put before Mr J. M. Robertson, the parliamentary secretary to the President of the Board, because 'the question of instituting proceedings is to some extent a question of policy'.[83] At the beginning of January 1912 Robertson discussed the case with the Hon. T. W. H. Pelham, the assistant secretary to the Board for the harbour department, and with Cunliffe. His internal file note was brief and to the point: 'I have consulted Mr Pelham and the Solicitor. It seems incumbent on us to proceed with the action.'[84] Robertson's minute of the meeting was fuller and revealed that he was aware that there were potential difficulties in pressing the claim and that he was doubtful in the light of these difficulties whether it was expedient to take proceedings given that the value of the foreshore was not large, and that more harm than good might be done to the crofters and cottars by such proceedings. However, having weighed it all up Robertson inclined, on the whole, to the view that proceedings should be taken. He took note of what the Royal Commission on Coast Erosion had said about the difficulties the Crown was under adequately to safeguard the proprietary rights of the Crown in the Scottish foreshore. He concluded his minute, which was sent to the President, by saying: 'where we are advised that we have a good case, as in the present instance, I suggest it is advisable to endeavour to preserve, if possible, the foreshore for the Crown against the claim of a private owner'. But Robertson was concerned to ensure that the duke was not upset by the actions of the Crown and that he should be told that the proceedings would be as friendly as possible and that the Board had no wish to act in a harsh or dictatorial manner; that it was obliged to act to safeguard the rights of the Crown where they were advised that those rights were good.[85] However, internal notes exchanged between the officials in the harbour department of the Board show that there was not a great deal of enthusiasm within that department for taking proceedings. Pelham questioned the expediency of such a step 'unless and until some pressure is brought to bear upon us by those interested'. On the other hand, he was concerned that further delay might weaken the Crown's case as regards future proceedings not only in Tiree, but also in other islands.[86] Pelham wrote to the duke in

[83] TNA:PRO, MT 10/1813, Minute, 30 December 1911.

[84] TNA:PRO, MT 10/1813, Minute, 4 January 1911.

[85] TNA:PRO, MT 10/1813, Note from Robertson to the President. Claim of the Duke of Argyll to the Foreshore of the Island of Tiree, 1 February 1912.

[86] TNA:PRO, MT 10/1813, Minutes, 27 November, 16 December, 30 December 1911, 4 January 1912.

March 1912. His letter followed the line that had been agreed by the Board. He told the duke that where there was a dispute over ownership of the foreshore, as there was here, the onus on proving title rested with the claimant, that is, the duke, not the Crown and that, on the basis of the evidence thus far produced by Lindsay Howe, the Crown's *prima facie* title had not been displaced. He explained the overriding public interest obligations of the Board and hoped that the duke would understand that the Board was not acting in an arbitrary manner, but that the Board felt it was necessary to bring the proceedings to establish the Crown's title; however, before such proceedings were brought, the Board would be glad to consider any observations which the duke might have.[87]

On receipt of this letter, the duke went to see Pelham, but, due to Pelham being unwell, the duke saw Cunliffe instead. It appears that the duke told Cunliffe that his rights to the Tiree foreshore had been granted to him by charter; but he held out an olive branch to Cunliffe, promising him that the Board could have, free of charge, all the materials they needed from the foreshore for the construction of the pier at Gott Bay. Lindsay Howe, writing to the Board on 27 March 1912, confirmed this offer but also went on to say that the duke would resist any attempt to deprive him of the foreshore. Lindsay Howe also expressed some surprise that the Board should have carried 'on a correspondence first with us and then write direct to His Grace'.[88] The conciliatory approach that the Board wanted to adopt with the duke, which was the reason for Pelham's personal letter to the duke, had not got off to a particularly auspicious start. Clearly, the letter of response to this would have to be carefully drafted. The letter that was finally sent by Pelham on 25 April was phrased rather more diplomatically than Cunliffe's rather blunt draft and politely, but firmly, reiterated the Board's position.[89] As to the duke's claim to have a Crown charter to the foreshore, the letter said that the Board had seen no evidence of this, but that if such a charter existed, asked for the Board to be supplied with particulars of it.

Lindsay Howe replied that the duke had not been referring to a charter that granted title in specific words, but to one that allowed a

[87] TNA:PRO, MT 10/1813, Copy letter Pelham to Argyll, 6 March 1912.

[88] TNA:PRO, MT 10/1813, Letter Lindsay Howe to Board of Trade, 27 March 1912.

[89] TNA:PRO, MT 10/1813. Compare the draft prepared by Cunliffe in the Memorandum dated 3 April 1912 with the copy letter Pelham to Lindsay Howe dated 25 April 1912.

claim to prescriptive possession to be made. The Board had already accepted this.[90] But Lindsay Howe re-emphasised the extent of the possession the duke had had through the collection of seaware for manure and kelp, such collection having been done by tenants on behalf of the duke under regulations made by him and by others under special leases. As to the extent of the kelp industry, Lindsay Howe said that £379 had been spent by the Argyll factor on the collection of seaware from the foreshore in the one season of 1875–6 and that the collection of seaware had gone on more or less in the same manner since before the nineteenth century. They also sent a copy of a notice that had been sent to tenants in 1822 as an example of how the kelp industry had been regulated by the 7th duke. This was a notice from James Maxwell, the duke's chamberlain, to the effect that the quality of kelp being made on the island was not up to standard and the tenants were warned that if they produced bad-quality kelp, they would be punished.[91] The Board seems to have regarded this letter and its enclosures, with its evidence of extensive possession through the kelp industry, to have been significant. Cunliffe agreed to submit the letter and its enclosures to James Pitman for his advice as to whether it would lead him to alter his views. Pitman responded that, while the 1822 Notice did, indeed, clearly show that the duke had asserted his right to the seaware, there was nothing in it to shake his opinion that because of the counter-possession of the public, the duke had not exercised possession which was sufficiently exclusive to establish his right to the foreshore. This was positive. However, Pitman ended his response on a negative note by saying: 'whether it will be possible to get the Tiree public to speak against the Duke is another question altogether'.[92] This issue was still a matter of concern.

There then followed, somewhat slowly, the necessary steps to bring the matter before the court. However, in June 1913 the attention of the Board was drawn to certain Scottish Land Court proceedings in Tiree. The proceedings concerned the creation of new, and the enlargement of existing, holdings at Hynish in Tiree by the BoAS under the Small Landholders (Scotland) Act 1911. The question of rights for the new tenants to seaware was, apparently, raised in the proceedings and the

[90] As we have noted earlier, the Office of Woods had seen a copy of the 1774 Crown charter and had commented on this aspect of it to the Board in February 1910, and the Law Officers and Pitman had been sent a copy of it.

[91] TNA:PRO, MT 10/1813, Letter Lindsay Howe to Pelham, 27 May 1912; copy Notice to the Tenants of Tiry, 12 April 1822.

[92] TNA:PRO, MT 10/1813, Letter Pitman to Davidson & Syme, 26 August 1912.

court was assured by the duke's counsel that any privileges or rights given to the new holders would not exclude those who were at present gathering seaware so that the position would not be that only the new holders would have the right to take seaware. The presiding judge, Lord Kennedy, also pointed out that, even if the duke had wanted to, the court was not in a position to prohibit those who were at present gathering seaware without, at the least, giving them a hearing.[93] Davidson & Syme informed Cunliffe of these proceedings because they believed them to have some bearing on the Crown's proposed action against the duke. It might, they suggested, be harder to persuade the crofters and cottars to give evidence if the duke had already publicly given assurances as to rights to seaware. This did not alter the Board's decision to press on. The Office of Woods, who still had responsibility for the mineral rights on the foreshore, appears to have been enthusiastic. The Office thought that the value of any possible minerals on the foreshore was an important matter (although admitting that the value was limited). It also appears that the Office of Woods thought that the policy of attempting to vindicate the Crown's right was a good one in the duke's case in view of the fact that the duke laid claim to several other foreshore areas such as Kintyre and Iona. It was the view of the Office of Woods that 'It would be well to show [the duke] the Crown is in earnest.'[94] The Office of Woods was concerned to know the attitude of the duke. Was he prepared to fight, or 'whether on a show of strength he will back down'? The Solicitor to the Office of Woods, Thomas Carmichael, thought the duke would be reluctant to enter into expensive litigation unless there was a financial interest at stake and he thought that 'very probably the action may not be keenly defended'.[95]

Work proceeded on drafting the summons of declarator. Cunliffe asked Davidson & Syme to ask Pitman to advise him whether there was any special point in the draft summons on which Cunliffe should see the Lord Advocate. Pitman thought that the Lord Advocate might

[93] See the report of the hearing in *The Scotsman*, 13 June 1913. For details of the BoAS Schemes in Tiree, see Cameron, *Land for the People?*, pp. 157–9.

[94] NRS, CR 11/152, Memorandum, 14 June 1913. The Memorandum stated that 'The attitude of this Dept should, I take it, be governed on the one hand by the value of the minerals and by the probable cost to this Dept. of the action if we are joined in.' As to the value of the minerals, the Office of Woods took the advice of Mr W. Forster Brown, a mining engineer. He reported that it was unlikely that there was much in the way of mineral value in the foreshore; see NRS, CR 11/152, Letter Forster Brown to Office of Woods, 11 July 1913.

[95] NRS, CR 11/152, Letter Carmichael to Office of Woods, 20 August 1913.

be reminded of the potential reluctance on the part of the crofters and cottars to give evidence and that the Lord Advocate might like to consider including words in the condescendence to make it clear that the Board was taking the action to protect the right of the public to take seaware, sand and gravel from the foreshore. This was something which was now, perhaps, even more important given that the BoAS schemes in Tiree were under attack from the crofters who were dissatisfied and disappointed with the size, character and locality of the holdings being offered. Instances of unfair preference and inequitable allotments of land were cited. At an open air meeting held in June 1913, a number of critical resolutions were passed including one that

> the people of Tiree are morally and religiously bound to take forcible possession of suitable and available land in the Island unless the Scottish Secretary undertakes to put the [Act] into operation in favour of all eligible applicants for new holdings.[96]

Relationships between the crofters and the Crown were not, it seemed, good. Pitman also thought that the Lord Advocate should have his attention drawn to the possible difficulty that 'although the real use of the foreshore had been public, the pecuniary profit in connection therewith was really derived by the Duke of Argyll from the kelp'.[97]

By the time the summons was issued in November 1913[98] the Law Officers had changed. Robert Munro was the Lord Advocate and T. B. Morison was the Solicitor General so neither of the Law Officers who had given the original opinion was in office.[99] The closed record in January 1914 shows that the duke's defence was based on the exclusive possession of the foreshore by the duke. The defenders, it said,

> have constantly and continuously, and without challenge, dealt with the said foreshore as their own property, and from time immemorial, or at least for [the prescriptive period of twenty years] exercised their proprietary rights by all the acts of possession of which the foreshore was capable. In particular they have systematically cut and gathered tangle and other seaware in large quantities for the manufacture of kelp and other purposes. The exercise of this valuable and important right of property has been carefully supervised

96 *Oban Times*, 28 June 1913.

97 TNA:PRO, MT10/1813, Letter Davidson & Syme to Cunliffe, 5 November 1912.

98 NRS, CS 257/393, Summons, 28 November 1913.

99 As we saw in Chapter 6, Munro and Morison were the Law Officers who advised the Board of Trade on the seaware and prescription clauses in the draft Coast Protection Bill in 1915.

and regulated by the defender and his predecessors in leases of agricultural land ex adverso of the sea, and has been separately leased by them to persons desiring to engage commercially in the manufacture of kelp.[100]

## THE CROWN ABANDONS ITS ACTION AGAINST THE DUKE

This defence should not have come as any surprise to the Board, but before the case was due to be heard on 16 June 1914, the Board abandoned the action. There is, unfortunately, an absence of papers or notes in the relevant files which go into this decision in any real depth, or which seek to explain it in terms other than the baldest of legal reasons. We know, of course, that the Law Officers were not the ones who had given the original opinion that the Board was in a position to commence proceedings, and a letter from the new Solicitor General, T. B. Morison, to the Lord Advocate gives his reasons for advising that the action should be abandoned:

> I point out that when the action was raised we had recovered none of the material documents. These now establish (1) that the Duke's title is *habile* to enable him to acquire right to the foreshore by prescriptive possession; (2) that he and his predecessors have asserted right to it for over 100 years and have occupied and used it in every possible way during that period; (3) that no counter right or claim of any kind has ever been asserted against this possession.
>
> I am clearly of opinion that in order to prevent such user, as the Duke and his tenants etc have made of the foreshore, from founding a good prescriptive right, it is necessary for us to establish some substantial adverse public use of the foreshore.
>
> I do not consider the use of the cottars on the Island – that is to say the Duke's cottars – as adverse use at all. They occupy their cottages at the pleasure of the Duke and the presumption is that that is the footing on which they took the kelp, sand and gravel etc. And there is evidence in fact which supports this legal presumption. The evidence of the use of the foreshore by outside people is of the most meagre and casual description and it is, in my view, wholly insufficient in character, quality and degree to interrupt the otherwise exclusive possession of the Duke.[101]

The Lord Advocate concurred with the views expressed by Morison and told Cunliffe that the Crown should not proceed with the case, mainly for the reasons given by Morison, but he also laid considerable

[100] NRS, CR 11/152, Closed Record – The Lord Advocate against Niall Diarmid Campbell, 20 January 1914.

[101] NRS, CR 11/152, Copy letter Morison to the Lord Advocate, 20 May 1914.

stress on the views of Lord Watson in Young v. North British Railway Company as to the value of the taking of loose or drift seaware as an act of possession. Lord Watson had, as we have noted above, said that the relative importance of taking drift seaware and cutting growing seaware depended not so much on the attachment or the non-attachment, but on the relative value. In the Tiree case, the value of the drift seaware had been considerable and was, therefore, of great significance in terms of acts of possession.[102] Pitman explained the views of the Solicitor General by saying that the 'law as to squatters in Scotland is I think the foundation of the opinion expressed by the Solicitor General'. Under Scots Law, he said, no length of time would give the cottars a title to their houses, and so there was no one in Tiree whose occupation of the foreshore could be founded on as being adverse to the duke. Pitman emphasised that the Crown's precognitions in this case had said that the principal collectors of tangle for kelp were the landless cottars all over the island. 'Whatever rights', he said, 'the cottars may have considered they had, or may have asserted, this certainly is clear, that all the kelp when manufactured was sold through the duke's agency.'[103]

We should consider this advice of Munro and Morison in the light of what had gone before. Morison's statement that when the action was started the Crown had not recovered any of the material documents is odd. The Board and all the lawyers had been well aware, from the outset, of the duke's title to the island of Tiree; the cases to Pitman and the Law Officers in 1910 and again in March 1911 had contained full details of the 1774 charter in favour of the then Duke of Argyll, a document that made it clear that the duke had a barony title that was *habile* and enabled him to acquire right to the foreshore by prescriptive possession. As to the documents that showed that the duke and his predecessors had asserted rights for over 100 years, while the Crown may not, before, have seen the leases granted by the duke, it can hardly be said that they were unaware of the extent of the duke's close involvement in the kelp industry or the terms under which that industry had been carried on, and the role of the crofters and, in particular, the

[102] NRS, CR 11/152, Copy letter Cunliffe to Davidson & Syme, 25 May 1914. See Young v. North British Railway Company (1887) 14 R (HL) 53 at p. 55, a case described by Rankine as being 'very instructive'; Rankine, *Ownership of Lands* (4th edn), p. 277.

[103] Was Pitman, perhaps, embarrassed that he had to explain the law behind the Solicitor General's point about the lack of security of the cottars for their houses, and that he had not spotted it himself? There is no indication that he was; NRS, CR 11/152, Copy letter Pitman to Davidson & Syme, 27 May 1914.

cottars. Furthermore, the previous Law Officers and Pitman would have known what Lord Watson had said in Young v. North British Railway Company and yet they did not mention it; nor, of course, did Cunliffe. But it is the advice given by Morison on the position of the cottars, and, in particular, the fact that they had no title to their houses but held them at the pleasure of the duke, that is the most significant. The status of the cottars and the manner in which they had contributed to the kelp industry had been dealt with in detail by Mackinnon's Report that made it clear, in particular, that the cottars were dependent for their houses on the goodwill of the duke. Indeed, it was the very precariousness of their position vis-à-vis the duke that had caused the concern over the gathering of evidence from them. Of course, it is true that Pitman had said in his original opinion in 1910 that there was no evidence of counter-possession and that the duke's claim was well founded; and that the Law Officers and Pitman had in 1910 asked for the further information before they were all able in 1911 to say that the duke did not have a right to the whole foreshore of the island and that the evidence of counter-possession was sufficient to oust the duke's claim; and that Pitman himself had asked, before the summons had been issued, for the Lord Advocate's attention to be drawn to the fact that the profits from the gathering of seaware by the cottars were wholly those of the duke. But on the whole it seems fair to say that on the same facts there was, as between Pitman, Ure and Hunter in 1911 and Munro and Morison in 1914, a fundamental difference of opinion as to the application of the law to those facts. Or, to be more generous to Pitman, Ure and Hunter, it might also be fair to say that they did, perhaps, have doubts but did not express them clearly; their 1911 opinion did not, after all, in terms, advise the Crown to bring an action against the duke but only that the appropriate steps, if the Crown wished to vindicate its rights, were to bring an action of declarator.[104] In any event, the advice left the Board with no alternative but to abandon the action. Cunliffe tried, as a last throw of the dice, to suggest that because the possession showed by the duke applied principally to the eastern side of the island, it might be argued that the duke did not have a title to all the foreshore of the island. Pitman, however, had no difficulty in dismissing this suggestion.[105]

[104] Munro's confidence in Pitman was not, however, shaken as he was later expressly to ask that Pitman should be instructed together with the Law Officers on the foreshore issues contained in the Coast Protection Bill discussed in Chapter 6; NRS, AF 43/60, Copy letter Milner Craig to Board of Trade, 8 October 1914.

[105] NRS, CR 11/152, Copy letters Cunliffe to Pitman, 25 May, Pitman to Cunliffe, 27 May 1914.

There then followed a damage limitation exercise. The duke's solicitors asked that the Board should agree to *absolvitor* being obtained in the action rather than that the action should be dismissed. The effect of *absolvitor* would be that the question of the ownership of the foreshore would be *res judicata* and no action on the same question could again be raised, whereas a dismissal would allow, at least theoretically, the Crown to raise a new action if it discovered new and additional evidence. The duke's solicitors also gave the Board to understand that if the Crown would not agree to *absolvitor* being obtained, the duke would, himself, bring an action against the Crown to have it declared that the foreshore belonged to the duke. Pitman's advice was that the duke was not entitled, in any event, to *absolvitor* and that if the duke did later bring an action that the Crown did not defend, the decree in absence thus obtained by the duke would be open to review in twenty years. The Crown could, therefore, to some extent protect its position or, at least, not put any claim it might have completely out of reach.[106]

And this is what happened. The Crown's action was abandoned[107] and the duke commenced his own action the next year, asking for a declaration that the whole of the Tiree foreshore was his property. The Law Officers advised that the duke's action should not be defended and a decree in absence was granted on 18 February 1915.[108] But this was not quite the end of the story. The Board again considered the ownership of the Tiree foreshore in 1983 in the context of the Tiree Long Range Radar Station. Officials at the Board wanted to be certain that the Crown had been right in abandoning its own action in 1914 and that it was not 'an internal office decision, based on unsound judgement that had led to the abandonment of the case'. The file was re-examined and the resulting file note drew a line under the whole issue. After summarising what had taken place, it confirmed that no challenge had been made after the decree in absence and concluded: 'It is clear that the Crown has been divested of this area of the foreshore and I recommend that my records be noted as per my minute of 23/11/83 [that the record

[106] TNA:PRO, MT 10/1813, Letter Davidson & Syme to Cunliffe, 2 June 1914.

[107] Reported in *The Scotsman*, 5 June 1914.

[108] TNA:PRO, MT 10/1813, Letter Milner Craig to Cunliffe, 4 February 1915; Summons, 27 January 1915. Duke of Argyll v. Lord Advocate (1915), NRS, CS 46/1915/3/2, Interlocutor signed by William Hunter finding, declaring and decreeing in absence against the Lord Advocate. It was, of course, the same William Hunter who had advised the Crown on its claim in 1911 as Solicitor General.

maps be noted "claim verified"].'[109] The pier at Gott Bay which gave rise to the dispute was eventually completed towards the end of 1914, some sixty-seven years after the idea for it was first mooted, and in roughly the same period of time which the legal manoeuvring between the duke and the Board had taken.

## CONCLUSIONS

The experiences of the Crown between 1857 and 1868 in the dispute between the 8th Duke of Argyll and the Crown over the Rosneath foreshore, as discussed in Chapter 4, had not been happy ones for the Crown. And the dispute over the Tiree foreshore had not ended any more successfully for the Crown. Indeed, we might conclude that the Crown had suffered a similarly humiliating defeat. What, then, was it that had motivated the Crown once again to take on a Duke of Argyll over a foreshore question? The ground rules had, of course, changed from the mid-nineteenth century when the Crown was attempting to have decided the main question as to the ownership of the foreshore. By the time the Tiree case was being considered it was accepted that the *ex adverso* proprietor with a suitable title could claim ownership of the foreshore if he could prove sufficient prescriptive possession. It was, as we saw in Chapter 6, the issue of prescriptive possession which, at the beginning of the twentieth century, was now the battleground for the Crown and that the Board (and, in particular, its solicitor Sir Ellis Cunliffe) believed that the rules regarding prescriptive possession and, in particular, the significance of the gathering of seaware for kelp and manure, needed to be changed in favour of the Crown. The Royal Commission on Coast Erosion had just recommended that the prescriptive period should be extended in relation to foreshore claims. The consideration by the Board of the Tiree case was, therefore, taking place at just the time when this issue was at the forefront of the minds of the permanent officials and the Board's advisers, and, indeed, the politicians. The parliamentary secretary to the Board had specifically referred to what the Royal Commission had said about the difficulties the Crown was under adequately to safeguard the property rights of the Crown in the Scottish foreshore. The officials and politicians recognised that the Board had a duty to protect those property rights and to challenge the duke if the Board was advised it had a case in law. Cunliffe must

109 NRS, CR 11/152, Minutes, 23 November–15 December 1983, Roslynne Falconer, S. Harvey, and Mrs Swanston.

have felt the ghost of Thomas Farrer hovering over his shoulder as he wrestled with the case.

The role the kelp industry played in the dispute and, in particular, the role in that industry of the crofters and cottars was fundamental. There can be no doubt that the eventual success of the duke in establishing title to the Tiree foreshore derived predominantly from the fact that, for the relevant period, the crofters and cottars had collected drift seaware for the manufacture of kelp and that the duke, and his predecessors, had purported to regulate this activity. This was truly a case where the foreshore became part of the Duke of Argyll's lands through, and because of, the kelp industry and the efforts of the crofters and cottars in that industry.

# 9

# 'A genuine opportunity to change the fabric of Scottish society'

## INTRODUCTION

The history of Scotland's foreshore thus far described in this book has been concerned with the hundred years or so between the mid-nineteenth and mid-twentieth centuries. It has largely engaged with the debate that centred on whether the shore was owned by the Crown or by adjacent proprietors. The ownership issue has been settled, but another part of the debate that has run through this book has been how, and by whom, the Crown-owned foreshore should be managed in the public interest, and this part of the debate is still a live issue. In this chapter we give an outline of modern developments in the responsibility for the management of Crown-owned foreshore, and proposals for changes in the law of the foreshore relating to public rights and crofters' rights to seaweed.

## MANAGEMENT OF SCOTLAND'S CROWN FORESHORE: EVOLUTION AND DEVOLUTION

### *Evolution*

The management of Scotland's Crown foreshore has been undertaken since 1833 by a number of different bodies in a manner that may be described as something of a merry-go-round. As we saw in Chapter 2, the management was transferred in 1833 from the Barons of His Majesty's Court of Exchequer in Scotland to the Office of Woods in London, and the Office of Woods were given the same powers with regard to Scotland's Crown foreshore as they had in England under the Crown Lands Act 1829. The Admiralty had responsibility for the protection of navigation over the foreshore until 1862 when this responsibility was transferred to the Board of Trade. In 1866 the management of Scotland's

Crown foreshore was, as we discussed in Chapter 3, transferred from the Office of Woods to the Board of Trade, thus uniting responsibility for the management of, and the protection of navigation over, the foreshore in the Board apart from certain parts of the foreshore that were excluded from the 1866 transfer; these were: the parts of the foreshore dealt with by lease by the Office of Woods before the end of 1866, the foreshore in front of government property above the high water mark, and mines and minerals under the foreshore (all of which remained with the Office of Woods). Crucially, as we saw in Chapter 3, the Board was given only the powers over the foreshore that the Office of Woods had under the 1829 Act. The exclusions from the 1866 Act meant that after 1866 there was still a split of responsibility for the excluded parts of the foreshore, a subject that was examined by the 1911 Royal Commission, as we discussed in Chapter 6. The Royal Commission recommended that provision should be made for the administration of all Crown foreshore by one department in the public interest, and that for this purpose a transfer of the management of the parts of the foreshore excluded from the 1866 transfer that remained with the Office of Woods should be made to the Board. The recommendation was to have been given effect by the Coast Protection Bill of 1929 but, as we saw in Chapter 6, the Bill failed to pass the House of Commons. The split of responsibility therefore continued.[1]

In 1927 the Office of Woods (renamed in 1924 as the Commissioners of Crown Lands[2]) became a body corporate under the name of the Commissioners of Crown Lands, and the powers of sale and leasing in the Crown Lands Act 1829 were replaced by provisions that provided sales and leases could only be made for the best consideration in money that could reasonably be obtained, thus making explicit what Farrer had said was implied by the spirit of the 1829 Act.[3] In 1939 the Board's responsibility for management of Crown foreshore passed to the Ministry

[1] Crown Lands Act 1906, section 2 did, in fact, provide for a transfer of management of foreshore between the Office and the Board (and vice versa) but it was only intended that this should be used to effect exchanges; PP, 1906, Select Committee on Crown Lands Bill, Paper No. 159, Minutes of Evidence, para. 6; PP, 1907, XXXIV, Royal Commission, vol. 1 (part 2), Cd 3684, Qs 96–7.

[2] By the Forestry (Title of Commissioners of Woods) Order 1924, SI 1924/1370.

[3] Crown Lands Act 1927, sections 3 and 5, which replicated the Settled Land Act 1925 provisions for trust property; PD, Fifth Series, vol. 204, House of Commons, col. 1302 (30 March 1927). Section 10 of the Act also introduced certain exceptions to the 'best consideration' requirement, again replicating the Settled Land Act 1925.

of Shipping when that department was created at the outbreak of war.[4] In 1941 there was another transfer of responsibility, from the Ministry of Shipping to the Ministry of War Transport.[5] In 1946 the title of the Ministry of War Transport was altered to the Ministry of Transport, and consideration was given to yet another transfer of responsibility for Crown foreshore. It was felt that the management of the bulk of the Crown's foreshore was not a function that was particularly appropriate to a department concerned with transport. The permanent secretary, Sir Gilmour Jenkins, said that

> the Ministry of Transport would like to be relieved of this work as soon as it could be arranged. Foreshore administration had been transferred to the Ministry for a number of historical reasons which had lost their force during the present century. It did not fit conveniently with the Ministry's organisation for its more important tasks and it would be a considerable convenience if this work could be taken over by the Commissioners of Crown Lands on an agency basis, until the necessary legislation could be secured.[6]

Consideration was given to a transfer of the management of the foreshore to either the Commissioners of Crown Lands, or the Ministry of Agriculture and Fisheries, or the Ministry of Town and Country Planning.[7] In the event, on 1 April 1947 it was the Commissioners of Crown Lands that assumed responsibility on an agency basis,[8] and legislative effect was given to the transfer in the Coast Protection Act 1949.[9] The reunification of the management of Crown foreshore that had been recommended by the Royal Commission in 1911 was thus, finally, achieved. In 1955 the Commissioners of Crown Lands were the subject of an inquiry into their activities from which major reforms resulted.[10] The resulting Crown Estate Act 1956 established a new board

[4] The Minister of Shipping (Transfer of Functions) Order 1939, SI 1939/1470.

[5] The Ministers of the Crown (Minister of War Transport) Order 1941, SI 1941/654. The Ministry of War Transport was formed by merging the Ministry of Shipping and the Ministry of Transport.

[6] TNA:PRO, T 227/1096, Crown Foreshore and Coast Protection. Meeting at the Treasury, 9 April 1946.

[7] TNA:PRO, T 227/1096, Cabinet. Machinery of Government Committee. Coast Protection and the Management of Crown Foreshore. Treasury Report. May 1946; TNA:PRO, MT 45/117, Memorandum for the Official Committee on the Machinery of Government – Crown Foreshore and Coast Erosion, June 1946.

[8] PD, Fifth Series, vol. 436, House of Commons Written Answers, col. 150 (25 April 1947).

[9] Sections 37–40.

[10] PP, 1955/56, Report of the Committee on Crown Lands, June 1955, Cmd

of Commissioners under the name of the Crown Estate Commissioners (CEC), and the remaining part of the reform, including the powers of management, was brought about in the Crown Estate Act 1961.[11]

So far, so unremarkable, apart from the rather unsatisfactory shuffling of responsibility for the foreshore. However, the issue that has run through this book, that of balancing the duty to administer the foreshore in the public interest with the perceived legal requirement not to part with property at less than full value, something that had so troubled Farrer when he wrote his memorandum in 1866, raised its head again in 1958. The legislative framework for the management of Crown foreshore had, since the Crown Lands Act 1829, been to prevent sales and leases at less than full value. This was the legacy left by the efforts of Skene & Peacock, the Association of Seaboard Proprietors of Scotland and individual proprietors in the House of Lords that had secured the amendments to the Crown Lands Bill of 1866 that had perpetuated the full value provisions for disposals of Crown foreshore discussed in Chapter 3. Farrer had believed, as we saw in Chapter 3, that changes would have to be made 'to enable the Board of Trade to deal more liberally with the title of the Crown in the case of works of public utility'.[12] But he had also expressed the hope that a 'liberal construction' of the legislative framework might enable the Board to manage the inherent conflict that this framework and the duty to act in the public interest created. The Crown Lands Act 1927 had made explicit what Farrer said had been implied by the spirit of the 1829 Act, and yet the Board and its successors, including the CEC, had all, it appears, managed to work within the legislative framework 'and had [yet] satisfied the requirements of the public interest', and they had done so because 'no rigorous policy of getting the best return had been pursued'.[13] But in 1958 it became apparent that the CEC were now pursuing a policy of getting the best return from the Crown foreshore without regard to the public interest. This came to a head over the proposal for development of the port at Milford Haven that was thought to be the first major exercise of the CEC's new policy. The controversy over the actions of

9483; M. E. Deans, 'The Crown Estate Commissioners: their role and responsibilities in respect of the foreshore and seabed around Scotland', *Journal of Energy and Natural Resources Law*, 4:3 (1986), p. 169.

[11] F. A. Enever, 'The Crown Estate Act 1961', *The Modern Law Review*, 25:4 (1962), pp. 442–5.

[12] Farrer Memorandum, p. 9.

[13] TNA:PRO, BT 243/95, Memorandum by Ports Division, Ministry of Transport – Foreshores and Seabed and the Crown Estate, 10 April 1958.

the CEC in dealing with rents and royalties for the foreshore and seabed at Milford Haven is well known.[14] What has not, however, been written about is that the concerns over the new policy of the CEC gave rise to the serious possibility that the responsibility for the foreshore would be removed from the CEC and moved back to the Ministry of Transport in much the same circumstances as had occurred in 1866, as we discussed in Chapter 3.

At a meeting of the permanent secretaries held in the Cabinet Office in November 1958 chaired by Sir Norman Brook[15] there was

> general agreement that the present policy of the Commissioners, although according to their statutory duty, was not, in relation to the foreshore ... compatible with the public interest ... [and] that it would not be possible for the Commissioners to retain jurisdiction over the foreshore ... within the present statutory framework ... [and] that this jurisdiction should be transferred to another body.[16]

There was also agreement recorded at a later meeting in the Cabinet Office that it was

> fundamentally illogical to equate the foreshore and seabed with [other Crown estate assets] which could be administered by reference to the ordinary criteria of sound and profitable estate management. The foreshore and seabed ... fell in a wholly different category and should be administered primarily by reference to the public interest.[17]

There then followed, over the next twelve months, discussions over the practicalities of the proposed transfer to the Ministry of Transport and the terms on which the transfer would be made. The choice of the Ministry of Transport was perhaps an odd one given what Sir Gilmour Jenkins had said in 1946 about the reasons for that Ministry giving up

[14] Deans, 'The Crown Estate Commissioners', pp. 182–3; PD, Fifth Series, vol. 643, House of Commons, cols 587–90 (28 June 1961).

[15] Brook was the Cabinet secretary, joint permanent secretary at the Treasury and head of the home civil service; he was '*the* great technician of cabinet government in mid-twentieth century Whitehall'; K. Theakston, 'Brook, Norman Craven, Baron Normanbrook (1902–1967)', in *Oxford Dictionary of National Biography*, Oxford University Press, available at <http://www.oxforddnb.com/view/article/32089> (last accessed 25 October 2017).

[16] TNA:PRO, BT 243/95, Cabinet – Foreshore and Seabed; record of meeting, 10 November 1958. As we see later in this chapter in relation to the devolution proposals, the conclusion reached by the Scottish Affairs Committee in 2012 as to the management practice of the CEC was remarkably similar to this conclusion of the permanent secretaries and Brook in 1958.

[17] TNA:PRO, BT 243/95, Record of meeting, 12 October 1960.

responsibility for the foreshore, but in a note written after the meeting, Jenkins had recorded:

> In discussion it became clear that there was no department more appropriate to administer the foreshore than the Ministry of Transport (who had indeed owned [sic] and administered it as a legacy from the Board of Trade, Ministry of Shipping and Ministry of War Transport up to 1948). Housing and Local Government own no estates and the only Ministry with substantial holdings is the Ministry of Supply, but they have no interest in the coastline. I said that if the transfer were decided upon, we would be prepared to take over again responsibility for the foreshore.[18]

There were also, crucially, discussions with the CEC about the possibility of involving the district valuer in negotiations for foreshore transactions.[19] In October 1960 Brook convened another meeting of the permanent secretaries at the Cabinet Office. He recalled the agreement that had been reached in the previous meeting in 1958 that ministers should be advised to approve the transfer of responsibilities from the CEC to the Ministry of Transport. But he now suggested that this conclusion should be reconsidered. He was concerned that legislation would be needed and 'it was always undesirable in principle to provoke Parliamentary discussion of the financial interests of the Crown unless it was absolutely necessary'. Furthermore, he said, the CEC could claim compensation for the transfer (as they had in 1866). But, significantly, the reconsideration seemed to be driven mainly by the fact that over the time since the proposal was first mooted, the CEC now appeared to be prepared to exercise their functions with respect to the foreshore with greater moderation than they had originally shown; they were prepared to employ the district valuer in assessing the consideration; and, most importantly, they were prepared to exclude any element of monopoly value in negotiating the consideration they would ask for. In these circumstances it was, Brook recorded, 'open to question whether it would be expedient for the Government to introduce legislation to transfer the administrative responsibility for the foreshore and seabed to the Ministry of Transport'.[20] And in the event, there was no forced transfer from the CEC. Although the CEC gave undertakings to involve the district valuer and to exclude any element of monopoly, the Crown Lands Bill of 1961 was amended in committee to include an express

[18] TNA:PRO, BT 243/95, Note by Jenkins, 11 November 1958.

[19] TNA:PRO, BT 243/95, Letter Edwards to Sharp, 20 October 1960.

[20] TNA:PRO, BT 243/95, Foreshore and Seabed. Record of meeting in the Cabinet Office, 26 October 1960.

provision that the requirement of the CEC to obtain 'the best consideration' was to 'exclude any element of monopoly value attributable to the extent of the Crown's ownership of comparable land'.[21]

The merry-go-round of shifting responsibility for the Crown foreshore had, pending devolution, turned full circle and it is fascinating to note, as we shall see, that the issue which had so troubled Farrer in 1866 and Brook in 1958 – that of balancing the duty to administer the foreshore in the public interest with the perceived legal requirement not to part with property at less than full value – was to be an important part of the debate over proposals to transfer to the Scottish Parliament the responsibility for the management of Scotland's Crown foreshore (and other Scottish Crown estate assets) and the terms on which the devolved management should be conducted.

### *Devolution*

The creation of the Scottish Parliament and the devolution settlement in the Scotland Act 1998 left in its wake a further confusion over the foreshore. The Crown's interest as proprietor of the foreshore and the public rights held by the Crown in trust for the public were not reserved matters but the management of Scotland's foreshore remaining in Crown ownership was reserved to the Westminster Parliament,[22] a split that was criticised in the debate on the 1998 Scotland Bill when a long-standing dissatisfaction with the operation of the CEC in Scotland was made clear.[23] In the aftermath of the creation of the Scottish Parliament, the Land Reform Policy Group (LRPG), set up to identify and assess proposals for land reform in rural Scotland, published a series of papers between 1998 and 1999.[24] Its initial paper noted that issues to do with the Crown estate and the CEC would be reserved matters dealt

[21] Crown Estate Act 1961, section 3(1); see PD, Fifth Series, vol. 643, House of Commons, cols 1818–38 (6 July 1961) for the debate on the amendment of the Bill to exclude the element of monopoly value. Sections 3(6) and 4 of the Act also preserved, and extended, the exceptions from the 'best consideration' requirement that had been in the 1927 Act.

[22] Scotland Act 1998, schedule 5, paras 1, 2(3), 3(1).

[23] PD, Sixth Series, vol. 309, House of Commons, cols 907–13 (30 March 1998); PD, Sixth Series, vol. 312, House of Commons, cols 806–13 (19 May 1998); A. McHarg, 'Crown estate devolution', *Edinburgh Law Review*, 20:3 (2016), p. 390.

[24] LRPG, Identifying the Problems, February 1998, available at <http://www.gov.scot/Resource/0045/00451950.pdf> (last accessed 25 October 2017); LRPG, Identifying the Solutions, September 1998, available at <http://www.gov.

with by the Westminster Parliament, but posed the question: 'Should the Scottish Executive press for change in the [CEC's] remit so as to strike a better balance between income generation and development'?[25] It became clear from the consultation conducted by the LRPG that most respondents felt that such a change should be pressed for to give more weight to the government's rural development objectives, and that the CEC should be accountable to the Scottish Parliament.[26] Further pressure for change in the administration of the foreshore came in 2006 with the publication of a report by the six local authorities covering the Highlands and islands, Highlands and Islands Enterprise and the Convention of Scottish Local Authorities. The report noted that there had long been criticisms of the CEC's approach to managing the Scottish Crown estate assets, in particular the adverse impact of the seabed and foreshore charges introduced by the CEC on public sector and community interests in the Highlands and islands. There was, the report noted, a stark contrast between the CEC approach to generate revenue from the resource and the ways in which the public interest in the Crown's ownership of the seabed and public foreshore could be managed to complement the Scottish Executive's policies designed to support rural, coastal and island communities and the public interest more generally. The report called for a review by the Scottish Executive of how the Scottish Crown estate assets could contribute more fully to the delivery of the Scottish Executive's policies and the well-being of the people of Scotland.[27] In 2009 the report of the Commission on Scottish Devolution (hereafter Calman Report) was published in which it was acknowledged that the Commission had received evidence calling for the CEC's Scottish responsibilities to be devolved 'to enable the Crown Estate to be made more accountable and to help ensure that its Scottish assets are managed in Scotland's interests'. It also noted that it had been argued that 'the current management of the Crown Estate focuses too narrowly on securing revenue'. Nevertheless, the Calman Report did not consider that 'legislative competence for the Crown Estate in Scotland should be devolved', instead pressing for Scottish ministers to ensure that the CEC had due regard to Scottish interests and recommending the

scot/Resource/0045/00453272.pdf> (last accessed 25 October 2017); LRPG, Recommendations for Action, January 1999, available at <http://www.gov.scot/Resource/0045/00454964.pdf> (last accessed 25 October 2017).

25 LRPG, Identifying the Problems, p. 6.

26 LRPG, Identifying the Solutions, p. 11.

27 Report of the Crown Estate Working Group, 2006, pp. 89–91.

appointment of a Scottish Crown Estate Commissioner,[28] a recommendation that was accepted in the government's response to the Calman Report. In 2010 the House of Commons Treasury Committee published a report on the management of the Crown estate that endorsed the government's response to the Calman Report and recommended that there should be a concordat between the Scottish government and the CEC to consolidate their working relationship. But the Treasury Committee did not recommend devolution.[29]

It seemed that devolution was stalled but its prospects received a boost with the publication in 2012 of a report by the House of Commons Scottish Affairs Committee on the Crown estate in Scotland. The report recommended that the CEC's responsibilities for Crown foreshore in Scotland should be devolved to the relevant local authorities. The Committee noted that many of its witnesses had stated that the CEC was largely driven by the pursuit of revenue, with very little regard to community benefits and the public interest. One witness in particular captured the inherent conflict between the public interest and a requirement to obtain full value. He said:

> The Crown Estate works within a commercial mandate, seeks a commercial return on them, but in doing so wishes to act as a good corporate citizen delivering business objectives in the wider public interest . . . that is a very difficult set of issues to weigh up by a body that is a public body. . . . [U] nder the terms of the legislation they have a difficult task to pull off of being commercial while working in the public interest all at the same time.[30]

The Committee was concerned about the very narrow interpretation of the Crown Estate Act 1961 that was employed by both the CEC and the Treasury, stating:

> part of the problem is one of an over-rigid and self-serving interpretation of the Act . . . If the Government and CEC continue to insist on this rigid interpretation of the Act, it reinforces our conclusion that the CEC is not the appropriate organisation to manage and administer . . . [ownership of the Crown foreshore].[31]

[28] Calman Commission on Scottish Devolution: Serving Scotland Better; Scotland and the UK in the 21st Century, Final Report June 2009, pp. 179–81.

[29] House of Commons Treasury Committee – The Management of the Crown Estate – Eighth Report of Session 2009–10, vol. 1, HC 325-1, pp. 48–51.

[30] David Wilson, director of energy and climate change, Scottish government, quoted in House of Commons Scottish Affairs Committee – The Crown Estate in Scotland – Seventh Report of Session 2010–12, HC 1117, p. 27.

[31] House of Commons Scottish Affairs Committee – The Crown Estate in Scotland – Seventh Report of Session 2010–12, HC 1117, pp. 25–8.

The government was not persuaded by this report.[32] The Scottish Affairs Committee revisited its proposals for devolution and concluded they remained correct, and urged the government to reconsider its position.[33] The tide was turning.

In May 2014 the report of the Land Reform Review Group set up by the Scottish government in 2012 was published. The report concluded that the responsibilities of the CEC in Scotland should be ended and recommended that its statutory responsibilities in Scotland should be devolved to the Scottish Parliament.[34] The momentum towards devolution built with the publication of the Smith Commission's proposal that 'Responsibility for the management of the Crown estate's economic assets in Scotland, and the revenue generated from those assets [be] transferred to the Scottish Parliament' and the subsequent white paper published in January 2015.[35] The Smith Commission's proposal was given legislative effect in section 36 of the Scotland Act 2016. After consultation[36] an interim body corporate was set up by the Scottish government in February 2017 to manage the Scottish Crown estate assets (including the foreshore), and the responsibility for the management of those assets was transferred to this body on 1 April 2017.[37] The devolution of management of the Scottish Crown estate assets had, finally, been achieved. In the words of Roseanna Cunningham, the Cabinet Secretary for the Environment, Climate Change and Land Reform, this was 'a genuine opportunity to change the fabric of Scottish society'.[38] How genuine this opportunity turns out to be will depend, in the main,

[32] HM Government, The Government's response to the Seventh Report of the Scottish Affairs Committee session 2012–13, Cmnd 8361.

[33] House of Commons Scottish Affairs Committee – The Crown Estate in Scotland: Follow up. Fifth Report of Session 2013–14, HC 889, p. 16.

[34] Land Reform Review Group Final Report – The Land of Scotland and the Common Good, May 2014, available at <http://www.gov.scot/Publications/2014/05/2852> (last accessed 25 October 2017), pp. 60–4.

[35] Report of the Smith Commission for further devolution of powers to the Scottish Parliament, 27 November 2014, p. 16; PP, 2014/15, Scotland in the United Kingdom: An enduring Settlement, Cm 8990, para. 5.5.

[36] Crown Estate – Consultation on Proposals for Establishing the Interim Body to manage the Crown Estate Assets in Scotland Post-Devolution, 2016, available at <http://www.gov.scot/Resource/0050/00502476.pdf> (last accessed 25 October 2017).

[37] The Crown Estate Scotland (Interim Management) Order 2017, SSI 2017/36; The Crown Estate Transfer Scheme 2017, SI 2017/524.

[38] Crown Estate – A Consultation on the Long Term Management of the Crown Estate in Scotland, 2017, p. 3.

on the basis on which the Scottish Crown estate assets that have been transferred will be managed. A consultation was launched in January 2017 to help the Scottish government shape the future management of these assets and how the revenue could be used to benefit Scotland and communities, the results being published in January 2018.[39] There had been a long history of antagonism between coastal and marine communities and the CEC,[40] and one of the design options for the long-term management framework involves communities taking more control of their local assets, especially in the context of the foreshore, an element of subsidiarity that the Smith Commission had proposed.[41] The vision for the future management of these assets will, however, be limited by the statutory constraints in the Scotland Acts of 1998 and 2016 and in the Scottish Crown Estate Bill introduced on 24 January 2018. The Bill disapplies the Crown Estate Act 1961 as regards the management of Scottish Crown estate assets, but continues the obligation to maintain and enhance the value of the assets and the 'market value' approach to transactions, although it introduces provisions that allow for a consideration of less than market value in certain defined situations to allow for the manager to manage the assets in a way which is likely to contribute to the promotion or the improvement of socio-economic and environmental factors. The Bill also gives Scottish ministers the power to transfer or delegate the function of management to a Scottish public authority, a local authority, or a community organisation.[42]

The future direction of the management of the Scottish Crown estate foreshore under the 2017 devolution settlement should become clear as the Scottish Crown Estate Bill, published as part of the Scottish government's legislative programme for 2017–18 to 'establish a framework for the management of Crown Estate assets to ensure Scotland's local communities, authorities and industry can benefit from [the devolution of the assets]', progresses through the Scottish Parliament.'[43] There is a

[39] Crown Estate – A Consultation on the Long Term Management of the Crown Estate in Scotland, 2017 and A Consultation on the Long Term Management of the Crown Estate in Scotland: Analysis of Consultation Responses, January 2018, <http://www.gov.scot/Publications/2018/01/3415> (last accessed January 2018).

[40] Wightman, *Poor Had No Lawyers*, pp. 140–1.

[41] Crown Estate – A Consultation on the Long Term Management of the Crown Estate in Scotland, 2017, p. 28; Report of the Smith Commission for further devolution of powers to the Scottish Parliament, 27 November 2014, p. 16; McHarg, 'Crown estate devolution', pp. 393–4.

[42] Scottish Crown Estate Bill SP Bill 24 Session 5 (2018).

[43] A Nation With Ambition: The Government's Programme for Scotland 2017–

common thread that links the transfer of responsibility for the management of Scotland's foreshore in 1866, the threatened transfer in 1958 and its devolution in 2017: it is the issue of balancing the duty to administer the foreshore in the public interest with the legal requirement not to part with property at less than full value. A fundamental question was put by the Scottish government for consultation:

> whether the estate should continue being managed on a primarily commercial basis, or whether there is a case for a wider set of considerations to be taken into account ... [and that] wider socioeconomic benefits, including community benefits [could] be taken into account.[44]

It is in this context that there is one document that it may be well worth Scottish ministers and the new body entrusted with the devolved foreshore taking down from the shelf and studying. It is the Farrer Memorandum. In a note prepared for the permanent secretary at the Ministry of Transport at the time of the debate in 1958 about the rigorous observation by the Commissioners of Crown Lands of their statutory duties, written nearly 100 years after the publication of the Farrer Memorandum, it was lauded as still providing 'excellent guidance'. Now, some sixty years further on, there is still much of value in it; in particular a warning to avoid 'the fatally erroneous [assumption] that the pecuniary interest of the public in the foreshore is the most important interest', a sentiment that was echoed in the 1960 Cabinet Office minute that recorded that the foreshore should be 'administered primarily by reference to the public interest' rather than 'by reference to the ordinary criteria of sound and profitable estate management'.[45]

## THE SCOTTISH LAW COMMISSION'S PROPOSALS FOR CHANGES IN THE LAW OF THE FORESHORE

As part of its general proposals for land reform in 1999, the LRPG recommended that the Scottish Law Commission (SLC) should be invited

2018, available at <http://www.gov.scot/Publications/2017/09/8468> (last accessed 25 October 2017), pp. 21, 30.

44 Crown Estate – A Consultation on the Long Term Management of the Crown Estate in Scotland, 2017, p. 18.

45 TNA:PRO, BT 243/95, Note for meeting with Sir Norman Brook, 11 October 1960; Farrer Memorandum, p. 6; TNA:PRO, BT 243/95, Record of meeting, 12 October 1960.

to review and revise the law of the foreshore and seabed.[46] In late 1999 the SLC received a reference from the then deputy first minister and minister of justice in the following terms: 'Taking account of the land reform action plan, to consider the existing law of the foreshore and seabed, and to advise on possible reforms with a view to improving clarity and consistency.'[47] The SLC published a discussion paper in 2001 and its report in 2003.[48] We now look, briefly, at two aspects of the SLC's deliberations that have resonance for this book: public rights and crofters' rights to seaweed.

### *Public rights*

Most of this book has been concerned with the dispute between private proprietors and the Crown over the ownership of the foreshore but as we noted at the outset in Chapter 1 and in subsequent chapters, the entire foreshore of Scotland, whether in Crown or private ownership, is subject to a number of rights that the Crown holds inalienably in trust for the public, and whatever the contending positions of the Crown and private proprietors may have been as to ownership, this fact has never really been in doubt or challenged. Private proprietors (with the notable exception of the Earl of Selkirk) and the Association had, as we saw in Chapters 2 and 5, conceded that the public had the right to use the foreshore for 'various purposes', but what, exactly, were these purposes? Did they include the right of bathing that the Earl of Selkirk denied in 1869, or indeed to hold religious services on the foreshore in the mid-1800s as discussed in Chapter 1? Lord Kinloch attempted, in 1859, to answer the question of what the 'various purposes' were, but without giving a definitive answer:

> The pursuer himself admitted that the right of property that he claimed was subject to certain public uses, and he specified those of fishing and navigation. But the Lord Ordinary would hesitate to find that the public uses were confined strictly to these. Has not the public, for instance, right to use the shores for the purpose of recreation, in walking and riding? May they not have a pic-nic on the beach, if not riotous, or use it for bathing, if decorous? There are many such questions which may be asked; and they are enough to make it hazardous to attempt a precise definition of the public uses of the sea-shore.[49]

[46] LRPG, Recommendations for Action, p. 33.
[47] SLC Discussion Paper, para. 1.1.
[48] SLC Discussion Paper; SLC Report.
[49] Nicol v. Blaikie (1859) 22 D 335 at p. 340.

The state of the law some years after the Free Church and Baptist ministers were holding their services on the foreshore and the Earl of Selkirk was objecting to the public bathing on his shores was still uncertain. The first edition of Rankine's work on land ownership published in 1879 recorded only an 1821 English case[50] which held that there was no common law right of bathing in the sea, but Rankine noted that this case had not been regarded as authoritative by a subsequent English case in 1864[51] and had been 'impugned by writers of merit', and he suggested that, on this basis, there would be 'less disinclination in Scotland to regard the point as an open one'. But in the final edition published in 1909, Rankine noted that the judgment in the 1821 English case might no longer be doubted in England, having now been followed in cases in 1899 and 1904.[52] As to the position in Scotland, Rankine concluded that

> the opinion may be hazarded that, as a general rule, the only public uses of the foreshore are for navigation and fishing, though there may be . . . 'numerous and extensive foreshores which the public cannot be hindered from using . . . as a public place open to all for pleasure and healthful resort.' These foreshores may probably be confined to such as are within burghs or within ancient liberties of burghs.[53]

The SLC said in its 2001 paper, discussed below, that 'Perhaps because it is obvious, there is no Scottish authority for the existence of a public right to swim in the sea.'[54] And as far as gatherings for religious services on the foreshore of the kind discussed in Chapter 1 are concerned, the only authority seems to have been an English one in 1899 in which preaching on the beach was held to be unlawful without permission even though it caused no obstruction and led to no breach of the peace.[55]

[50] Blundell v. Catterall (1821) 5 B & Ald 268.

[51] Mace v. Philcox (1864) 15 CB (NS) 600.

[52] Llandudno Urban District Council v. Woods (1899) 2 Ch 705; Brinckman v. Matley (1904) 2 Ch 313.

[53] Rankine, *Ownership of Lands* (1st edn, Edinburgh, 1879), pp. 214–15; (4th edn), pp. 270–2; see also Officers of State v. Smith (1846) 8 D 711 at p. 719 in which the public right was described as the 'common use by the subjects for the purpose of passage from port to port, or of mere enjoyment and healthful exercise'.

[54] SLC Discussion Paper, para. 4.25, n. 189. The Supreme Court in Newhaven Port and Properties Ltd v. East Sussex CC [2015] UKSC 7 referred to the SLC Discussion Paper at paras 117 and 118 and seemed to suggest at paras 47 and 49 that on the basis of Officers of State v. Smith (1846) 8 D 711 there was a right in Scots Law for the public to use the foreshore for bathing.

[55] Rankine, *Ownership of Lands* (4th edn), p. 271; Ferguson, *Law of Water*, p. 68; Llandudno Urban District Council v. Woods (1899) 2 Ch 705.

The nature and extent of the common law public rights over the foreshore are still matters of disagreement although it is uncontroversial that there is a public right of navigation and of fishing for white fish and shellfish. It may also be taken as settled that the public has a right of recreation; what, however, this word actually encompasses is less clear, and it is said that it is easier to state what the word does not include than what it does. It does not, for example, include the right to erect a tent or a beach hut, the right to collect seaware (hence the significance of the 1891 Sea Ware Bill discussed in Chapter 7),[56] or to sell refreshments. It does, however, in the view of the SLC,[57] include the rights of walking, running, having a picnic or a barbecue, sunbathing and swimming, and shooting wildfowl. It may also be taken as settled that there is a public right of passage along and through the foreshore. These public rights may be enforced at the instance of the Lord Advocate or in an *actio popularis*.[58] The SLC drew attention to the potential for a conflict of interest between the Crown as beneficial owner and its role as guardian of the common law public rights.[59] We should also note that the CEC who have responsibility to manage the Crown foreshore (and presumably also since April 2017 the interim body with responsibility for Scotland's devolved Crown foreshore) have no statutory duty to protect the public's rights to use the foreshore.[60] The commercial use of the foreshore by the public is prohibited where it interferes with proprietary rights. Public rights on the foreshore cannot at common law be exercised unless there is access to the foreshore by public road, by public right of way, or from the sea. But there is a statutory public right of access to, and of being on, the foreshore for recreational and other purposes under the Land Reform (Scotland) Act 2003.[61]

The SLC recommended that the common law public rights described above should be abolished and replaced by statutory public rights held

[56] Paterson v. Marquis of Ailsa (1846) 8 D 752; Lord Saltoun v. Park (1857) 20 D 89.

[57] SLC Discussion Paper, para. 4.25.

[58] SLC Discussion Paper, paras 3.14–3.15, 4.1.

[59] SLC Discussion Paper, para. 3.16.

[60] SLC Discussion Paper, paras 3.9–3.11.

[61] Sections 1 and 2, which do not define 'recreational purposes', and section 9, which provides exclusions from them. For the modern law concerning public rights over the foreshore, see Reid, *Law of Property in Scotland*, paras 524–6; Robbie, *Private Water Rights*, paras 2.96, 2.97, 2.100–2.102; SLC Discussion Paper, Part 4. The Royal Commission on Coast Erosion had, as we saw in Chapter 6, made various recommendations about public rights on the foreshore; PP, 1911, XIV, Royal Commission, vol. 3 (part 1), Cd 5708, pp. 116–17.

directly by the public rather than by the Crown as trustee, enforceable in the sheriff court, and that these statutory public rights should only be exercisable in a way that is lawful and reasonable and takes proper account of the rights of others and the features of the land and water over which they are exercised, with reciprocal duties on land owners.[62] The SLC also recommended that the statutory public rights should be in addition to the statutory access rights under the Land Reform (Scotland) Act 2003 but that they should not be exercisable in relation to any land in respect of which access rights under the 2003 Act are not exercisable.[63] It was the intention of the SLC that the scope of the statutory public rights, when combined with access rights, should be at least as extensive as that of the public rights at common law.[64] In the draft Bill produced by the SLC, these statutory public rights included the right to use the foreshore for the purposes of recreation which were listed, on a non-exclusive basis, as including bathing, swimming, sunbathing; making sandcastles and playing games; having picnics, lighting fires and cooking food; and beachcombing. There was also a statutory public right to gather shellfish and to fish for sea fish from the foreshore. The common law right to shoot wildfowl was also included, provided the wildfowl are on or over the foreshore when shot.[65]

### *Crofters' rights to seaweed*

We looked, in Chapter 1, at how seaware was regarded by custom as a communal asset in Gaelic Scotland, and in Chapter 7 at the debate in 1886 and 1891 over whether crofters, and the public, should be given legislative rights to seaweed. We now look at the deliberations of the SLC over whether crofting tenure should carry with it any special rights in relation to the foreshore, specifically a right to gather seaweed. The responses to the LRPG's consultation papers had established that there was a particular interest in the right to gather seaweed on the foreshore given its value as fertiliser both for use on the croft and for commercial

62 SLC Report, paras 3.7, 3.8, 3.40, 3.30.

63 SLC Report, para. 3.10.

64 SLC Report, para. 3.7, p. 40.

65 SLC Report, paras 3.12–3.17, pp. 40–2. The SLC's recommendations have not, yet, been implemented, but the Scottish Green Party's 2016 Holyrood Manifesto advocated their enactment; Scottish Green Party's Holyrood 2016 Manifesto – A better Scotland needs a bolder Holyrood, available at <http://greens.scotland-can> (last accessed 25 October 2017).

purposes.[66] The SLC stated that the collection of seaweed was the main example of a right which may be held by crofters over the foreshore that is not held by the general public and that this right of crofters, where it existed, was a right held by crofters as a pertinent of their lease and not as a statutory or common law right, as we discussed in Chapter 7. The SLC considered whether a general statutory right should be introduced for all crofters to take seaweed from the foreshore but concluded that there were no convincing grounds 'within the context of this law reform project'[67] for such a right. It was a particular objection that any extension of the pertinential rights could 'be at the expense of private rights of ownership'.[68] As to the exercise of the pertinential right, the SLC examined whether crofters should be entitled to exploit such a right for commercial benefit, and accepted that 'it may . . . be possible to argue that the right to collect seaweed extends to commercial exploitation'.[69] However, while the SLC noted the complaints and concerns of crofters in North Uist referred to in Chapter 7, the SLC's consultation 'did not suggest any legal reasons'[70] why this pertinent should permit commercial use when the general rule for pertinents did not, and recommended that unless otherwise stated it should be made clear that this right should be restricted in extent to what was necessary for the reasonable purposes of the croft.[71] There was no recognition or, indeed, any mention by the SLC of any of the customary communal rights to seaware discussed in Chapter 1.

Finally, we return to the issue that has been prominent in this book. As we saw in Chapter 6, the Commissioners of Crown Lands had decided in 1947 that the question of the period that was required to establish prescriptive possession of the foreshore in Scotland should be shelved indefinitely but that if a legislative opportunity should arise in the future concerning land in Scotland generally, the question should be borne in mind. The Land Reform (Scotland) Act 2003 might have been such an opportunity as, also, might the reference to the SLC, although given that the SLC considered that the question whether the Crown should continue to have full ownership of the foreshore was outwith the scope of its remit, which was 'to advise on reforms which would clarify,

66 SLC Report, para. 4.2.
67 SLC Report, para. 4.4.
68 SLC Discussion Paper, para. 6.15.
69 SLC Discussion Paper, para. 6.17.
70 SLC Report, para. 4.7.
71 SLC Discussion Paper, paras 6.17, 6.18, p. 39; SLC Report, para. 4.8.

and bring consistency to, the existing law', and that the SLC could not, within their remit, 'consider or make recommendations on more wide-ranging aspects of land reform which may be considered politically controversial', this was always improbable.[72] And the foreshore only featured in the deliberations of the Land Reform Review Group in 2014 that gave rise to the Land Reform (Scotland) Act 2016, in the context of devolution of management of the Crown foreshore. While the legislation that underlay the devolution of the management of Crown estate lands in Scotland may have provided, in the words of Roseanna Cunningham, an opportunity to change the fabric of Scottish society, it was not taken as an opportunity to reconsider the prescriptive period question. The horse that had bolted at the end of Chapter 6 may now be taken to have disappeared over the horizon and is unlikely to be retrieved.

[72] SLC Report, para. 1.10; SLC Discussion Paper, para. 1.11.

# *Envoi*

THIS BOOK BEGAN WITH the observation that the ownership of Scotland's foreshore had been a matter of prolonged controversy in Scotland. In telling the story of the battle that took place during the nineteenth century and into the early twentieth century between the Crown and private proprietors over the ownership of the foreshore; in examining the different motivations of the Crown and proprietors towards the ownership of land; and in discussing the issues that have arisen concerning which body should manage the Crown-owned foreshore, and how the responsibilities should best be carried out, in particular the importance of managing the foreshore in the public interest, this book has shown the extent of the controversy and shone light on the important issues that have been at the heart of the debate that culminated in early 2017 in responsibility for the management of Scotland's Crown-owned foreshore being devolved to the Scottish Parliament. The examination of the crucial role played by the Association of Seaboard Proprietors of Scotland, its law agents and counsel in the battle and their interaction with the Office of Woods and the Board of Trade, and of the deliberations and opinions of Crown lawyers and officials over the handling of foreshore cases, and over proposed changes to the law as to how prescriptive possession of the foreshore could be established, based as it is on material that has not previously been examined, has provided new and valuable insights into the controversy and further informed our understanding of how the modern law as to ownership of the foreshore was forged in the crucible of the battle.

As to the future, it is to be hoped that the exciting possibilities for the ongoing management of Scotland's Crown-owned foreshore that were suggested by the positive words of Roseanna Cunningham that formed the title to the final chapter of this book will be realised. If the history told by this book is anything to go by, it will be important that the new management body does not, in the words of Thomas Farrer, act 'simply as a matter of £. s. d.'.

# *Select Bibliography*


## MANUSCRIPT SOURCES

### *Estate papers*

Dunvegan Castle, Isle of Skye (DVGN):
  Macleod Muniments
    Section 2
      Foreshores, 543–74.

### *National Records of Scotland, Edinburgh ('NRS')*

Court of Session Records:
  Warrants of the Register of Acts and Decreets, 5th Series, CS 46.
  Unextracted processes, 3rd Arrangement Outer House E office, CS 257.
Crown Estate Commissioners – Foreshore Files, CR11.
Private papers:
  Lothian Muniments, GD 40.
  Seaforth Papers, GD 46.
  Records of the Scottish Landowners Federation, GD 325.
Records of the Department of Agriculture and Fisheries for Scotland:
  Board of Agriculture, Miscellaneous Files, AF 43.
  Crofting Files, AF 67.
  Education, Research and Intelligence, AF 70.
  Estate Management Files, AF 83.
Scottish Home and Health Department – Miscellaneous Files, HH 1.
Scottish law officers draft opinions, AD 54.

### *National Register of Archives for Scotland ('NRAS')*

Maclean Family of Ardgour, NRAS, 3583/Bundle 10.

### *The National Archives, London (TNA:PRO)*

Board of Trade and successors:
  Establishment Department. Correspondence and Papers, BT 13.

Ministry of Transport: Marine Department: Registered Files, BT 243.
Foreshores – Registered Files and Miscellaneous, BT 297.
Board of Trade Harbour Department: Correspondence and Papers, MT 10.
Ministry of Transport and successors, Establishment and Organisation: Correspondence and Papers, MT 45.
Office of Woods, Forests and Land Revenues and successors: General Department and successors: Registered Files, CRES 36.
Treasury:
General Registered Files (G Series), T 163.
Social Services Division: (SS and 2SS series) Files, T 227.
Civil List; reports, Civil List Act 1910: Crown Lands Bill, papers, memoranda, amendments, T 250.

## PRINTED PRIMARY SOURCES

### *Parliamentary Papers (PP) and official papers*

PP, 1841, VI, Reports from the Select Committee on Condition of the population of Islands and Highlands of Scotland, and Practicability of affording Relief by means of Emigration.
PP, 1847–8, XXIV and 1849, XX, Reports from the Select Committee on the Woods, Forests and Land Revenues of the Crown.
PP, 1852, XXVI, Twenty-ninth report of the Commissioners of Her Majesty's Woods, Forests and Land Revenues.
PP, 1863, L, Copy of any Petition by Sir James Matheson, Baronet, to the Treasury, for a Grant of Foreshore in Stornaway [sic], in the Island of Lewis; of any Report by the Crown Agent in Scotland; and of any Disposition by the Crown of such Foreshore, in favour of Sir James Matheson.
PP, 1866, LVIII, Copies of the Correspondence which took place in the course of last Year between His Grace the Duke of Argyll and the Lords Commissioners of Her Majesty's Treasury.
PP, 1866, LX, Return of Correspondence between the Treasury and the Board of Trade as to the transfer of the Management of certain rights of the Crown in Tidal Lands.
PP, 1867/68, LVII, Copy of Memorandum as to Board of Trade's Dealings with Foreshore and Bed of the Sea.
PP, 1884, XXXII–XXXVI, Report of Her Majesty's Commissioners of Inquiry into the Condition of the Crofters and Cottars in the Highlands and Islands of Scotland.
PP, 1902, LXXXIII, Report by the Crofters Commission on the Social Condition of the People of Lewis in 1901.
PP, 1906, Select Committee on Crown Lands Bill, Paper No. 159.
PP, 1907, XXXIV and 1911, XIV, Reports of the Royal Commission on Coast Erosion and Afforestation, Cd 3683, 3684, 5708, 5709.

PP, 1914, XXXII, Report to the Board of Agriculture for Scotland on Home Industries in the Highlands and Islands, Cd 7564.
PP, 1953/54, VIII, Report of the Commission of Enquiry into Crofting Conditions, Cmd 9091.
PP, 1955/56, XIII, Report of the Committee on Crown Lands, June 1955, Cmd 9483.
PP, 2014/15, Scotland in the United Kingdom: An enduring Settlement, Cm 8990.

Crofters Commission Annual Reports.
Hansard, Parliamentary Debates (PD).
House of Commons Journals.
House of Lords Journals.
Scottish Land Court Reports as to Proceedings.

Land Reform Policy Group (LRPG), Identifying the Problems, February 1998, <http://www.gov.scot/Resource/0045/00451950.pdf> (last accessed 25 October 2017).
Land Reform Policy Group (LRPG), Identifying the Solutions, September 1998, <http://www.gov.scot/Resource/0045/00453272.pdf> (last accessed 25 October 2017).
Land Reform Policy Group (LRPG), Recommendations for Action, January 1999, <http://www.gov.scot/Resource/0045/00454964.pdf> (last accessed 25 October 2017).
Scottish Law Commission Discussion Paper on Law of the Foreshore and the Seabed, No. 113, April 2001.
Scottish Law Commission Report on the Law of the Foreshore and Sea Bed (Scot Law Com No. 190), March 2003.
Report of the Crown Estate Working Group, 2006, <http://www.orkney.gov.uk/Files/Council/Publications/2007/CERWG07MAR22.pdf> (last accessed 25 October 2017).
Calman Commission on Scottish Devolution: Serving Scotland Better; Scotland and the UK in the 21st Century, Final Report June 2009.
House of Commons Treasury Committee – The Management of the Crown Estate – Eighth Report of Session 2009–10, vol. 1, HC 325-1.
House of Commons Scottish Affairs Committee – The Crown Estate in Scotland – Seventh Report of Session 2010–12, HC 1117.
HM Government, The Government's response to the Seventh Report of the Scottish Affairs Committee Session 2012–13, Cmnd 8361.
House of Commons Scottish Affairs Committee – The Crown Estate in Scotland: Follow up. Fifth Report of Session 2013–14, HC 889.
Crown Estate – Scotland Report 2014.
Land Reform Review Group Final Report – The Land of Scotland and the

Common Good, May 2014, <http://www.gov.scot/Publications/2014/05/2852> (last accessed 25 October 2017).

Report of the Smith Commission for further devolution of powers to the Scottish Parliament, 27 November 2014.

Crown Estate – Consultation on Proposals for Establishing the Interim Body to manage the Crown Estate Assets in Scotland Post-Devolution, 2016, <http://www.gov.scot/Resource/0050/00502476.pdf> (last accessed 25 October 2017)

Scottish Green Party's Holyrood 2016 Manifesto – A better Scotland needs a bolder Holyrood, <http://greens.scotland-can> (last accessed 25 October 2017).

Crown Estate – A Consultation on the Long Term Management of the Crown Estate in Scotland, 2017, <http://www.gov.scot/Publications/2017/01/8661> (last accessed 25 October 2017).

A Nation With Ambition: The Government's Programme for Scotland 2017–2018, <http://www.gov.scot/publications/2017/09/8468> (last accessed 25 October 2017).

A Consultation on the Long Term Management of the Crown Estate in Scotland: Analysis of Consultation Responses, January 2018, <http://www.gov.scot/Publications/2018/01/3415> (last accessed 29 January 2018).

## *Newspapers*

*City Press.*

*Daily Telegraph.*

*Edinburgh Evening Courant.*

*Inverness Courier.*

*Oban Times.*

*Pall Mall Gazette.*

*The Scotsman.*

*Scottish Highlander.*

*The Times.*

*West Highland Free Press.*

## *Contemporary books, pamphlets and articles*

Anon., 'Fraser-Mackintosh, M.P. and the Duke of Argyll', *The Celtic Magazine*, 10 (1885), pp. 42–8.

Anon., 'The right of the Crown to foreshores', *The Scottish Law Magazine*, 5:12 (1866), pp. 82–4.

Anon., *The Solicitor's Journal*, 33 (1888–9), pp. 313–14.

Anon., 'Title of the Crown to the seashore', *The Law Magazine and Law Review*, 6 (November 1858–February 1859), pp. 99–116.

Argyll, The Dowager Duchess (ed.), *George Douglas, Eighth Duke of Argyll: Autobiography and Memoirs*, vol. I (London, 1906).

Argyll, Duke of, *Crofts and Farms in the Hebrides* (Edinburgh, 1883).

Barron, J., *The Northern Highlands in the Nineteenth Century*, vol. 1 (Inverness, 1903).

Barron, J., *The Northern Highlands in the Nineteenth Century*, vol. 2 (Inverness, 1907).

Bateman, J., *The Great Landowners of Great Britain and Ireland* (London, 1883).

Bell, G. J., *Principles of the Law of Scotland* (10th edn, Edinburgh, 1899).

Beveridge, E., *Coll and Tiree: Their Prehistoric Forts and Ecclesiastical Antiquities* (Edinburgh, 1903).

Blackie, J. S., *The Scottish Highlanders and the Land Laws* (London, 1885).

Boase, F., *Modern English Biography*, vol. II (Truro, 1897).

Botfield, B., *Journal of a Tour through the Highlands of Scotland during the Summer of 1829* (Norton Hall, 1830).

Brown, The Rev. T., *Annals of the Disruption* (Edinburgh, 1884).

Buchanan, W., *Reports of Certain Remarkable Cases in the Court of Session* (Edinburgh, 1813).

Cameron, J., *Celtic Law* (Edinburgh, 1937).

Carr, Sir J., *Caledonian Sketches on a Tour through Scotland in 1807* (London, 1809).

Craigie, J., *Principles of Conveyancing: Heritable Rights* (3rd edn, Edinburgh, 1899).

Cregeen, E. R. (ed.), *Argyll Estate Instructions* (Edinburgh, 1964).

Ferguson, J., *The Law of Water and Water Rights in Scotland* (Edinburgh, 1907).

Goodrich-Freer, A., *Outer Isles* (London, 1902).

Grant, F. J. (ed.), *The Faculty of Advocates in Scotland 1532–1943* (Edinburgh, 1944).

Groome, F. H. (ed.), *Ordnance Gazetteer of Scotland: A Survey of Scottish Topography* (London, 1893–5).

Hall, R., *Rights of the Crown and the Privileges of the Subject in the Sea-shores of the Realm* (n.p., 1830).

Henderson, Rev. G. (ed.), *Memoirs of a Highland Gentleman, Being the Reminiscences of Evander Maciver of Scourie* (Edinburgh, 1905).

Innes, C., *Lectures on Scotch Legal Antiquities* (Edinburgh, 1872).

Johnston, T., *Our Scots Noble Families* (Glasgow, 1909).

Loch, G., *The Family of Loch* (Edinburgh, 1934).

Macculloch, J., *A Description of the Western Islands of Scotland* (London, 1819).

Macdonald, J., *General View of the Agriculture of the Hebrides or Western Isles of Scotland* (Edinburgh, 1811).

Mackay, Ae, 'The foreshore question', *Journal of Jurisprudence*, 11 (1867), pp. 75–88.

Mackenzie, W. C., *History of the Outer Hebrides* (Paisley, 1903).

Macleod, Canon R. C., *The Book of Dunvegan*, vol. 2 (Aberdeen, 1939).

Macleod, The Rev. R. C., *The Macleods: Their History and Traditions* (Edinburgh, 1929).

Mitchell, J., *Reminiscences of my Life in the Highlands (1884)*, vol. II (London, 1884).

Moore, S. A., *A History of the Foreshore and the Law Relating Thereto* (London, 1888).

Napier, Lord, 'The Highland crofters: a vindication of the report of the Crofters' Commission', *The Nineteenth Century*, 17 (1885), pp. 437–63.

Omond, G. W. T., *The Lord Advocate of Scotland from the Close of the Fifteenth Century to the Passing of the Reform Bill* (Edinburgh, 1883).

Pycroft, J. W., *Arena Cornubiae* (London, 1856).

Rankine, J., *A Treatise on the Rights and Burdens Incident to the Ownership of Lands and Other Heritages in Scotland* (1st edn, Edinburgh, 1879).

Rankine, J., *A Treatise on the Rights and Burdens Incident to the Ownership of Lands and Other Heritages in Scotland* (4th edn, Edinburgh, 1909).

Skene, W. F., *Celtic Scotland: A History of Ancient Alban. Volume III: Land and People* (Edinburgh, 1880).

Stanford, E. C. C. and W. M. Wood, 'On the economic applications of seaweed', *Journal of the Society of Arts*, 32:1646 (1884), pp. 717–30.

## SECONDARY SOURCES

### *Books, pamphlets and articles*

Agnew, Sir C., *Crofting Law* (Edinburgh, 2000).

Ansdell, D., *The People of the Great Faith: The Highland Church 1690–1900* (Stornoway, 1998).

Bathurst, B., *The Lighthouse Stevensons* (London, 1999).

Bennion, T., M. Birdling and R. Paton, *Making Sense of the Foreshore & Seabed* (Wellington, 2004).

Bumsted, J. M., *The People's Clearance: Highland Emigration to British North America 1770–1815* (Edinburgh, 1982).

Cameron, E. A., *Land for the People?: The British Government and the Scottish Highlands, c. 1880–1925* (Edinburgh, 1996).

Cameron, E. A., *The Life and Times of Fraser Mackintosh, Crofter MP* (Aberdeen, 2000).

Campbell, J. L., *Canna: The Story of a Hebridean Island* (Edinburgh, 1994).

Coull, J. R., 'The island of Tiree', *Scottish Geographical Magazine*, 78:1 (1962), pp. 17–32.

Davis, J., 'Farrer, Thomas Henry, first Baron Farrer (1819–1899)', in *Oxford Dictionary of National Biography*, Oxford University Press, <http://www.oxforddnb.com/view/article/9194> (last accessed 25 October 2017).

Deans, M. E., 'The Crown Estate Commissioners: their role and responsibilities in respect of the foreshore and seabed around Scotland', *Journal of Energy and Natural Resources Law*, 4:3 (1986), pp. 166–87.

Devine, T. M., *Clanship to Crofters' War: The Social Transformation of the Scottish Highlands* (Manchester, 1994).

Devine, T. M., 'The emergence of the new elite in the western Highlands and islands, 1800–60', in T. M. Devine (ed.), *Improvement and Enlightenment* (Edinburgh, 1989).

Devine, T. M., *Exploring the Scottish Past* (East Linton, 1995).

Devine, T. M., *The Scottish Nation, 1700–2000* (London, 1999).

Drever, W. P., 'Udal law and the foreshore', *Juridical Review* (1904), pp. 189–202.

Duncan, A. (ed.), *Hebridean Island: Memories of Scarp* (East Linton, 1995).

Edwards, J. Ll. J., *The Attorney General, Politics and the Public Interest* (London, 1984).

Edwards, J. Ll. J., *The Law Officers of the Crown* (London, 1964).

Enever, F. A., 'The Crown Estate Act 1961', *The Modern Law Review*, 25:4 (1962), pp. 442–5.

Evans, R. J., *The Pursuit of Power: Europe 1815–1914* (London, 2016).

Fenton, A., *The Shape of the Past 2: Essays in Scottish Ethnology* (Edinburgh, 1986).

Gibson, J., 'Foreshore: a concept built on sand', *Journal of Planning and Environment Law* (1977), pp. 762–70.

Gray, M., *The Highland Economy* (Edinburgh, 1957).

Gray, M., 'The kelp industry in the Highlands and islands', *The Economic History Review*, 4 (1951), pp. 197–209.

Hamilton, J. A., 'James, Sir William Milbourne (1807–1881)', rev. H. Mooney, in *Oxford Dictionary of National Biography*, Oxford University Press, <http://www.oxforddnb.com/view/article/14630> (last accessed 25 October 2017).

Hillyard, B., 'Moir, George (1800–1870)', in *Oxford Dictionary of National Biography*, Oxford University Press, <http://www.oxforddnb.com/view/article/18891> (last accessed 25 October 2017).

Hunter, J., 'The emergence of the crofting community: the religious contribution 1789–1843', *Scottish Studies*, 18 (1974), pp. 95–116.

Hunter, J., *The Islanders and the Orb* (Stornoway, 2001).

Hunter, J., *Last of the Free* (Edinburgh, 1999).

Hunter, J., *The Making of the Crofting Community* (Edinburgh, 1976).

Hunter, J., *On the Other Side of Sorrow* (Edinburgh, 1995).

Johnston, D., *Prescription and Limitation* (Edinburgh, 1999).

Jones, M., 'Udal law', in M. A. Mulhern (ed.), *Scottish Life and Society: A Compendium of Scottish Ethnology. Vol. 13: The Law* (Edinburgh, 2012).

Kelly, F., *Early Irish Farming* (Dublin, 1997).

Kelly, F., *A Guide to Early Irish Law* (Dublin, 1988).

Kenicer, G., S. Bridgewater and W. Milliken, 'The ebb and flow of Scottish seaweed use', *Botanical Journal of Scotland*, 52:2 (2000), pp. 119–48.

Law Society of Scotland, *Glossary: Scottish Legal Terms and Latin Maxims* (Edinburgh, 1992).

Lee, G. A., 'The right to take seaweed from the foreshore', *Northern Ireland Legal Quarterly*, 18:1 (1967), pp. 33–43.

MacArthur, A., *The Tiree Crofters' Struggle* (Tiree, 1986).

MacAskill, J., 'Foreshore', in M. A. Mulhern (ed.), *Scottish Life and Society: A Compendium of Scottish Ethnology. Vol. 13: The Law* (Edinburgh, 2012).

MacAskill, J., 'The Highland kelp proprietors and their struggle over the salt and barilla duties, 1817–1831', *Journal of Scottish Historical Studies*, 26:1–2 (2006), pp. 60–82.

MacAskill, J., '"The most arbitrary, scandalous act of tyranny": the Crown, private proprietors and the ownership of the Scottish foreshore in the nineteenth century', *The Scottish Historical Review*, 85:2:220 (2006), pp. 277–304.

McGlashan, D. J., 'Udal law and coastal land ownership', *Juridical Review* (2002), pp. 251–60.

McGlashan, D. J., R. W. Duck and C. T. Reid, 'The foreshore: geographical implications of the three legal systems in Great Britain', *Area*, 3 (2004), pp. 338–47.

McHarg, A., 'Crown estate devolution', *Edinburgh Law Review*, 20:3 (2016), pp. 388–94.

Macinnes, A. I., 'From clanship to clearance in Argyllshire', in T. M. Devine (ed.), *Scottish Elites* (Edinburgh, 1994).

Macinnes, A. I., 'Scottish Gaeldom: the first phase of clearance', in T. M. Devine and R. Mitchison (eds), *People and Society in Scotland: Volume I 1760–1830* (Edinburgh, 1988).

Macinnes, A. I., 'Scottish Gaeldom from clanship to commercial landlordism, c. 1600– c. 1850', in S. Foster, A. I. Macinnes and R. Macinnes (eds), *Scottish Power Centres from the Early Middle Ages to the Twentieth Century* (Glasgow, 1998).

MacLean, A. J., 'The 1707 Union: Scots Law and the House of Lords', *The Journal of Legal History*, 4:3 (1983), pp. 50–75.

Macleod, J., *No Great Mischief if you Fall: The Highland Experience* (Edinburgh, 1993).

MacNeill, E., *Celtic Ireland* (Dublin, 1921).

MacPhail, I. M. M., *The Crofters' War* (Stornoway, 1989).

MacQueen, H. L,, 'Lawyers' Edinburgh 1908–2008', *Book of the Old Edinburgh Club*, new series 8 (2010), pp. 27–53.

Malcolm, C. A., 'The Solicitor-General for Scotland', *Juridical Review*, 54 (1942), pp. 67–79, 125–43.

Marston, G., *The Marginal Seabed: United Kingdom Legal Practice* (Oxford, 1981).

Mason, J. W., 'The Duke of Argyll and the land question in late nineteenth century Britain', *Victorian Studies*, 21:2 (1978), pp. 149–70.

Matthew, H. C. J., 'Campbell, George Douglas, eighth Duke of Argyll in the peerage of Scotland, and first Duke of Argyll in the peerage of the United Kingdom (1823–1900)', in *Oxford Dictionary of National Biography*, Oxford University Press, <http://www.oxforddnb.com/view/article/4500> (last accessed 25 October 2017).

Meek, D. E., 'The Baptists of the Ross of Mull: evangelical experience and social change in a West Highland community', *Northern Studies*, 26 (1989), pp. 28–42.

Meek, D. E., 'The preacher, the press-gang and the landlord: the impressment and vindication of the Rev. Donald McArthur', *Records of the Scottish Church History Society*, 35 (part 2) (1994), pp. 256–87.

Meek, D. E., 'The role of song in the Highland land agitation', *Scottish Gaelic Studies*, 16 (1990), pp. 1–53.

Meek, D. E., *Tuath is Tighearna* (Edinburgh, 1995).

Meston, M. C., W. D. H. Sellar and Lord Cooper (eds), *The Scottish Legal Tradition* (Edinburgh, 1991).

Miller, G. F., 'Young, George, Lord Young (1819–1907)', in *Oxford Dictionary of National Biography*, Oxford University Press, <http://www.oxforddnb.com/view/article/37074> (last accessed 25 October 2017).

Morrison, A., 'The Grianam case 1734–1781, the kelp industry and the clearances in Harris, 1811–1854', *The Transactions of the Gaelic Society of Inverness*, 52 (1980), pp. 20–89.

Neeson, J. M., 'Coastal commons: custom and the use of seaweed in the British Isles, 1700–1900', in S. Cavaciocchi (ed.), *Ricchezza del Mare, Ricchezza dal Mare Secc. XIII–XVIII. Atti della 'Trentasettesima di Studi', Istituto Internazionale di Storia Economica 'F. Datini', Prato, 11–15 aprile 2005* (Florence, 2006).

Officer, L. H. and S. H. Williamson, 'Five ways to compute the relative value of a UK pound amount, 1270 to present', *MeasuringWorth*, 2017, <https://www.measuringworth.com/ukcompare/> (last accessed 25 October 2017).

O'Neill, T. P., 'Some Irish techniques of collecting seaweed', *Folk Life*, 8 (1970), pp. 13–19.

Pryce, H. and G. Owen, 'Medieval Welsh law and the mid-Victorian foreshore', *The Journal of Legal History*, 35:2 (2014), pp. 172–99.

Pugh, R. B., *The Crown Estate: A Historical Essay* (London, 1960).

*Register of the Society of Writers to Her Majesty's Signet* (Edinburgh, 1983).

Reid, K. G. C., *The Law of Property in Scotland* (Edinburgh, 1996).

Richards, E., *The Highland Clearances* (Edinburgh 2000).

Richards, E., *A History of the Highland Clearances*, vol. 1 (London, 1982).

Richards, E., *A History of the Highland Clearances*, vol. 2 (London, 1985).

Richards, E., 'The landed agent', in G. E. Mingay (ed.), *The Victorian Countryside* (London, 1981).

Ritchie, L. A., 'The floating church of Loch Sunart', *Records of the Scottish Church History Society*, 22 (1985), pp. 159–73.

Robbie, J., *Private Water Rights* (Edinburgh, 2015).

Rubinstein, W. D., 'New men of wealth and the purchase of land in nineteenth century Britain', *Past and Present*, 92 (1981), pp. 125–47.

Rymer, L., 'The kelp industry in North Knapdale', *Scottish Studies*, 18 (1974), pp. 127–32.

Rymer, L., 'The Scottish kelp industry', *Scottish Geographical Magazine,* 90:3 (1974), pp. 147–52.

Stein, P., 'Law and society in eighteenth-century Scottish thought', in N. T. Phillipson and R. Mitchison (eds), *Scotland in the Age of Improvement* (Edinburgh, 1970).

Stephenson, W. A., *Seaweed in Agriculture and Horticulture* (London, 1973).

Theakston, K., 'Brook, Norman Craven, Baron Normanbrook (1902–1967)', in *Oxford Dictionary of National Biography*, Oxford University Press, <http://www.oxforddnb.com/view/article/32089> (last accessed 25 October 2017).

Thomas, B., '"The Clach": Alexander Mackenzie and the land question in the late-nineteenth century Highlands and islands', *Northern Scotland*, 8 (2017), pp. 68–86.

Thomson, D. S. (ed.), *The Companion to Gaelic Scotland* (Glasgow, 1994).

Tindley, A. M., '"Actual pinching and suffering": estate responses to poverty in Sutherland, 1845–1886', *Scottish Historical Review*, 90:2 (2011), pp. 236–56.

Tindley, A., *The Sutherland Estate 1850–1920: Aristocratic Decline, Estate Management and Land Reform* (Edinburgh, 2010).

Walker, D. M., *A Legal History of Scotland*, vol. II (Edinburgh, 1990).

Walker, D. M., *A Legal History of Scotland*, vol. V (Edinburgh, 1998).

Walker, D. M., *A Legal History of Scotland*, vol. VI (Edinburgh, 2001).

Walker, D. M., *The Oxford Companion to Law* (Oxford, 1980).

Walker, D. M., *Principles of Scottish Private Law* (Oxford, 1989).

Wardale, G., 'Jenkins, Sir (Thomas) Gilmour (1894–1981)', in *Oxford Dictionary of National Biography*, Oxford University Press, <http://www.oxforddnb.com/view/article/66858> (last accessed 25 October 2017).

Whatley, C. A., *Scottish Society 1707–1830* (Manchester, 2000).

Whetstone, A. E., *Scottish County Government in the Eighteenth and Nineteenth Centuries* (Edinburgh, 1981).

Whitty, N., 'Water law regimes – the foreshore', in K. Reid and R. Zimmerman (eds), *A History of Private Law in Scotland*, vol. 1 (Oxford, 2000).

Wightman, A., *The Poor Had No Lawyers* (Edinburgh, 2010).

Withers, C. J., '"Give us land and plenty of it": the ideological basis for land and ownership in the Scottish Highlands', *Landscape History*, 12 (1990), pp. 46–54.

Withers, C. J., *Urban Highlanders: Highland–Lowland Migration and Urban Gaelic Culture 1700–1900* (East Linton, 1998).
Youngson, A. J., *After the Forty-Five* (Edinburgh, 1973).

### *Theses*

MacAskill, J., '"A silver fringe?" The Crown, private proprietors and the Scottish kelp shores and the Scottish foreshore generally, c. 1800–c. 1940' (PhD thesis, University of Aberdeen, 2003).
Mulhern, K. M., 'The intellectual duke – George Douglas Campbell, 8th Duke of Argyll' (PhD thesis, University of Edinburgh, 2006).
Thomson, G. W., 'A Hebridean industry: kelp manufacture in the Western Isles, c. 1760–1846' (MPhil thesis, University of Strathclyde, 1994).

# Index

CPSIA information can be obtained
at www.ICGtesting.com
Printed in the USA
BVHW061554300620
582685BV00002B/15

9 781474 436922